The Paradox of Power

For sale by the Superintendent of Documents, U.S. Government Printing Office
Internet: bookstore.gpo.gov   Phone: toll free (866) 512-1800;   DC area (202) 512-1800
Fax: (202) 512-2104 Mail: Stop IDCC, Washington, DC 20402-0001

ISBN 978-0-16-089760-3

The Paradox of Power
Sino-American Strategic Restraint in an Age of Vulnerability

By David C. Gompert and Phillip C. Saunders

Published for the
Center for the Study of Chinese Military Affairs
Institute for National Strategic Studies
By National Defense University Press
Washington, D.C.
2011

Opinions, conclusions, and recommendations expressed or implied within are solely those of the contributors and do not necessarily represent the views of the Defense Department or any other agency of the Federal Government. Cleared for public release; distribution unlimited.

Portions of this book may be quoted or reprinted without permission, provided that a standard source credit line is included. NDU Press would appreciate a courtesy copy of reprints or reviews.

Cover image: USS *Mustin* conducts emergency breakaway drill while on patrol in South China Sea. Photo courtesy of U.S. Navy/Kenneth R. Hendrix.

Library of Congress Cataloging-in-Publication Data

Gompert, David C.
  Paradox of power : Sino-American strategic restraint in an era of
vulnerability / by David C. Gompert and Phillip C. Saunders.
      p. cm.
  Includes bibliographical references.
  1. United States--Foreign relations--China. 2. China--Foreign
relations--United States. 3. Strategic culture--United States. 4.
Strategic culture--China. 5. Deterrence (Strategy) I. Saunders,
Phillip C.
(Phillip Charles), 1966- II. Title.
  JZ1480.A57C6 2011c
  327.73051--dc23

                              2011041137

NDU Press publications are sold by the U.S. Government Printing Office. For ordering information, call (202) 512–1800 or write to the Superintendent of Documents, U.S. Government Printing Office, Washington, D.C. 20402. For GPO publications on-line, access its Web site at: http://bookstore.gpo.gov.

For current publications of the Institute for National Strategic Studies, consult the National Defense University Web site at: http://www.ndu.edu.

In the hope of a safer world for Audrey Gompert, Kofi Burke, Anoushea Burke, Miles Saunders, and Linnea Saunders

Contents

List of Illustrations.. ix

Foreword xi

Preface... xiii

Acknowledgments... xvii

Executive Summary... xix

Chapter One
Introduction... 1

Chapter Two
U.S. Views on Strategic Power, Vulnerability,
and Restraint.. 19

Chapter Three
Chinese Views on Strategic Power, Vulnerability,
and Restraint.. 39

Chapter Four
Mutual Nuclear Restraint... 71

Chapter Five
Mutual Restraint in Space.. 95

Chapter Six

Mutual Restraint in Cyberspace 115

Chapter Seven

Integration and Implications 153

Chapter Eight

Conclusions and Recommendations 185

About the Authors 197

Illustrations

Figures

Figure 1–1. Cost by Type of Attack.. 10

Figure 1–2. Deaths by Type of Attack... 11

Figure 4–1. Cost of Offense Dominance in Missile and
Intercept Systems.. 75

Figure 5–1. Costs of Offense and Defense in Space
Domain..106

Figure 6–1. China's Internet Usage (1990–2009)......................122

Figure 6–2. China's Foreign Direct Investment Flows...........124

Figure 6–3. Diminishing Returns on Investment in Cyber
Security..133

Figure 6–4. Cyber Attack: Offensive Capability Versus
Vulnerability..137

Figure 6–5. Deterrence in the Cyber Domain...........................139

Tables

Table 1–1. Human and Economic Costs of Strategic
Warfare Compared.. 11

Table 5–1. U.S. and Chinese Investment in Space.................... 97

Table 6–1. Economic Cost of Cyber Attack by Sector...........119

Table 6–2. Cyber Deterrence: Possible Versus Necessary.....139

Table 8–1. Levels of Mutual Trust and Cooperation
in Strategic Domains 187

Foreword

The second half of the 20th century featured a strategic competition between the United States and the Soviet Union. That competition avoided World War III in part because during the 1950s, scholars like Henry Kissinger, Thomas Schelling, Herman Kahn, and Albert Wohlstetter analyzed the fundamental nature of nuclear deterrence. Decades of arms control negotiations reinforced these early notions of stability and created a mutual understanding that allowed U.S.-Soviet competition to proceed without armed conflict.

The first half of the 21st century will be dominated by the relationship between the United States and China. That relationship is likely to contain elements of both cooperation and competition. Territorial disputes such as those over Taiwan and the South China Sea will be an important feature of this competition, but both are traditional disputes, and traditional solutions suggest themselves. A more difficult set of issues relates to U.S.-Chinese competition and cooperation in three domains in which real strategic harm can be inflicted in the current era: nuclear, space, and cyber.

Just as a clearer understanding of the fundamental principles of nuclear deterrence maintained adequate stability during the Cold War, a clearer understanding of the characteristics of these three domains can provide the underpinnings of strategic stability between the United States and China in the decades ahead. That is what this book is about.

David Gompert and Phillip Saunders assess the prospect of U.S.-Chinese competition in these domains and develop three related analytic findings upon which their recommendations are built. The first is that in each domain, the offense is dominant. The second is that each side will be highly vulnerable to a strike from the other side. And the third is that the retaliating side will still be able to do unacceptable damage to the initiating party. Therefore, the authors make an important recommendation: that the United States propose a comprehensive approach based on mutual restraint whereby it and China can mitigate their growing strategic vulnerabilities. Unlike the Cold War, this mutual restraint regime may not take the form of binding treaties. But patterns of understanding and restraint may be enough to maintain stability.

Earlier this year, then-Secretary of Defense Robert Gates called upon China to begin a dialogue with the United States on nuclear, space, and cyber issues. A first discussion was held in May that focused primarily on cyber issues. This book can help to inform the ongoing dialogue. With a clearer understanding of mutual vulnerabilities in these domains, the authors hope that competition will give way to greater U.S.-Chinese cooperation.

Hans Binnendijk
Vice President for Research and Applied Learning
Institute for National Strategic Studies

Preface

During 2010, several seemingly unrelated events involving China occurred. In January, a Chinese rocket intercepted and destroyed a high-speed object in space. Soon thereafter, Google reported that its subsidiary in China had suffered a computer network intrusion exfiltrating a vast amount of data. Around that time, the U.S. Government released a new Nuclear Posture Review that cast its nuclear relationship with China in more or less the same terms as its nuclear relationship with Russia—in essence, based on strategic stability and, by implication, on mutual deterrence.

Although we were working separately at that time—one of us as a government official and the other in research—we both made essentially the same observation: the United States is increasingly exposed to China's growing strategic offensive capabilities. One of us had previously written an exploratory treatment of the possible implications. The other resolved to study the Sino-U.S. strategic relationship upon leaving government. When our paths crossed at National Defense University, it was natural that we should collaborate.

This study is the product of that collaboration. We readily confess to having a preconception, albeit a vague one: that the United States and China are *both* increasingly vulnerable to each other in strategic domains—nuclear, space, and cyberspace—where great harm can be done. Because capabilities to do such harm are growing and defenses against them are difficult and costly, it follows that the world's leading power and its fastest rising power each must look to the other to exercise restraint in using strategic offensive capabilities. This study looks deeply into the matter of strategic vulnerability. More than that, it addresses prescriptively the questions that that vulnerability poses: Do conditions exist for Sino-U.S. mutual deterrence in these realms? Might the two states agree on reciprocal restraint? What practical measures might build confidence in restraint? How would strategic restraint affect Sino-U.S. relations as well as security in and beyond East Asia?

The search for answers to these questions demanded research on both sides of the Pacific. Interestingly, our Chinese contacts seem less acutely aware than their Americans counterparts of what we call the "paradox of power," whereby growing power is accompanied by growing vulnerability. While the paradox is partly explained by the interdependence of security that grows with the integration of the world economy, technology, and infrastructure, it also has a historical precedent. When the Americans and Soviets came to realize that nuclear weapons brought a degree of vulnerability unknown in human experience, they entered a relationship of mutual strategic deterrence based on the fear of retaliation and the futility of defense. Although space and especially cyberspace do not fit neatly into the Cold War version of deterrence theory, the core principle of mitigating vulnerability through mutual restraint still stands.

Of course, early 21st-century Sino-American relations are fundamentally different and more textured than mid-20th-century Soviet-American relations. True, China and the United States have divergent interests; if they did not, the idea of strategic restraint would be uninteresting and unnecessary. But they also have convergent interests as well as interactions that go far beyond mere Cold War–style "coexistence." This raises the possibility of mutual strategic restraint based not just on fear but also, with work and patience, on growing trust and cooperation.

Implicit in this study is the idea that China and the United States both face vulnerabilities of the sort that will characterize human affairs under conditions of globalization and rapid technological change as nuclear weapons proliferate, as space becomes more essential, and as cyberspace unites economies and societies worldwide. Beyond fear of the harm that the other power can inflict, perhaps China and the United States can be motivated by awareness that vulnerability is a shared problem, that their chances of developing a constructive relationship can be advanced if they can deal with the problem cooperatively, and that with great power comes great responsibility.

Even with such lofty hopes, relations between the United States and China are clouded by mutual suspicion about intentions—whether China wants to displace the United States as the world's premier power, and whether the United States aims to frustrate China's legitimate ambitions. While leaders of both countries understand that armed conflict between them could be extremely damaging, such a contingency cannot be excluded in a region where China has outstanding territorial claims and growing military power and reach. Consequently, military modernization and operational-contingency planning are intensifying, stoked by technological change.

Herein lies the challenge, analytical as well as political: Despite divergent interests, probable frictions, and the possibility of conflict, can an established power and a rising one credibly pledge not to threaten or strike the other in these strategic domains? If they cannot, their relationship may be defined increasingly by the dangers they pose to each other. If they can, those dangers can be tamed, and the relationship can be more constructive for both countries, for the Asia-Pacific region, and for the world.

Acknowledgments

Of the many persons who in one way or another helped the authors conduct this study and write this book, several stand out. First and foremost is research assistant Ross Rustici, whose exceptional knowledge of both China and strategic affairs is matched by his inquisitiveness, discipline, and energy as an analyst. The best way to sum up his contribution is to say that this book would not exist without him. When Ross left us to join the U.S. Government, his place was taken by Roxanne Bannon, our indispensable research assistant for the final stage of work. We thank them both profoundly. Institute for National Strategic Studies (INSS) Research Analyst Isaac Kardon also assisted in gathering materials, especially for chapter three.

Throughout this work, we relied on our colleague and counselor Hans Binnendijk, INSS Vice President for Research and Applied Learning, for both strong encouragement and intellectual challenge, drawn from his extraordinary career as a public servant, strategic thinker, and executive.

One of the keys to successful research is to engage merciless reviewers. Ours were James Mulvenon, Elaine Bunn, and Jonathan Pollack. Having worked with them before, we expected and got painstakingly thorough and tough reviews, with James concentrating especially on cyber issues, Elaine on nuclear and strategic issues generally, and Jonathan on China and Sino-American relations. The book is better because of them. We also benefited from feedback received on a December 2010 research trip to China and from comments following presentations for Office of the Secretary of Defense and Joint Staff audiences.

We are also especially grateful to Dennis Blair and Terry Pudas for sharing their wisdom on one of the thornier issues we faced: how to reconcile a seemingly unstoppable extension of conventional military conflict into cyberspace with a compelling need to avoid general cyber war. While the book's ideas in this regard are ours to defend, they were influenced and improved by our exchanges with Blair and Pudas. Equally important was our access to Martin Libicki and his fertile mind. Bruce MacDonald, Michael Swaine, Dean Cheng, and Timothy Thomas were also generous with their time, informed comments, and valuable insights.

National Defense University provided the setting and support that made this work possible. The United States is blessed to have an official institution that makes possible diverse, dispassionate, and innovative research and analysis in the interest of national security, and we hope that this book will be a credit to it.

While these and other individuals and this institution enabled us to produce this book, the views are ours alone, not those of National Defense University, the Department of Defense, or the U.S. Government. We alone stand behind its content.

Executive Summary

The United States and China each have or will soon have the ability to inflict grave harm upon the other by nuclear attack, attacks on satellites, or attacks on computer networks. Paradoxically, despite each country's power, its strategic vulnerability is growing. Particularly since September 11, 2001, Americans have sensed this vulnerability. The extent to which the Chinese sense it is unclear.

Vulnerability to nuclear attack is familiar to both countries. But the United States and China are also becoming exposed to damage in space and cyberspace because of their growing reliance on those domains for their prosperity and security, as well as each side's increasing antisatellite (ASAT) and cyber war capabilities. For China, economic integration, production, and commerce—and thus, sustained growth and perhaps political stability—depend vitally on data sharing, making networks and satellites as strategic as they are for the United States.

All three strategic domains are "offense dominant"—technologically, economically, and operationally. Defenses against nuclear, ASAT, and cyber weapons are difficult and yield diminishing results against the offensive capabilities of large, advanced, and determined states such as the United States and China. Nuclear weapons are patently offense dominant because a single explosion can destroy a city. Moreover, it is easier and cheaper for China to improve the survivability of its strategic missile launchers, to multiply deliverable weapons, and to penetrate U.S. missile defenses than it is for the United States to maintain a nuclear first-strike capability. Though it has yet to admit it, the United States cannot deny the Chinese the second-strike nuclear deterrent they are determined to have.

Satellites are inherently vulnerable: conspicuous, easy to track, and fragile. Destroying them or degrading their performance is easier than protecting them. ASAT interceptors are much cheaper than satellites. Likewise, defending computer networks becomes harder and more expensive as the scale and sophistication of the attacker increase. The woes of the cyber defender are compounded by integrated global markets and supply chains for digital components and equipment—in which U.S. and state-affiliated Chinese corporations are leading competitors—increasing the potential for strategic degradation of network infrastructure and disruption of services. In general, strategic offense dominance gives each country an incentive to invest in offense, which in turn spurs the other to keep pace.

Apart from offense dominance, the advance of technology has slashed the costs in lives and treasure of strategic attack, as capabilities have graduated from mass invasion to heavy bombing to nuclear weapons to ASAT and cyber war. If one ignores possible deaths resulting from disruption of public services, ASAT and cyber war might even be considered "nonviolent." As the number of expected casualties from strategic attack options drops, so could international opprobrium and the inhibitions of decisionmakers. Absent deterrence, thresholds for war in space and cyberspace could become perilously low as offenses improve.

Establishing Mutual Strategic Restraint

Curbing these dangers through Sino-U.S. nuclear, ASAT, or cyber war disarmament is largely impractical and unverifiable. Because of this, along with the futility of strategic defense and the plunging costs of attack, the United States and China must consider ways of mitigating their growing vulnerabilities in these domains by mutual restraint in the *use* of strategic offensive capabilities. The bedrock of such restraint would be mutual deterrence in each domain, based on the fear of devastating retaliation and the limits of defense. Preconditions for mutual deterrence—namely, risks of retaliation that outweigh expected gains of attacking first—exist in all three domains, although this may not be fully recognized by both the United States and China.

Augmenting deterrence, Sino-U.S. mutual restraint should include reciprocal pledges to refrain from attacking first; regular high-level communications about capabilities, doctrine, and plans; and concrete confidence-building measures (CBMs) to provide reassurance and avoid misperceptions. Because China and the United States have both convergent and divergent interests, mutual strategic restraint is both possible and necessary. Without convergent interests, there would be no hope for genuine mutual restraint; without divergent interests, conflict would be implausible, and vulnerability would not matter.

As a logical starting point, the United States should acknowledge the reality and accept the legitimacy of China's nuclear retaliatory capability, endorse mutual deterrence, and be prepared in principle to explore a bilateral understanding not to use nuclear weapons first against the other or its allies. However, given its severe vulnerability in space and cyberspace and the growing importance of those domains, the United States should insist on a broad and integrated approach to mutual restraint.

Mutual ASAT restraint should take the form of agreeing not to be the first to try to deny the other country's use of space, in peace or war. Mutual restraint in cyberspace, the most complex domain, should entail a pledge by each country not to be the first to attack networks critical to the other's well-being—that is, "strategic cyberspace." This would not encompass non-critical networks or intelligence collection. In the event of armed conflict, Chinese and U.S. forces are likely to conduct attacks on military networks, the infrastructure for which may also support civilian networks, involving a danger of escalation. Therefore, both governments bear responsibility to exert tight political control, to not escalate, and to avoid harm to noncombatants—in effect, to create a firebreak between tactical cyber war, where deterrence may be weak, and strategic cyber war, where it ought to be strong. Only in this way can the utility of military cyber war and the imperative of avoiding general cyber war be reconciled.

Because mutual strategic restraint does not necessitate elimination of offensive capabilities, there is no guarantee that it will hold in the event of a Sino-American crisis, much less actual hostilities. Since surprise attacks in any of these domains are improbable, strategic restraint that is doomed to fail in crises is hardly worth having. If either side suspects that the other intends not to exercise agreed restraint at a moment of tension, crises could be all the more unstable. So it is fair to raise concerns about the breaching of strategic restraint. Keep in mind, however, that in all three domains, objective conditions of mutual *deterrence* are either already in place (nuclear and space) or forming (cyberspace). While mutual restraint is superior to simple deterrence because it includes reciprocal acknowledgment and confidence-building, it can be counted on in crises or conflict only if it rests squarely on mutual deterrence based on fear of retaliation.

While the United States should take an integrated three-domain approach to mutual strategic restraint, doing so could be complicated and might encounter Chinese skepticism, raise regional concerns, and take patience and persistence. The main obstacles are the potential warfighting utility of different types of strategic weapons; the risks of weakening deterrence by pledging not to escalate beyond conventional combat; allied security and reactions; and asymmetric U.S. and Chinese motivations.

Warfighting Utility

Neither the United States nor China regards nuclear weapons as militarily useful, against each other or in general. China has a longstanding nuclear no-first-use policy, and the United States now seeks to reduce the role of nuclear weapons in world affairs and warfare. Moreover, regardless of whether the two sides agree on mutual restraint, U.S. nuclear attack will be deterred by China's improved retaliatory capabilities, even if U.S. conventional forces may be defeated.

In contrast, ASAT weapons could play a role in Sino-American military combat. The Chinese know that U.S. Armed Forces rely critically on space-based command, control, communications, computers, intelligence, surveillance, and reconnaissance (C⁴ISR) for operations in the sprawling Pacific, just as the United States knows that the People's Liberation Army's (PLA's) reliance on satellites will grow as it extends its military reach eastward. Yet because many satellites serve both military and civilian purposes (for example, communications, global positioning, and Earth observation), there is no clear firebreak between tactical and strategic ASAT war. The United States would be better off preserving its own use of space than denying China's during a conflict and thus should rely on ASAT weapons only for deterrence, not warfighting. Given its current conventional military disadvantages and awareness of U.S. military use of space, the PLA may hesitate to part with the option of initiating ASAT attacks.

While deterrence may not apply against many cyber threats, it could be relevant between large and capable states, especially at times of crisis. Due to the limits and costs of network defense, strategic cyber deterrence between China and the United States is not only necessary but also possible. Because each country relies vitally on vulnerable computer networks, each has reason to fear retaliation. Determining the source of a large cyber attack would be aided by circumstances and by the fact that very few actors, all of them states, are currently capable of large and sophisticated attacks. Even without certainty of an attack's origin, the prospective attacker would be gambling its economic health by betting against retaliation and escalation to general cyber war.

While both the United States and China might be deterred and accept mutual restraint in strategic cyberspace, neither one can or will exclude attacking computer networks that enable enemy forces and weapons performance in combat. The PLA knows that U.S. reliance on networked C⁴ISR for waging expeditionary warfare and conducting precision strikes is a critical vulnerability. Likewise, the U.S. military knows that the PLA will depend increasingly on systems linked through cyberspace to target U.S. strike forces (for example, aircraft carriers) and so will not want to foreclose cyber attack options in the event of war.

A firebreak between military and civil-commercial cyberspace is theoretically possible. While network hardware used in military operations is partly dual use, it may be possible to discriminate on the software level between military and strategic-civilian programs that use this common infrastructure. Though this would require exceptional network intelligence, precise targeting, and tight command and control on both sides, it could prevent escalation to general cyber war without requiring that military cyber attacks be forbidden.

Maintaining Deterrence in the Region

Mutual restraint, broadly cast, means that neither China nor the United States will attack the other in any of the three strategic domains; nor will either one escalate to strategic attacks in the event of military hostilities. Although it is in the U.S. interest to avoid strategic conflict with nuclear weapons or in space and cyberspace, there is some risk that deterrence of Chinese conventional aggression in East Asia could be weakened by easing China's fear of escalation—an effect known as *strategic decoupling*. Such risks could be aggravated by trends in the western Pacific conventional military balance favoring China, owing particularly to its expanding missile and submarine forces (also offense dominant) and its growing ability to strike U.S. aircraft carriers and air bases in the region.

Regardless of agreement on mutual strategic restraint, the U.S. ability to rely on the threat of nuclear escalation to deter Chinese attack on Taiwan is already slight and will decline as China improves its nuclear retaliatory capabilities. While U.S. threats to escalate to attacks on Chinese satellites and strategic computer networks are more credible, the risks and consequences of escalation argue against relying on such threats to deter Chinese conventional aggression. Instead, the United States should strengthen deterrence of Chinese aggression by conventional means—for example, conventional strikes on mainland military (but nonstrategic) targets and bringing U.S. worldwide general purpose forces to bear in a protracted conflict.

If Sino-American relations were to become fundamentally unfriendly, mutual strategic restraint might either break down or make aggression and conflict in the region more probable below the strategic level. As the local conventional military balance shifts in its favor, China could become more inclined to try to settle territorial disputes on its terms, including over Taiwan, by use or threat of force. However, joint acceptance of mutual strategic restraint could help prevent relations from deteriorating, reduce the likelihood of armed conflict, and make the shifting conventional balance less deleterious to regional security and U.S. interests.

Protecting and Reassuring Allies

Key regional states, notably Japan and South Korea, may be ambivalent about Sino-U.S. accords on mutual restraint. On the one hand, they do not want Sino-U.S. tensions or an arms race, much less conflict in any of these strategic domains; after all, they share U.S. and Chinese vulnerabilities in space and cyberspace and are part of the same integrated economy. Moreover, U.S. allies should appreciate that mitigating U.S. strategic vulnerabilities could help ensure American steadfastness in the event of any Chinese challenges. On the other hand, Japan and South Korea already are sensitive to signs of reduced U.S. commitment, and they would not want Chinese fear of escalation to be relieved by Sino-U.S. mutual strategic restraint. In the worst case, Japan could be more inclined either to accommodate China or to develop offensive strategic capabilities of its own, neither of which would be good for U.S. interests or regional stability.

The United States can and should assuage allied concerns about its strategic commitments by reaffirming its regional security bonds, maintaining its presence, and improving conventional deterrence capabilities in light of Chinese force enhancements. It should also insist that Sino-U.S. mutual strategic restraint apply to allies, which would mean that China is bound not to attack U.S. allies in any of these domains and, by implication, that the United States would be justified to retaliate in kind if it did. U.S. extended nuclear deterrence of Chinese nuclear threats to U.S. allies would thus be unaffected. Moreover, in ensuring that allies are covered by mutual strategic restraint, and thus by deterrence based on the threat of U.S. retaliation, the approach recommended here would improve allied security against Chinese strategic attack by extending the U.S. strategic umbrella to cover space and cyberspace as well as nuclear attack.

Gaining Chinese Acceptance

It is unclear how fully Chinese leaders comprehend that their country's economic growth and political stability could be endangered by warfare with the United States in space and cyberspace. China, the PLA especially, might want to confine mutual restraint to no first use of nuclear weapons—in effect, to "pocket" mutual nuclear deterrence while keeping open options to strike first in space and cyberspace. A rising sense of China's own vulnerabilities in space and cyberspace, along with the chance to obtain U.S. acceptance of nuclear no first use, should in time make Chinese leaders more receptive to mutual restraint across all three domains.

However, the PLA could see agreement not to initiate attacks on satellites and computer networks as foreclosing China's only way to neutralize U.S. military advantages by degrading U.S. C^{4}ISR and strike capabilities—

thus, its best chance to avoid defeat. Unless China's political leaders are convinced of the need for mutual restraint and prepared to overrule military objections, the United States may encounter Chinese civil-military discord, stalemate, or opposition regarding restraint in space and cyberspace. China does not yet have effective mechanisms for making unified national security policy, as warranted by its expanding interests and role in international security.

The United States can sway China toward acceptance of mutual restraint in space and cyberspace by having effective ASAT and cyber war capabilities, by making clear its will to retaliate with those capabilities if attacked, and by insisting that nuclear no first use be accompanied by similar restraint in these other two domains. Still, it may be unrealistic to expect China to embrace agreement on mutual strategic restraint, broadly defined, until the reality of growing vulnerabilities fully registers or until political and economic leaders prevail over PLA interest in gaining operational advantages over U.S. forces.

Sooner or later, a clear U.S. strategic deterrent posture, coupled with China's inescapable vulnerabilities, should convince Chinese leaders that their country is in fact deterred in space and cyberspace, just as the United States is in the nuclear domain. The PLA will not have feasible solutions to address this reality. Recent U.S. policy statements stressing deterrence in these new domains are a good start.

The prospect that initial Chinese resistance will yield to growing interest in mutual strategic restraint argues for the United States to lay out an integrated three-domain approach early in the process. By doing so, it can frame the way the Chinese conceive the strategic vulnerability problem, the reality of offense dominance, the extension of deterrence concepts to space and cyberspace, and the wisdom of general strategic restraint with nuclear restraint as an element.

Building Confidence

To buttress and sustain mutual restraint, the United States should propose CBMs in each domain: transparency in nuclear forces and doctrines; launch notification and other forms of space cooperation; and warning of and cooperation against third-party cyber threats. Additionally, regular high-level civilian-military dialogue on capabilities, plans, doctrines, and the strengthening of mutual restraint is essential. Such exchanges will let U.S. policymakers sensitize Chinese counterparts to growing vulnerabilities, the dangers of conflict in space and cyberspace, and the need for effective political control of decisions that risk escalation.

While mutual deterrence is a sine qua non of mutual restraint, deterrence by itself may do little more than describe conditions of equilibrium based on presumptions of prudence in the face of retaliatory threats. By institutionalizing those conditions and agreeing on terms, mutual restraint can be more adaptable, enduring, and better for Sino-American relations than threat-based deterrence alone. Deterrence relies on reciprocal fear; restraint adds and fosters shared responsibility and trust. By embracing mutual restraint, China and the United States can place themselves in a position to convince others (for example, Russia) to accept the need for caution in the use of offensive capabilities in all three domains.

Prospects and Recommendations

Agreement with China to exercise mutual restraint across these strategic domains would serve U.S. interests in mitigating critical vulnerabilities; reducing the importance of nuclear weapons; permitting full and productive exploitation of space and cyberspace; and unburdening Sino-American relations of the threat of strategic conflict. Accordingly, the United States should propose such restraint, founded on mutual deterrence, in all three domains, including reciprocal pledges not to be the first to use nuclear weapons, to interfere with access to space, or to attack the other nation's strategic cyberspace. The United States should insist that these pledges also proscribe such attacks on allies, thus preserving its right to retaliate if an ally were attacked. In light of risks that China might try to exploit bilateral strategic restraint to seek regional dominance, the United States should state its expectation that such restraint will strengthen prudence and security at all levels.

It may be neither realistic nor essential to get agreement on all terms soon. Nonetheless, the United States should lay out its complete framework with China, after first consulting with U.S. allies, and then pursue it patiently and persistently. It would be good to share U.S. analysis of common vulnerabilities in space and cyberspace with Chinese counterparts at an early date. The United States could also indicate that it is willing to discuss bilateral no first use of nuclear weapons if China is willing to discuss comparable ideas concerning space and strategic cyberspace. In parallel, the United States should reiterate that its purpose in all three domains is deterrence and that its retaliatory capabilities and resolve should not be doubted.

Regardless of the pace of progress in negotiating terms of mutual restraint, it is important to ensure strong political oversight of operational decisions that could lead to escalation in any of these strategic domains.

The United States should update its protocols for delegating authority under peace and war conditions and should implore Chinese civilian leaders to do the same. Strict control is especially important for cyber war, given the relative lack of inhibition to attack.

A framework for mutual strategic restraint should be pursued not with undue urgency but with care and conviction that such restraint is right for the United States, for the security of a vital region, and for putting Sino-American relations on a stable strategic footing. Because the United States and China are in a formative stage in what will be the world's most important relationship for generations to come, the United States should not be reactive. The need for the United States to speak with one voice on these matters argues for civilian-military, executive-congressional, and bipartisan discussions.

This study is not the last word on mutual strategic restraint. Like most research, it ends with an appeal for more work on a number of questions:

- What missile defense capabilities would afford assured protection against small, hostile nuclear weapons states or unauthorized missile launches without raising doubts about Chinese deterrence?

- How can computer networks used for military C^{4}ISR be partitioned from those that enable civilian and commercial information-sharing, even with common infrastructure, so that more robust firebreaks can prevent escalation to strategic cyber war?

- What CBMs beyond those proposed here could bolster trust in Chinese and American mutual restraint in the use of offensive capabilities?

- What methods of Sino-American notification of third-party or ambiguous attacks in space and cyberspace could prevent mistakes, miscalculations, and inadvertent conflict?

- What other forms of Sino-American cooperation in space and cyberspace could inculcate a sense of shared interests and complement restraint?

- How could other states, such as Russia, be brought into a regime of mutual strategic restraint?

- How will advances in science and technology affect strategic offense dominance and the logic of mutual restraint?

Even with a need for more study and debate, there may be no better time than now for the United States and China to start together down a path toward greater safety for themselves and the world.

Chapter One

Introduction

For all their power, the United States and China are increasingly vulnerable. Each faces strategic dangers, from nuclear weapons to disruption of critical computer networks and space links.[1] Because their relationship is at once interdependent and potentially adversarial, the United States and China are especially vulnerable to *each other*: interdependence exposes each to effects of the other's activities, malicious or not, while the potential for conflict impels each to acquire offensive capabilities against which defenses can be futile. Strategic vulnerability cannot be eliminated, only mitigated.

Of the two countries, the United States is stronger in offensive strategic capabilities, notably nuclear, antisatellite (ASAT), and cyber weapons. Yet it is also highly exposed to danger in these domains, confirming that power does not necessarily reduce vulnerability. If Americans thought before the 9/11 attacks that being the only superpower made them safer, they think otherwise now. Even its $600-billion-plus annual defense budget does not let the United States buy its way out of vulnerability.

Meanwhile, China's striking economic and technological development is enabling it to acquire all forms of power, including offensive strategic capabilities. But China's development is also making it more vulnerable, as it becomes more integrated at home and with the world and thus more susceptible to economic disruption. While the Chinese have long felt, based on their history, that weakness breeds vulnerability, they are learning that greater vulnerability can also accompany greater strength.

This book confronts the paradox that as power grows, so can vulnerability. The basic reason for this is that the same factors that produce modern power—technological advancement and economic integration—also increase exposure to risk. The book suggests a way to mitigate U.S. and Chinese strategic vulnerabilities to each another. It is written from an American perspective, with U.S. interests foremost in mind. But because the United States cannot escape its growing vulnerability to China unilaterally, Chinese agreement is needed. The book's core idea is that mutual strategic vulnerability calls for mutual strategic restraint. Whether Sino-American distrust will preclude agreed restraint is one of the questions it tackles. But even with distrust, self-interest in avoiding harm—in a word, deterrence—can move both powers in this direction.

In becoming more vulnerable, the United States and China are not alone. With global economic integration and information networking, most nations are increasingly susceptible to disturbances and damage caused by other nations and transnational actors. The 300-year-old model of nation-states controlling their territory, vulnerable only to invasion, was shaken by the advent of strategic bombing and then nuclear weapons. On the chessboard where nations play, queens with stunning speed and unlimited range now endanger sovereign kings (and their realms). Against strategic offense, defense is getting more costly but not more effective, leaving fear of retaliation as the surest way to avert disaster. This has been the essence of nuclear deterrence, though neither the problem nor the remedy is confined any longer to the nuclear domain.

The increased vulnerability of sovereign states that began in the mid-20th century with strategic bombing and nuclear weapons has been compounded by two factors that mark passage to the 21st century: integration and information networking. The former has increased the exposure of states to each other's products, services, data, money, ideas, surveillance, migrants, and travelers, including terrorists. Integration has also opened new domains in which nations interact: no longer just at sea, on land, and in the air but now also in space and cyberspace. While economic integration has brought growth to those nations that participate, it has also reduced their ability to escape risk.

Information networking has accelerated economic integration not only internationally but internally as well, as China's transformation from a fragmented to a national economy shows. It is also demolishing the ability of sovereigns to control what their populations know. This heightens the potential for political upheaval, which is of more concern to Chinese than to American leaders.

Information networking increases vulnerability in another way: improved military targeting. It has yielded dramatic enhancements in sensors, data processing and sharing, geolocation precision and coverage, navigation, and guidance—thus, in the ability to deliver weapons at any distance with great speed and accuracy, and to defeat defenses. Information technology has made objects—fixed and moving, on land, at sea, and in the air—increasingly observable and vulnerable. Such advances are also evident in space and cyberspace, which are susceptible to targeting and also can serve as media for novel weapons, including electromagnetic and energy-based ones.

Although growing strategic risk affects weak and strong states alike, those that face the power/vulnerability paradox are the strong ones. Recall that the United States and the Soviet Union were simultaneously at their most powerful and their most vulnerable during the Cold War because the capacity of each to visit nuclear destruction made it the other's primary target. Today, the conventional military superiority of the United States incentivizes adversaries, real and potential, to target its strategic vulnerabilities.[2] For all its power, the United States is hard pressed to protect its territory from nuclear attack, its satellites from ASAT attack, and its computer networks from cyber attack.

The United States and China are not mortal enemies, as the United States and the Soviet Union were. But their growing capacity to inflict strategic harm, when combined with the possibility of conflict, motivates each to be capable of striking at the other's vulnerabilities, at least for deterrence. Fortunately, there are enough positive aspects of Sino-American relations that the two should be able to find ways to mitigate their mutual vulnerabilities. After all, even the United States and Soviet Union, despite their animosity, were able to manage their nuclear vulnerabilities through mutual deterrence. But while Soviet-American strategic peace was kept by reciprocal fear, there is reason to think—at least to hope—that China and the United States can manage their vulnerabilities with a quotient of reciprocal trust.

The distinction between *mutual deterrence* and *mutual restraint* is crucial. Although mutual restraint depends on mutual deterrence, it is less fragile and more likely to contribute to wider cooperation than fear-based deterrence alone. It implies that the parties are not fundamentally adversarial and that each seeks a relationship based on more than canceling out the other's strategic threat. While mutual restraint does not depend on faith in good intentions, it can ease fears of hostile intent, thus reducing the danger of miscalculation and the collapse of restraint during crises. It also invites—indeed, requires—earnest dialogue and understanding regarding the shared problem of strategic vulnerability, as well as concrete steps to reinforce restraint.

There is no guarantee that both China and the United States would abide by agreements to exercise strategic restraint—that is, to refrain from escalation—in the event of conflict. This is why mutual deterrence is a prerequisite for mutual restraint. Even in the midst of war, the prospect of retaliation can prevent escalation if accords reached in peacetime cannot.

Conditions for mutual deterrence exist in all three domains. At the same time, Sino-American agreement on the concept of mutual strategic restraint may help the two countries create a more cooperative relationship in general and thus reduce the likelihood of conflict.

Noting both the certainty of mutual fear and the aspiration of mutual trust, this book contends that the United States and China have both a need and an opportunity to adopt and apply the principle of strategic restraint as the best way to mitigate their vulnerabilities to one another. Present conditions in China, in the United States, and in Sino-American relations may or may not offer fertile ground for the book's proposals for mutual strategic restraint. The time horizon of this study is about a decade, and it may take that long for awareness of strategic vulnerability to impel both nations toward an accord. Nevertheless, the ideas offered here can be grist for discussion within each nation and between them, looking toward the time when conditions will be ripe for their adoption.

The United States and China in an Age of Vulnerability

The United States and China will be the world's most powerful states for at least the next decade, and probably longer. Though it is premature to proclaim the world bipolar, China has an impressive package of modern power: economic scale and productivity, technological prowess, spreading political influence, military capabilities, and human capital and creativity. Though their nuclear force is small compared to those of the United States and Russia, the Chinese believe that possessing more than an assured minimal deterrent is unnecessary and wasteful. Only the United States can match China's ASAT and cyberwar potential.[3]

However, China's expanding power will not prevent its vulnerability from expanding, any more than U.S. power has reduced U.S. vulnerability. Whether China's leaders appreciate that its vulnerabilities are growing along with its power will determine whether they will have an incentive to accept mutual restraint with the United States. While the Chinese have long sought mutual restraint with respect to nuclear weapons, it is unclear whether they will accept mutual restraint in space and cyberspace. Given their strong advocacy of no first use of nuclear weapons, they clearly understand the concept.

Meanwhile, China's growing offensive power in space and cyberspace is making the United States all the more determined to acquire offensive capabilities to disable Chinese satellites and computer networks, at least for deterrence. Because China will find it at least as hard as the United States does to defend its satellites and networks, its offensive power makes it a target for U.S. offensive capabilities. Conversely, because the Chinese will not tolerate U.S. monopolies in ASAT weapons and cyberwar, and because the United States will find it hard to protect its satellites and networks, it too will become more vulnerable.

How the United States and China manage their strategic vulnerabilities depends on their larger relationship, which combines convergent and divergent interests. The two share interests in an open, orderly, and expanding world economy; the stability of resource, product, and financial markets; international security as a condition for economic growth; effective multilateral institutions; and controlling violent extremism and other nonstate threats. They also have an immense stake in each other's economic health, which encourages strategic restraint.

Yet U.S. and Chinese interests can also be at odds and occasionally collide. This is especially so in East Asia, a region vital to both nations, where China aspires to be the preeminent power but where the United States will not abandon its stabilizing presence and influential role. China is not content to let the United States obstruct its national unification or, regardless of Taiwan's fate, its access to the Pacific. China may see the United States as a barrier to its regional ambition and potentially to the world's seas, trade routes, resources, and markets. Although history teaches that established powers and rising ones do not inevitably clash (think of Great Britain and America), it also teaches that clashes are more likely when the rising power sees the established one as posing obstacles to its material interests (think of Germany and Great Britain or of imperial Japan and America).

One of this book's load-bearing assumptions is that neither hegemonic struggle nor harmonious interdependence can fully explain present and future Sino-American relations.[4] The former ignores weighty shared interests that encourage accommodation; the latter relies on a romantic notion that sovereigns lose their urge for advantage when their economies become interdependent. Because reality lies in the middle, relations will be a mix of cooperation and competition, understanding and suspicion, partnership and rivalry. This duality in Sino-American relations is crucial for the idea of mutual restraint: a relationship that combines divergent and convergent interests supplies both the *necessity* and the *opportunity* for accord to limit the use of strategic power against one another. A relationship without conflict would not require such an arrangement, whereas one fraught with conflict would not permit it.

This book is not about Sino-American relations in general but about mutual restraint in using strategic power. By *strategic power*, we mean the ability to harm the other nation's essential well-being for purposes of imposing one's will by threat or attack. *Essential well-being* includes homeland security, population safety, state viability, and economic health (that is, productivity, employment, and availability of goods and services). With the deep involvement of both countries in the world economy, essential well-being extends to access to resources and markets, the ability to use both traditional and new lanes of trade and communications—oceans, space, and cyberspace. Of all the dangers to the well-being of the United States and China, offensive nuclear, space, and cyberspace capabilities have strategic significance because of the harm they could do.

Nuclear conflict can cause unspeakable destruction, knocking out satellites can cause widespread and lingering economic disruption, and degradation of critical information networks can cause major economic and societal shocks. Any of these sorts of attacks can be regarded as a deliberate blow to vital functions of the other nation, intended to weaken its resolve or ability to resist the attacker's designs (yet another way to define *strategic*). A premise of this book is that both the United States and China will have enough offensive power in these domains to cause grave harm. Although the United States is and could remain superior to China in each of these three domains, there is no evidence that it can dissuade China from gaining greater offensive power in all of them.[5] Quite the opposite is true: nuclear retaliatory forces, ASAT weapons, and cyber warfare are high priorities in China's military modernization.

At a minimum, the Chinese believe they need offensive capabilities in these categories to deter and avoid being bullied by the United States.[6] This is clearly the case with respect to nuclear weapons. More ominously for the United States, the Chinese, or at least the People's Liberation Army (PLA), may be motivated in space and cyberspace not as much by deterrence as by a belief that U.S. vulnerabilities can be exploited to China's advantage in the event of conflict.

In sum, the advantages the United States has in offensive strategic capabilities do not reduce its vulnerability to China's growing offensive strategic capabilities. Likewise, China's efforts to reduce U.S. advantages will leave it no less exposed to U.S. offensive capabilities. Because neither China nor the United States will forego these forms of strategic power, and because divergent interests may cause frictions, crises, or conflicts, the security of each nation depends on the other's restraint in the use of such power. Obviously, neither one would agree to restrain itself unilaterally. Moreover, because it is unrealistic if not risky to assume that understandings of reciprocal restraint can be negotiated in the heat of a crisis, it follows that some attempt should be made to fashion terms of restraint before crises occur. Given the nontrivial potential for Sino-American discord and confrontation, such an attempt should begin sooner rather than later.

Offense Rising

Defenses against nuclear, ASAT, and cyber weapons are difficult, costly, and yield diminishing returns versus offensive capabilities of large, advanced, and determined states like the United States and China. This offense dominance gives an edge to the side that invests comparatively more in offense. It gives both sides an incentive to invest in offense instead of defense, which in turn compounds the strategic vulnerability of both.

After 25 years of U.S. work on ballistic missile defense, it is as clear as ever that defenses can be overwhelmed with modest numbers of missiles and sophisticated attacks. The offense-dominant character of nuclear warfare also stems from the fact that a single weapon on a missile that penetrates a missile defense system can do horrendous damage (for example, destroy a city). If successful defense is defined as avoiding such damage, defense must stop *all* incoming missiles.[7] By the same standard, offense succeeds if *any* missile penetrates.[8] With known technology, the odds of one missile penetrating improve sharply with increases in the size and complexity of attack.

Satellites—delicate objects moving predictably and conspicuously against the background of space—are much easier to destroy than to defend. Moreover, high-performance satellites cost much more than ASAT interceptors. Therefore, as the performance of interceptors improves and the cost of every additional one declines, it is far cheaper to multiply interceptors than to replace satellites. Once developed, interceptors can be readily increased in number.

Likewise, protecting information networks becomes increasingly difficult and costly as the scale and sophistication of the would-be attacker grow. After years of heavy investment in making networks more secure from intrusion, they are for the most part less secure. Hacking is far cheaper than network defense. After all, networks are meant to accommodate users' needs for access, sharing, and collaboration. Strong forces of supply responding rapidly to demands for connectivity and convenience generally trump security. Short of undoing information-sharing, with huge negative economic consequences, defense must compete with the very purposes and virtues of networking.

Meanwhile, markets, firms, and supply chains for networks and their components have become global and integrated, with the United States and

China top players in both production and demand. U.S. concerns about dependence on Chinese sources have grown as China graduates from making chips to making supercomputers, often based on technology of U.S. origin. Now that Chinese state-affiliated firms are competitive in network infrastructure—for example, data and cellular networks—U.S. concerns about insecure supply chains have merged with worries that made-in-China hardware and software within U.S. networks could be manipulated or disrupted for strategic purposes.[9]

Across all three strategic domains, as well as in conventional military capabilities, offense dominance and vulnerability are the result of advances in information sensing, processing, and sharing that facilitate *targeting*. Industrial-age military power swung between offense and defense dominance, depending on the physics of speed, distance, armor, weapons accuracy, and the like. In the digital age, however, offense dominance is persistent and even getting more pronounced, given the accuracy, timeliness, and distance of targeting.[10] Using space and information technology, networked targeting capabilities are increasingly global, and they can deliver physical weapons and electronic agents alike. The United States is a world leader in the very technologies that underlie strategic offense dominance, and China is on its heels.

U.S. and Chinese military priorities reflect judgments on both sides that investments in offense are rewarding. The United States has declared that it will maintain the qualitative superiority of its strategic nuclear offensive forces (as long as nuclear weapons exist) and that its missile defense system is intended only for protection against small threats, such as Iran and North Korea.[11] China concentrates investment in offensive strategic nuclear forces in order to have a credible deterrent. Neither the United States nor China can count on protecting its satellites; both are developing systems that can destroy or disable satellites. While neither country will divulge specific information about its cyberwar capabilities or operations, China is plainly active in network attack, and the United States is formidable in offense as well as defense.

Unless and until nonlinear scientific advancements make defense feasible against large nuclear, space, and cyberspace attacks, strategic vulnerabilities will persist and increase. Whether offense dominance will last is taken up later in this book. Because of the role and power of information technology and continuing integration of the world economy, it is almost sure to last for at least another decade.

Declining Costs of Strategic Attack

In addition to favoring offense over defense, technology is drastically reducing the costs of strategic attack. Until the mid-20th century, any powerful state determined to bring about the collapse or capitulation of another state might decide to launch a massive land invasion, at great cost in lives and treasure to itself, not to mention to the victim. Napoleonic France and Nazi Germany tried, unsuccessfully, to conquer Russia; the North was compelled to invade the South to win the American Civil War, with huge casualties; Germany defeated France by invasion in the Franco-Prussian War and World War II, but lost World War I when its invasion stalled; neither Napoleon nor Hitler could subdue Great Britain because they could not invade it. The advent of strategic air forces gave strong states the option of bombing other states into submission, at substantially lower cost to the attacker. Although World War II and the Vietnam War revealed the limits of heavy bombing against states and peoples with the fortitude to endure, champions of strategic bombing can cite evidence that strong states can defeat weak ones from the air—Germany's conquest of the Netherlands in World War II, the U.S. defeat of Iraq in the Gulf War, and the North Atlantic Treaty Organization's defeat of Serbia.

Nuclear weapons provided those possessing them with a decisive way to impose strategic will on another state—at least a nonnuclear one—at very low cost to the attacker in either human or economic resources. However, the cost to the victim would be more apocalyptic than that incurred by invasion or heavy bombing. Even if not deterred by the threat of nuclear retaliation, states with nuclear weapons have shown great inhibition to use them as a substitute for the higher cost alternatives of invasion and conventional bombing. Only in the case of the U.S. nuclear attack on Japan was a state prepared to accept such high enemy casualties, given that invasion would have caused enormous American casualties.

With technologies available to destroy satellites and crash computer networks, states in possession of such capabilities can inflict immense harm, if not total defeat, on other states. Satellite and cyber attacks have the capacity to damage the essential well-being of those on the receiving end, at modest economic cost to the attacker—minor cost in the case of cyber attack—and with negligible immediate loss of life on either side.

The following three graphics depict the sharply declining costs of producing enough strategic damage to defeat another state. Figure 1–1 shows, in orders of magnitude, the economic and human costs of strategic attack as technology has evolved from land warfare to air warfare to nuclear warfare to antisatellite and cyber warfare. For purposes of illustration, it is assumed that all these strategic attack options have the same effect: to destroy the ability and/or sap the resolve of a state to resist an attacker. As technology has progressed from mechanized armies to long-range bombers to nuclear-armed missiles to information systems, the costs to the attacker have declined in both economic resources and lives.

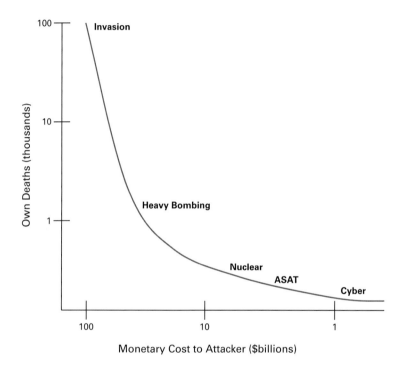

Figure 1–1. Cost by Type of Attack

Figure 1–2 shows that the same technological developments have reduced the expected casualties of not only the attacker but also of the attacked.[12] The most striking implication of this is that inhibitions about attacking due to expected loss of life on both sides may not apply with regard to satellite and cyber attacks. Anticipating no bloodshed and the resulting outrage, the threshold of justification for attack would be lower.

Table 1–1 summarizes how the five classes of strategic warfare compare in regard to the attacker's expected casualties, the economic cost of delivering the attack, and the expected casualties of the state being attacked. In a

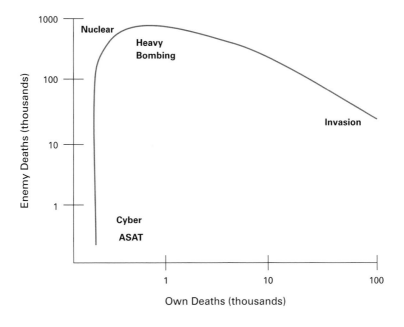

Figure 1–2. Deaths by Type of Attack

nutshell, technological "progress" is making it cheaper and easier to harm another nation. This is another way of saying that even the most powerful states are becoming increasingly vulnerable to those who command those technologies. Conversely, powerful states, including China and the United States, could become less restrained about inflicting harm on one another as the costs to the attacker and expected deaths on both sides sharply decline—unless, of course, mutual deterrence and restraint take effect.

	Invasion	Heavy Bombing	Nuclear	ASAT	Cyber
Own Deaths	High	Medium	Low	Low	Low
Cost	High	High	Medium	Medium	Low
Enemy Deaths	High	High	High	Low	Low

Table 1–1. Human and Economic Costs of Strategic Warfare Compared

Table 1–1 suggests that technology has created options for practically "nonviolent" forms of strategic attack. Yet the potential economic damage done by denying the use of space or cyberspace is on the same order of magnitude as the economic damage from invasion or bombing. Because causing an economic shock and corresponding hardship could be strategically effective without causing death and destruction, those in possession of these new means of attack could be less hesitant to use them if they have important interests at stake.

The Case for Deterrence and Restraint

China and the United States are in the vanguard of these technological and economic trends. The dominance and declining cost of strategic offense and the resulting investment of both China and the United States in offensive capabilities compound their mutual vulnerability. Yet attempting to limit and reduce such capabilities through negotiated disarmament would not be fruitful. China will not negotiate away its hard-earned ability to maintain a credible retaliatory nuclear force, and antisatellite and computer network attack capabilities do not lend themselves to meaningful or verifiable limits and reduction. With both defense and traditional arms control being so unpromising, vulnerability will have to be mitigated by mutual deterrence—better yet, by agreed and institutionalized mutual strategic restraint.

Despite great differences in the circumstances, the way U.S.-Soviet nuclear peace was kept during the Cold War offers a starting point for how the United States and China can manage their growing mutual strategic vulnerabilities. A wider application of mutual deterrence to Sino-U.S. strategic relations is not without complications: although mutual nuclear deterrence is straightforward, deterring attacks on satellites and even more so on computer networks is different, conceptually and technically. How mutual deterrence and restraint apply across the domains will vary as much as the domains do.

Again, the stakes in Sino-American strategic relations are not ideological or existential, as those in the U.S.-Soviet relationship were. Therefore, the danger of actual strategic strikes by either against the other is less acute, at least in the nuclear domain. Moreover, while interdependence makes China and the United States more vulnerable, it also gives them both reasons not to harm the other's well-being and thereby their own. For instance, China's trade and financial interests would suffer badly from the loss of U.S. satellites or critical U.S. computer networks. Thus, deterrence by threat of retaliation could be reinforced by the risks of self-inflicted harm.[13]

Just as cooperative aspects of Sino-American relations could help mitigate strategic vulnerabilities, failure to mitigate those vulnerabilities could disturb those relations. The risks and fears of new forms of U.S. and Chinese strategic power and of unmitigated vulnerability could make it harder for the world's two leading powers to work together. China could calculate that one or more forms of strategic offensive power could offset U.S. conventional military advantages and thus reduce its susceptibility to coercion, defeat, and humiliation. At the same time, the United States could come to rely increasingly on strategic escalation to ensure deterrence as China increases its military capabilities and its boldness in East Asia.

Thus, it cannot be assumed that mutual strategic restraint will happen spontaneously as conditions of mutual deterrence are met. It will come about only through Sino-American dialogue about vulnerabilities, capabilities, and intentions. It could take years before a dialogue bears fruit: even with shared awareness of the need for prudence, common assessments, concepts, and vocabularies will be needed before substantial accords can be reached. Meanwhile, new offensive capabilities are being developed, increasing vulnerabilities. So the process should begin now. Washington appears to have reached that conclusion. Whether Beijing has is unclear.

Issues and Analytic Approach

In sum, growing strategic vulnerabilities of the United States and China, given the dominance of offense over defense and the declining costs of attack, suggest that mutual strategic restraint is an important goal. But the path to that goal is paved with quandaries and risks. The chapters that follow will address these quandaries and risks, pointing to specific terms for mutual restraint in all three strategic domains as the book unfolds.

Because restraint in using strategic power must be reciprocal, the first hurdle is that the United States and China both must accept it. Divergent interests and competitive impulses in Sino-American relations are strong enough that whatever arrangements one side might judge to be advantageous, the other might suspect. If, for example, the Americans fear that China aims to dominate the western Pacific, and the Chinese fear that the United States aims to control their freedom of action in the region and their access beyond it, one or the other could be concerned that restraint at the strategic level might embolden the other to risk conflict below that level. The Americans may be hesitant to relieve Chinese fears of nuclear escalation, and the Chinese may be reluctant to relieve American fears of war in space or cyberspace.

As the established power with superior strategic offensive capabilities, the United States theoretically stands to lose more than China by excluding their use. U.S. strategic advantages give it the potential for so-called escalation dominance: the upper hand in a crisis or conflict by virtue of having less to lose from escalation than the adversary does. Weighed against this is the growing U.S. vulnerability, in absolute terms, to Chinese strategic offensive capabilities, and the prospect that escalation could cause great harm to the United States, irrespective of the harm it also causes China. This dilemma is addressed in chapter two, which examines U.S. views on China, Sino-American relations, the role of force, global security challenges, and long-term interests in East Asia.

China has a different calculus. It is presently at a disadvantage in strategic offensive power and also is increasingly vulnerable. Therefore, in theory, it stands to gain by mutual strategic restraint. Yet facing U.S. conventional military superiority, the Chinese may believe that they can exploit U.S. fears of strategic hostilities in space and cyberspace. Therefore, China might want to preserve its freedom of action and give the United States reason to fear escalation. On the other hand, with the United States preoccupied with threats elsewhere (such as terrorism), and with trends in the East Asian conventional military balance starting to favor China, mutual strategic restraint could prove advantageous for China, perhaps enabling it to dominate the region or at least to settle territorial disputes on its terms. Chapter three examines how the Chinese could weigh these factors in the context of Sino-U.S. and regional relations; it also examines how the views of China's politicians and military could differ, while lacking the experience and mechanisms that the United States has to reconcile those views.

Chapters four, five, and six analyze how the concept of mutual strategic restraint might apply in the three domains. The answers depend in part on whether mutual deterrence, which assured Soviet-U.S. nuclear peace, can apply to space and cyberspace. On this, it is important to distinguish between nuclear deterrence, as practiced during the Cold War and since, and the deeper logic of deterrence that, although crystallized by the arrival of nuclear weapons, dealt with transcendent observations about human rationality in the face of danger.[14] The core idea, that fear of retaliation may be the best way to avoid the use of strategic weapons when defense is futile, is not peculiar to the nuclear domain. Forms of deterrence not only apply but also are needed in space and cyberspace, given offense dominance and the declining costs of attack. Chapters four, five, and six develop these ideas in the three domains of Sino-American strategic relations.

Even if the United States cannot deny China the ability to deter a U.S. nuclear attack, it could be risky for the United States formally to accept mutual nuclear deterrence at a time when the conventional military balance in East Asia is starting to tilt in China's favor. However, the United States has little chance of getting the Chinese to accept restraint in space and cyberspace if it will not do so in the nuclear domain.

The surest way of mitigating U.S. and Chinese vulnerability in space is through mutual restraint, founded on deterrence. Yet hostilities between Chinese and U.S. conventional forces cannot be ruled out; indeed, the potential for such conflict is one of the main reasons for concern about escalation to strategic domains. The fact that satellites play an increasingly critical role in military operations, especially for U.S. forces but increasingly for the PLA as well, raises a serious question: is Sino-American mutual restraint in space possible if one or both sides want to retain the option of disabling satellites that support combat against their forces? What complicates this is that many satellites that support military operations also perform important economic functions, leaving no sharp firebreak between the tactical and the strategic.

There are even higher hurdles to the pursuit of mutual restraint in cyberspace. Attacks on networks that enable opposing military forces to perform their missions can escalate rapidly and unpredictably into full-scale cyber war, with enormous damage to the U.S., Chinese, and world economies. Yet it is unrealistic to expect military forces not to attack networks used by the adversary to target and strike their forces. This might imply that Sino-American acceptance of restraint in cyber warfare would apply only when the countries are at peace; but this would fail to address the fact that the most likely scenario for general cyber war is via escalation from tactical-military cyber war.

While chapter four finds that neither country is interested in using nuclear weapons for warfighting, chapters five and six find that attacking satellites and computer networks may have warfighting utility. Yet the dangers in those domains of strategic escalation and harm to both nations are clear. This tension between military-operational necessity and national-strategic risk is an analytic conundrum and potential impediment to mutual strategic restraint. It may create tension between the needs of military commanders and the fears of national leaders in both China and the United States.

If warfighting utility is the greatest obstacle to mutual strategic restraint, the greatest risk may be that removing the danger of escalation to conflict in any or all of these strategic domains could weaken deterrence and make at least East Asia "safer" for the use or threat of conventional military force, particularly by China. Of special concern is the potential for conflict over Taiwan. Even if China is unlikely to use or threaten force in East Asia, Japan and South Korea might feel that the combination of declining U.S. conventional superiority and mutual strategic restraint could shift the region's power-political balance toward China. This could disturb the equilibrium that the United States has sought for a century to preserve in this vital region. Chapter seven assesses the risks of conflict and instability resulting from strategic decoupling, how to mitigate such risks, and how to weigh them against the benefits of mutual strategic restraint.

Chapter seven also integrates the three strategic domains. China may see much to gain by locking the United States into mutual nuclear deterrence and no first use. But Chinese military commanders may believe that locking themselves into similar restraint in space and cyberspace is unwise. U.S. leaders may take the opposite view. Consequently, from a U.S. vantage point, it is advisable to link these domains as part of a general understanding on mutual strategic restraint.

Finally, chapters seven and eight suggest practical steps that the United States and China can take to converge on the goal of mutual strategic restraint, build confidence that each is committed to that goal, and avoid miscalculation. Chapter eight also examines what could happen if China and the United States do not adopt mutual strategic restraint, as well as whether such restraint would hold up if technology makes strategic defense more promising. It concludes by suggesting questions in need of further study.

It could take years before the world's two strongest powers, each with its own experience and outlook, are both ready to seize the advantages, adopt the terms, and manage the risks associated with strategic restraint. This book is not meant to be the final word on this idea. Rather, it is intended to inform a journey that the United States and China must take together because of their common interests and despite their differences.

Notes

   [1] Other, "softer" dangers, such as environmental damage, disrupted energy supplies, and turmoil in financial markets, are also exacerbated by interdependence but lie outside the scope of this study.

   [2] Russia, for instance, is showing renewed interest in nuclear weapons and unabashed enthusiasm for cyber weapons as its inferiority to U.S. conventional military strength grows. In China's case, the appeal of asymmetric capabilities could work against acceptance of restraint in space and cyberspace.

[3] While capable of conducting sophisticated cyber attacks and of developing antisatellite (ASAT) weapons, Russia lacks the resources and technological depth to match China. This is not to say that principles of mutual restraint cannot prevail in Russian-American (or Sino-Russian) strategic relations—a possibility that is touched on but not developed in this study.

[4] Another view of what is driving Sino-American relations can be found in Charles Glaser, "Will China's Rise Lead to War?" *Foreign Affairs* 90, no. 2 (March–April 2011). It argues that even the "realist" view of Sino-American relations does not necessarily imply a likelihood of conflict because the current international system, more than that of the past, provides constraints on the use of power and mechanisms for resolving disputes peacefully. This view would seem consistent with the idea that China and the United States could agree on mutual strategic restraint.

[5] The goal of dissuading China from attempting to compete strategically with the United States was pronounced early in the administration of George W. Bush. However, China's increased allocation of resources for military capabilities in the ensuing years suggests that the Chinese were determined to become more, not less, prepared for the contingency of conflict with the United States.

[6] As one of our Chinese interlocutors said, if the United States is seen as keen on certain capabilities, China will more likely than not emulate the United States, even if it is not sure how it would use the capabilities.

[7] For a primer on understanding of the effects of nuclear war, including single weapons, we recommend Hans M. Kristensen, Robert S. Norris, and Matthew G. McKinzie, "Simulated U.S. and Chinese Nuclear Strikes," in *Chinese Nuclear Forces and U.S. Nuclear War Planning* (Washington, DC: Federation of American Scientists and Natural Resources Defense Council, November 2006), 173–196.

[8] Missile defenses might still have some value in limiting damage in a nuclear conflict, but such dire circumstances would constitute a failure of both deterrence and policy.

[9] Thanks to Martin Libicki of RAND for sharing this assessment.

[10] Targeting depends on wide-area, high-resolution, and continuous sensing, on rapid data processing, on tracking, and on sharing target data among sensors and "shooters." The cost performance of these capabilities has improved and should continue to improve as microelectronics and digital networking do. Consequently, those being targeted must rely increasingly on interference, hiding, deception, and mobility, involving considerable cost, operational inconvenience, and mixed results. It is unlikely that targeting improvements will be reversed in the next decade with known technology.

[11] Department of Defense, *Nuclear Posture Review* (Washington, DC: Department of Defense, 2010).

[12] This discounts possible casualties resulting indirectly from the disruption of services—for example, health and public safety—caused by cyber or satellite attack.

[13] In addition to the disruption of space-based and other networks of common interest to the United States and China, space debris from ASAT could be harmful to all spacefaring nations.

[14] Thomas Schelling, in particular, applied game theory and other economic analysis to the particular (and pressing) problems of avoiding nuclear war and managing nuclear crises. But his reasoning could apply to any dreadful weapons in opposing hands against which defense is difficult, leaving fear of retaliation as the best way to avoid the harm from their use out of proportion with the matter in dispute. The right question is not whether space and cyberspace fit the nuclear deterrence case but how the general theory applies to those cases. In an excellent summary of lessons learned in a recent U.S. wargame involving deterrence in space and cyberspace, then–Maj Gen Susan Helms, USAF, writes: "Nuclear deterrence concepts that worked very well during the Cold War and still work extremely well today do not always translate in practice to the space and cyber domains. At the same time, the fundamental behavioral principles on which classical deterrence theory is based are still valid when applied to the nuclear as well as cyber and space domains." "Schriever Wargame 2010: Thoughts on Deterrence in the Non-Kinetic Domain," *High Frontier* 7, no. 1 (November 2010).

Chapter Two

U.S. Views on Strategic Power, Vulnerability, and Restraint

The U.S. attitude toward the idea of mutual strategic restraint with China will reflect U.S. views on China and Sino-American relations, on the use of force in general, and on nuclear weapons, space, and cyberspace in particular. This chapter analyzes these views and draws conclusions about whether the United States could accept limits on its strategic freedom of action contingent on Chinese reciprocity. It also examines whether and how tensions between military-operational and national-strategic objectives could complicate U.S. views on mutual restraint.

At one level, U.S. policy on strategic matters is literally an open book. In the year or so prior to this study, the U.S. Government issued the *National Security Strategy, Quadrennial Defense Review, Nuclear Posture Review, National Space Policy of the United States of America,* and *Cyberspace Policy Review.* Very broadly speaking, these documents reflect U.S. preoccupation with the threat of violent extremism, counterinsurgency campaigns in Iraq and Afghanistan, and turmoil throughout the Middle East and South Asia. China has not been the center of U.S. strategic attention—the proverbial elephant in the corner of the room. It is depicted as a rising giant to be engaged, not an adversary to be countered. If there is a common theme to U.S. policy statements, it is that the United States wants to meet global challenges in partnership with others, including "new centers of power," among which China looms largest.

Current U.S. Views on China and Sino-American Relations

Most Americans would agree that forging a stable and productive relationship with China is as important as any foreign policy challenge for generations to come—a challenge that calls for a combination of accepting the reality of Chinese power, discouraging its irresponsible use (as defined by the United States), and safeguarding U.S. interests and friends in East Asia. The possibility of armed conflict with China appears remote, especially with recent improvement in China-Taiwan ties. The United States is preoccupied with more pressing security problems and more likely contingencies: wars in Iraq and Afghanistan, terrorist attacks on the United States, dangers within and surrounding Pakistan, the prospect that North Korea and Iran will both be able to deliver nuclear weapons to the United States and its allies in a few years, and Mexico's deadly battle with drug cartels, to name a few. These external dangers compete on the national agenda with the need to restore U.S. economic strength by balancing the Federal budget and creating jobs in the short term, and by overhauling national infrastructure and reinvigorating public education in the long term. With this agenda, the problem of Sino-American strategic vulnerability is not an urgent U.S. concern.

Strategic vulnerability must even compete for attention in Sino-American relations. Because of China's multifaceted power, spreading influence, and deep interdependence with the global and U.S. economies, Sino-American relations are exceedingly complex, far more so than Soviet-American relations ever were. The bilateral agenda is crowded enough without elevating the importance of strategic issues. Yet this is not necessarily deleterious to the prospects for mutual strategic restraint. The two countries now have an *opportunity* to set conditions for a stable strategic relationship that engenders mutual trust, obviates worst-case planning, averts costly arms races, fosters prudent behavior, prevents miscalculation, and reinforces the kind of relations the United States wants in general with China. Better to begin addressing these matters calmly in today's environment than to wait until conditions are less conducive or until strategic vulnerability and competition make it harder to discuss and set rules. This sentiment appears to lie behind Washington's call for a wide-ranging bilateral strategic dialogue to advance the goal of "strategic reassurance."[1]

Strategic matters aside, Sino-American ties are controversial in the United States because of frictions that accompany China's stunning growth and the complex interdependence of the two economies. Americans are concerned with China's failure to allow the yuan to appreciate sufficiently to remedy imbalanced trade, with unsatisfactory Chinese protection of intellectual property rights, and with an array of barriers to the immense and growing Chinese domestic market. As long as the U.S. unemployment rate stays high, China will be regarded, fairly or not, as the chief culprit. Add to this American disappointment with slow Chinese progress on human rights, especially the heavy-handed treatment of Tibet and religious movements, and China is gaining detractors on both the American left and right.

Yet both the political left and right also have interests in improved Sino-U.S. relations—the former to promote peace, and the latter to promote business. There is little stomach in the United States for trying to frustrate China's rise, encircle it with alliances and forces, or start a Sino-American cold war. Voices a few years back advocating that the United States seize the "unipolar moment," establish "benevolent hegemony," and contain China have been drowned out by pragmatic and broad opinion that the United States needs the cooperation of others, including China, to meet 21st-century challenges.[2] Of late, U.S. economic woes, combined with recognition that the Nation's prosperity is inextricably linked to the world economy, have settled the matter of whether the United States can or should try to command the international landscape and impose its will. Moreover, China's relentless growth, manufacturing prowess, and attendant demand for resources are increasingly shaping the global economy as well as the global ecology. In these conditions, theories of great sovereign states vying for relative power and hurtling toward conflict have become inadequate if not obsolete.

An adversarial Sino-American relationship, in President Barack Obama's words, is not predestined.[3] At the same time, China's increasing power and international influence, perhaps coupled with a mistaken perception of U.S. decline in the midst of the financial crisis, have translated into an increased confidence and assertiveness that are common among emerging great powers.[4] China is now energetically protecting and pursuing its national interests on issues ranging from sanctions on Iran and handling of tensions on the Korean Peninsula to climate change and coddling of Burma, Sudan, and other odious states. If China is now an American partner, it is hardly a malleable one.

Nonetheless, the emerging consensus view in the United States is that it is worth trying to obtain China's cooperation in tackling global problems while being vigilant toward Chinese misconduct, especially in East Asia. In essence, the United States is predisposed to Sino-American partnership, contingent on China behaving as a "responsible stakeholder" in the global system.[5] Coupled with awareness of national vulnerability, this predisposition is conducive to U.S. pursuit of Sino-American mutual strategic restraint. At the same time, uncertainty about how China will use its newfound power will cause the United States to approach Sino-American strategic relations warily and conditionally.

East Asian stability is of pivotal concern in U.S. considerations of its global interests, with Europe at last peaceful and the Middle East so unstable. It is easy to see how an increasingly strong and demanding China could destabilize East Asia but harder to envision how it could do so in other regions, which it can influence but not dominate. Indeed, it is in Asia in particular far more than in global affairs in general that Chinese and U.S. goals could be at odds, with China suspected by Americans of wanting to become the dominant East Asia power at the expense of U.S. influence and interests. The United States is determined to continue to play a prominent and stabilizing role in this vital region, but many Americans see China as wanting to marginalize the U.S. position. While it is possible to imagine an East Asia that accommodates both China's growing power and a robust role for the United States, Americans are not inclined to regard Chinese regional aims as benign, especially in light of increased Chinese assertiveness vis-à-vis its neighbors and U.S. presence.

From the U.S. perspective, there are three potential problems that China could create in East Asia. The first is the use or threat of force to gain control over Taiwan, or at least to pressure Taiwan into a union on Chinese terms. The second is Chinese use or threat of force to settle territorial disputes on its terms and to assert a privileged position, if not virtual sovereignty, in the South China and East China Seas. The third is that the relentless growth and extension of Chinese power, even if not misused, could destabilize the region, perhaps causing Japan to remilitarize, act unilaterally, and possibly acquire nuclear weapons.

The combination of a vital U.S. interest in the economic and political stability of East Asia and the potentially destabilizing effects of unchecked Chinese power will require the United States to maintain its regional military presence and security relationships. There is no strategic or political argument about this within the United States. Far from receding with the end of the Cold War, U.S. military activities and ties in East Asia have continued and expanded in some respects, largely in response to regional anxiety about China. It is a matter of simple geography that U.S. presence in support of its interests in a region of vital importance stands within waters that China believes are key to its security, continued growth, and future.

Unlike in the Cold War, U.S. and Chinese forces will increasingly occupy the same western Pacific space, each considering it to be strategically important and keeping a sharp eye on the other. Repeated U.S. efforts to engage China in sustained military-to-military dialogue and practical cooperation have been rebuffed or canceled in retaliation for U.S. arms sales to Taiwan. Prospects for cooperation instead of rivalry between U.S. and Chinese military forces are dimmed by PLA suspicion that the United States seeks to contain and encircle China. Under these conditions, the potential for competition, confrontation, miscalculation, incidents, and even hostilities in East Asia will condition U.S. attitudes toward concepts of strategic restraint with China. U.S. views toward China and competitive dynamics in East Asia make mutual restraint important but difficult to achieve.

U.S. Defense Attitudes and Efforts

The possibility of a U.S. military conflict with China may be remote, but outside East Asia, military conflict has been more common than peace since the end of the Cold War. The United States has been involved in five wars involving Kuwait, Serbia, Iraq, Afghanistan, and Libya. With the exception of the invasion of Afghanistan in the aftermath of 9/11, the United States entered or started these conflicts without having been attacked. It has organized and led international coalitions, some grand and some small. Major U.S. military operations in Iraq lasted 8 years, and in Afghanistan, 9 years and counting. (The other three ended quickly owing to decisive application of U.S. capabilities.)

A number of observations about U.S. attitudes toward force that bear on this study can be mined from this history. First, the United States is willing to go to war if its interests are threatened, even if it has not been attacked. Contrary to earlier conventional wisdom, Americans are not averse to taking—much less inflicting—casualties, and they have considerable stamina. Second, the United States is sensitive to both domestic and international political demands to act within multilateral coalitions, unilateralism having been discredited by the U.S. invasion of Iraq. Third, notwithstanding early difficulties adjusting to counterinsurgency (COIN), U.S. forces have proved very capable and have earned national confidence and international respect. No country wants to test U.S. expeditionary and strike capabilities. Fourth, the United States has threatened escalation to strategic warfare only when necessary to deter an enemy (Iraq) from using nonnuclear "weapons of mass destruction" against U.S. forces.[6] Fifth, and related, it is sufficiently confident in its ability to prevail with conventional forces that it has deemphasized the military value of nuclear weapons.

In the course and as a consequence of these wars, the United States has been spending nearly as much on defense as the rest of the world. It has military-technological supremacy, has forces hardened and honed by experience, is unrivaled in capabilities for regular warfare, and has sufficient conventional strike power to defeat any state. It has also expanded and improved its capabilities for irregular warfare, including large and superb Special Operations Forces. The U.S. military is in a league of its own in computer network–based command, control, communications, computers, intelligence, surveillance, and reconnaissance (C⁴ISR) systems, giving it both an advantage and a vulnerability. Although the emphasis since 9/11 has shifted from capabilities for decisive regular warfare to COIN, the United States is and will remain prepared for a wide spectrum of contingencies globally—as it must be, given the high uncertainty about what sorts of conflicts it will face and where. At present, there is a yawning gap between U.S. and Chinese military capabilities, especially in the ability to deploy and sustain combat forces far from national borders. While the United States expresses concern about China's military enhancement programs, U.S. investment (over $100 billion per year) in developing and acquiring improved capabilities is approximately 10 times that of China, which effectively assures stronger U.S. military capabilities for many years to come.[7]

Although the superiority of U.S. Armed Forces across a range of contingencies is not in doubt, three factors could affect their ability to respond to the growth in Chinese military capabilities in the western Pacific: downward pressure on U.S. defense spending, growing Chinese antiaccess capabilities, and higher U.S. priorities elsewhere.

The *National Security Strategy* issued in 2010 by the Obama administration makes explicit that U.S. security depends on the restoration of national economic strength.[8] Shrinking the Federal budget deficit will require some combination of politically painful cuts in domestic programs, entitlements, *and* defense spending. Pentagon spending, off-limits since 9/11, is now fair game. Even with reductions on the order of $400 billion over the next decade (as requested by President Obama), the U.S. defense budget would still be roughly three times more than Chinese official defense spending. However, with heavy demands of spending due to current operations and rising personnel costs, investment in major platforms and weapons systems—that is, increasingly expensive naval and air forces—are especially inviting targets. Thus, pressure on the Defense Department's budget could disproportionately fall upon capabilities of particular importance to countering expanding PLA capabilities.

The second problem in maintaining U.S. military superiority in the western Pacific is the growing difficulty of operating near China and its growing array of extended-range sensors and weapons. As will be covered in depth elsewhere in this book, U.S. strike forces that depend on aircraft carriers and air bases in the region are falling within range of Chinese short- and medium-range ballistic and cruise missiles. Increasing the numbers and improving the range and accuracy of these missile forces are high priorities in Chinese military investment, as are the extended-range sensor and communications systems that will enable the PLA to locate, track, and target U.S. forces far from China—potentially farther away than the range of U.S. carrier-based airpower. Of particular concern is the PLA's antiship ballistic missile (ASBM) with maneuverable guidance that, when supported by extended-range sensors, can potentially strike and disable U.S. aircraft carriers that would come to Taiwan's defense.[9] In light of these developments, a 2010 Pentagon report to Congress assesses the cross-Strait military balance to be shifting in China's favor.[10]

As China's short- and medium-range ballistic missile arsenal grows, the United States will find it difficult to defend and thus employ its surface naval forces and land-based air forces in the western Pacific. In parallel, the PLA is building a large attack submarine fleet and seeking capabilities to degrade the C⁴ISR networks that enable U.S. forces to surge and conduct integrated operations against China and its forces, which explains Chinese interest in the means to attack U.S. computer networks and satellites. What Chinese missiles, submarines, and network attacks have in common is that defense against them becomes less cost-effective as the scale and sophistication of offensive capabilities grow.[11] These developments will raise the difficulty, cost, and risks to the United States of intervening in the event that China attacks Taiwan. Finally, the PLA's strategy of striking suddenly and confining the conflict in time, geographic scope, and weaponry is designed to limit the ability of the United States to bring its full conventional power to bear.

The third factor contributing to the potential for military instability in the western Pacific is that China and the United States are both able to commit resources to countering the other's forces in the region in roughly the same volume. Given the size of the annual U.S. and Chinese defense budgets—about $600 billion and $150 billion, respectively—this is counterintuitive.[12] Even if U.S. defense spending is flat (in constant dollars) and Chinese defense spending grows by 10 percent annually, it would take about 15 years for China to close the gap in annual spending; by then, the United States would have outspent China on defense by a factor of 2 (roughly $12 trillion to $6 trillion), thus accumulating more capabilities.

However, unlike China, the United States must allocate its defense resources to meet *worldwide* security interests and responsibilities and must prepare for a full spectrum of military contingencies. Continued upheaval in Arab and other Muslim lands from North Africa to South and Central Asia, compounded by terrorist and nuclear proliferation threats, will likely keep those areas the main theater of U.S. defense. If the next two decades resemble the last two, the biggest claimant on U.S. forces and resources will not be U.S. Pacific Command (USPACOM) but rather U.S. Central Command (USCENTCOM). By a RAND estimate, of the portion of the Pentagon's budget that can be attributed to meeting global requirements, USPACOM demands account for about 20 percent, compared to 60 percent for USCENTCOM.[13] So great is the requirement for U.S. military capabilities and resources in the greater Middle East that even a 25 percent increase in capabilities for USPACOM in response to the growth in Chinese capabilities would result in USPACOM requirements still less than half those of USCENTCOM. And of course, the prospect of reduced overall U.S. defense spending on the order of $400 billion over the coming decade makes such a shift problematic, as long as Middle East unrest remains a major challenge.

In contrast, over the last 15 years, China's defense modernization has focused primarily on the need to develop weapons, doctrine, and training to counter a prospective U.S. military intervention in a conflict over Taiwan, with most other missions being treated as "lesser included cases." China's resolution of most of its land border disputes and improved relations with most of the countries on its borders have greatly reduced the potential for a major land war, a shift reflected in PLA emphasis on modernization of its naval, air, and missile forces. As a result, while the United States must prepare for myriad missions around the world, the Chinese military emphasizes building the capability to fight and win local wars, with a potential Taiwan conflict as the central focus. This is beginning to change somewhat as China's expanding national interests prompt a reconsideration of appropriate military roles, but most of the new missions being discussed (such as peacekeeping, humanitarian assistance and disaster relief, and noncombatant evacuation operations) do not require expensive new capabilities. (The exception would be if China decided to make a serious effort to contest U.S. naval dominance, which is unlikely over the next 10 to 15 years.)

Assuming the above spending projections, and assuming China does not seek to build large expeditionary forces for contingencies in other regions, China should be able to devote equivalent resources as the United States to military capabilities for the same region and the same contingency. Chinese defense spending is already at rough parity with USPACOM's claim on U.S. defense spending, and the former is growing rapidly, while the latter is not growing at all.

For all these reasons, it will be difficult for the United States to stop the erosion of the ability of its forces to prevail over Chinese forces near

China, especially in a conflict that follows the PLA's script of a brief, intense, and confined conflict. This puts pressure on the United States to consider its escalation options, both to strengthen deterrence and to frustrate the PLA's strategy of a short and confined war—pressure that could affect U.S. attitudes toward strategic restraint. While the United States is most unlikely to consider using nuclear weapons if conventional defense falters, it may be hesitant to say so lest it weaken deterrence by relieving Chinese fears of nuclear war. This may cause the United States to be reticent about acknowledging mutual nuclear deterrence or accepting mutual nuclear restraint.

Options to take out satellites and computer networks on which the PLA increasingly relies for targeting U.S. intervention forces will be of growing military interest to U.S. military planners. Even as U.S. political leaders may be interested in constraining China from attacking the United States in space and cyberspace, U.S. military commanders may be interested in enabling forces to attack the PLA in those same domains. This tension between tactical exigency and strategic caution will weigh on U.S. attitudes about mutual restraint.

Generally speaking, the United States tends to be coy about its military options, both to bolster deterrence and to plant doubts in the opponent's mind. Because of the wide spectrum of threats and unpredictability it faces, the U.S. military is disinclined to exclude options. This attachment to flexibility is an operational strength as well as a strategic one: whereas the Chinese want a conflict to go according to the PLA's blueprint, the Americans want to confront the Chinese with uncertainty about the direction a conflict could take and their ability to control and confine it. The U.S. preference to keep military options open and to be mum about plans may become even more evident as trends in conventional force balances tip toward China, perhaps causing reluctance to be specific about strategic restraint.

U.S. Attitudes and Policies Regarding Strategic Capabilities and Vulnerability

Guarded by two vast oceans, the United States has been the world's least vulnerable power for 200 years. Yet its citizens have experienced heightened vulnerability in the period of greatest American power. From 1950 to 1990, they lived in the shadow of Soviet nuclear capability to destroy their country, offset by their own country's ability to destroy the Soviet Union. For most Americans and their leaders, this vulnerability became increasingly abstract after the fears of the 1950s, culminating in the

Cuban missile crisis of 1962. Americans' sense of vulnerability returned abruptly on September 11, 2001, and since then, even failed minor terrorist attacks, such as the 2009 Christmas Day and 2010 Times Square scares, have heightened national anxiety.

Fear of the threat of terrorist attack has been accompanied by a general sense of increased U.S. vulnerability due to unprecedented exposure to the outside world: the spread of weapons of mass destruction and long-range ballistic missiles, infectious diseases, drugs, porous borders, international crime, and, of late, cyber attack. The perception and reality of vulnerability, despite unmatched power, could predispose the American people and their government in favor of policies designed to contain and reduce vulnerability.

U.S. strategic vulnerability, policy, and potential interest in mutual restraint vary from domain to domain.

Nuclear

In the words of President Obama, the U.S. Government is "taking specific and concrete steps to reduce the role of nuclear weapons while preserving [U.S.] military superiority, deterring aggression and safeguarding the security of the American people."[14] While this policy is allowed by U.S. conventional military superiority, it is motivated mainly by the objective of retarding the proliferation of nuclear weapons. Fundamentally, it reflects growing U.S. comfort with the idea that the sole purpose of nuclear weapons should be to deter the use of nuclear weapons—thus, that only nuclear retaliation is permissible.[15]

At this juncture, the U.S. Government is not prepared to declare universally that the "sole purpose" of nuclear weapons is to deter nuclear attack. But it has stated that it "will work to establish conditions under which such a policy could be safely adopted."[16] The United States also has proclaimed that a world without nuclear weapons is its ultimate objective. Because that world is such a remote possibility, U.S. goals, broadly stated, are twofold: further strategic arms reductions, and restraint in using nuclear weapons among those countries that possess them. In parallel, the U.S. military's interest in nuclear warfighting has waned since the disappearance of the Soviet threat to Europe. U.S. conventional capabilities now offer alternatives to using nuclear weapons for some strategic missions, potentially including long-range conventional strike options with extraordinary precision owing to advanced sensor and guidance technologies.[17]

Nuclear weapons do not figure prominently in U.S. thinking about war with China, as they did in regard to the Soviet Union, mainly because China is less threatening to U.S. vital interests than the Soviet Union was.

The 2010 U.S. *Nuclear Posture Review* (NPR) calls for "strategic stability" with China, as well as with Russia.[18] This could be read as acknowledgment of mutual deterrence with China.[19] This implied willingness to live with vulnerability to Chinese nuclear retaliation reflects a judgment that a U.S. nuclear response to Chinese conventional aggression is not needed and not a credible threat as China improves the survivability of its retaliatory force. Residual U.S. reservations about a universal nuclear no-first-use policy, according to the NPR, make no reference to China, which could be inferred to mean that the United States already recognizes de facto Sino-American mutual nuclear restraint and does not feel a need expressly to reserve the option of using nuclear weapons first against China.

The NPR's implicit acquiescence regarding China's nuclear deterrent has evoked no domestic public concern or political criticism. This suggests that the United States as a whole is not particularly troubled by the ability of the Chinese to deter a U.S. nuclear attack, given that the United States can be confident of its ability to deter a Chinese nuclear attack. Even as American concern has grown about improved Chinese military capabilities in the western Pacific, there is little or no apparent interest in relying on nuclear threats to deter Chinese conventional aggression.

The United States is much more concerned about Iranian and North Korean nuclear weapons, as evidenced by its development of a missile defense system specifically intended to block those threats. Although there is not unanimity in the United States that missile defense should not apply to China, the capabilities currently programmed will not be able to defend the country against a missile force of the sort and size China is committed to have, much less a force that China *could* have. This tends to confirm that the United States accepts mutual deterrence as the way to mitigate its vulnerability to Chinese nuclear weapons, even if it has not said so.

Space

While not a matter of great public interest, the U.S. Government is seriously concerned about the vulnerability of satellites, on which the country increasingly depends. The 2010 *National Space Policy* declares that "free access to [space] is a vital national interest."[20] Presumably, then, foreign interference with U.S. use of space would be considered a hostile strategic act to be prevented.

Given its stated expectation that space will be a "contested environment," the United States wants to make satellites more resilient and redundant, including the use of commercial and foreign space capabilities.[21] However, satellites are hard to defend and expensive to replicate. Therefore, deterrence figures importantly in U.S. thinking about how to mitigate vulnerability to attacks on satellites. In fact, the policy issues a thinly veiled retaliatory warning that "the United States views its space assets as a vital national interest . . . [and] will respond accordingly to attacks on them."[22] This posture is consistent with U.S. development and possession of an ASAT capability. While the United States does not preclude retaliating for a Chinese ASAT attack by means other than in kind, a reciprocal deterrence policy, as well as equivalent retaliation, has advantages of credibility, proportionality, and legitimacy.

Although U.S. policy calls for enhancing American advantages in space, it does not aim to deny others the use of space for "peaceful purposes." By implication, the United States does not rule out denying others the use of space for nonpeaceful purposes. Evidently, U.S. use of space to support military operations is deemed to be "peaceful," whereas U.S. adversaries' uses of space for military operations against U.S. forces receive no such benefit of the doubt. This implies that U.S. ASAT weapons could be used in wartime even in the absence of an attack on U.S. satellites—for example, if an enemy is using space nonpeacefully—and thus, not only for deterrence.

Generally speaking, because the United States relies more than any other country on satellites while knowing it cannot adequately protect them, it would prefer to make space a sanctuary from warfare. On this point, the *National Space Policy* is clear: "We believe it is in the interest of all space-faring nations to avoid hostilities in space." While it has not ruled out being the first to use ASAT weapons, the United States is clearly worried about the harm that could result from ASAT conflict and escalation. Of course, U.S. acceptance of mutual strategic restraint in space—implying a pledge not to use ASAT weapons first—would be in conflict with keeping open the option of halting an enemy's use of space for nonpeaceful purposes.

In no case is U.S. ambivalence about ASAT capability more apparent than in regard to China. In contrast to the nuclear domain, where new nuclear states are the main concern, China is considered the principal (and still growing) threat to U.S. satellites.[23] Yet China's increasing reliance on satellites to target U.S. forces and guide Chinese weapons in the event of conflict could cause the U.S. military to want to take out Chinese satellites, certainly if the Chinese had attacked U.S. satellites but perhaps even if they had not.

Notwithstanding some ambiguity and possible tension regarding ASAT weapons in U.S. declaratory policy, the overarching U.S. interest is to maintain its access to space, both in peacetime and wartime and for both military and economic purposes. Given China's development of ASAT weapons, the United States could find itself deterred from initiating attacks on satellites, even in hostilities with China. Presumably, it would have no inhibition in using ASAT weapons in retaliation for attacks on U.S. satellites; indeed, it has essentially warned that it might do so. Thus, U.S. interests might best be served by mutual deterrence and mutual restraint in space.

The same space policy statement also reveals the U.S. Government's interest in expanded partnership with commercial providers of space assets and services.[24] This implies that the United States has a growing stake in and commitment to the security of not only government satellites, but also all satellites that serve important national functions. Greater reliance on commercial providers to meet government needs in space also means it will become increasingly difficult to draw a line separating U.S. official use of space and commercial use of space. Thus, the absence of an escalatory firebreak in the event of ASAT weapons use could weigh in favor of U.S. support for mutual restraint.

Cyberspace

In no strategic domain is the United States more concerned about vulnerability and yet more vague about intent than in cyberspace. This is partly because U.S. capabilities, activities, and plans in this domain are secret for technical reasons. But it is also because the United States wants to keep open all its options, including offensive ones, but at the same time does not want to lend legitimacy to cyber war.

The President himself has declared that "America's economic prosperity in the 21st century will depend on cyber-security."[25] More specifically, according to then–Deputy Secretary of Defense William J. Lynn III, "Cyber-attacks offer a means for potential adversaries to overcome overwhelming U.S. advantages in conventional military power and to do so in ways that are instantaneous and exceedingly hard to trace. Such attacks may not cause the mass casualties of a nuclear strike, but they could paralyze U.S. society all the same."[26]

While the President has stated that protecting cyberspace will be a national security priority, Deputy Secretary Lynn correctly observed that "offense has the upper hand" in cyberspace. This implies that the United States must rely on deterrence to limit its vulnerability to attacks on important computer networks. The United States has stressed that retaliation for such attacks need not be in the form of reciprocal attacks. However, the threat and execution of equivalent retaliation have the advantages of credibility, proportionality (depending on scale), and legitimacy. Thus, if only as a deterrent, the United States should be capable of conducting substantial cyber attacks on a wide range of adversary networks.

In its clearest statement to date about its doctrine on cyber security, the U.S. Government has in effect equated cyber attack with physical attack—both potentially being an act of war. Consistent with this standard, the United States warns that it may respond with means of its choosing, which could mean conventional retaliation. This could be viewed as escalation (even though a cyber attack could actually do more harm overall). Therefore, the U.S. warning can also be interpreted to mean retaliation in cyberspace. Statements from Beijing depicting this U.S. position as dangerous indicate that the warning was heard and thus may be heeded.

Apart from deterrence, the United States could be interested in operations against foreign computer networks for several reasons: to gather intelligence, neutralize threats, and capitalize on an opponent's reliance on such networks in support of military operations against U.S. forces. This suggests an acute U.S. quandary akin to the one it faces in space, in which China again figures prominently. Former Defense Secretary Robert Gates surely had China in mind when he spoke of a "huge future threat."[27]

Given the difficulty of defending U.S. cyberspace against such threats, deterrence could be critical. Yet Chinese strategy calls for the PLA to rely increasingly on computer networks—"informationization," to use their term—to defeat U.S. forces, which impels the United States to consider initiating cyber war in the event of war. This places the United States on the horns of a dilemma: whether to threaten retaliation in order to deter Chinese cyber attacks, implying restraint in initiating such attacks, or to exploit its own prowess in these technologies for operational advantage.

Simply stated, the United States would like to have it both ways: mutual restraint in attacks on networks critical to the Nation, its population, and its economy, but without foreclosing military options to conduct and possibly initiate attacks. Put differently, U.S. interests would be optimized by being able to limit cyber war to the battlefield, thus advantaging U.S. forces in combat without the risk of escalation to the strategic level. While the U.S. dilemma can be stated simply, its resolution is exceedingly complex.

Differences in Civilian and Military Perspectives

Strong civilian control over the armed forces has been a constant throughout U.S. history, with the uniformed military as committed to it as their political superiors and the American public are insistent upon it.

Strong civilian control applies in peacetime, crisis, and conflict. Although forces and their commanders must be able to operate with flexibility and speed, especially in today's fluid and information-rich hostilities, war aims are set, plans reviewed, strategy approved, and risks weighed by the civilian chain of command.[28]

The well-developed principles and practices governing U.S. civilian-military relations do not preclude differences in perspectives on priorities, options, risks, targeting, forces engaged, and so on, within established intent and constraints. Though rarely public, such differences are to be expected. After all, the military has a professional and constitutional duty to advise policymakers, and their advice would be less objective, credible, and valuable if it was skewed to align with what policymakers already thought or wanted to hear. In addition, military leaders are obliged to provide unvarnished assessments and judgments of military matters to Congress, whether or not these converge with administration policies.

It is therefore not surprising that U.S. military commanders may have different perspectives than U.S. policymakers on necessary capabilities and preparations for military contingencies involving China. The commanders have been charged with deterring or defeating Chinese aggression at the lowest possible cost and without prejudging choices that are rightly the civilian leadership's to make. In view of what is arguably a worsening conventional military balance in the western Pacific, military commanders may be inclined to hold open (if not expand) escalation options, for deterrence or victory.

This is unlikely to revive the U.S. military's interest in fighting a nuclear war, but it could lead to a preference to wage war in space or cyberspace—if not as strategies, then as natural extensions of military operations. Given their narrower focus, commanders may be less sensitive than policymakers to the risks of national harm that could come from hostilities in these domains. Consequently, military leaders may be less inclined than political leaders to embrace mutual strategic restraint with China, particularly in space and cyberspace.

The U.S. military can be counted on to fall in line with civilian policy. But the civilians have to take operational military views and requirements seriously. If the admirals and generals advise that there are operational risks to foreclosing options to attack satellites and computer networks that enable the PLA to operate against U.S. forces, policymakers will need to be confident that such risks are outweighed by the risks of escalation. In the end, political leaders, mindful of the totality of national interests at stake, will have to balance the advantages of disabling satellites or computer networks that enable Chinese warfighting against the dangers that such attacks could lead to general war in space and cyberspace, where the United States is vulnerable.

The need to balance civilian control with military agility is especially critical during operations. In regard to nuclear weapons, civilian control has always taken precedence over military need. Only the President can order the use of nuclear weapons, whatever the conditions, objectives, or targets. An issue that civilian and military leaders must now confront is how tightly to control attacks on satellites and computer networks. Conflict in both space and cyberspace is highly unpredictable, so much so that attacks in these domains could be considered indiscriminate in their effects. This suggests that tight civilian control should also be exercised over such escalatory decisions or when civilian harm could result, even at some cost in operational agility. While this should be workable in regard to attacking satellites, it could be increasingly problematic as computer network operations for C⁴ISR become inextricably woven into the fabric of military routine.

U.S. Armed Forces already operate according to a paradigm that balances battlefield needs with requirements to avoid civilian harm and unwanted escalation. Authority to strike targets with weapons that could cause collateral damage is not delegated as freely as authority for decisions with purely military effects. Likewise, actions that escalate or could trigger enemy escalation are taken up the chain of command in proportion to the degree of risk. Decisions to use nuclear weapons are so fateful that only the President can take them. Decisions to use ASAT or cyber weapons may take if not Presidential, then at least high-level civilian, approval.

At the same time, the requirement for control needs to be balanced with U.S. military commanders' needs for operational and tactical flexibility, which will become increasingly important in the face of improving Chinese capabilities in the western Pacific. As protocols are set for managing conflict in space and cyberspace, differences between military and civilian perspectives on mutual restraint in these domains can and must be reconciled.

Without adequate controls, Sino-American mutual strategic restraint could break down in the event of conflict. Confidence in compliance with Sino-American understandings governing warfare in strategic domains, especially in space and cyberspace, may be more justified for the U.S. side than the Chinese one, where limits on the PLA's freedom of action are at least not transparent and at most not tight. An advantage for the United

States in engaging Chinese civilian and military leaders on matters of strategic restraint is to sensitize them to the importance of strict control.

Conclusions and Key Issues

In principle, the United States may be—in the authors' view, ought to be—ready to accept Sino-American mutual nuclear restraint if coupled with similar reciprocal restraint in space and cyberspace, depending on the terms. Doing so would serve U.S. interests in mitigating growing strategic vulnerabilities, in fostering a constructive relationship with China, and in enabling the United States to concentrate on various other national security priorities.

At the same time, the United States has many problems with China: unfavorable trade, exchange rate, and intellectual property rights; discord over global climate change; and disappointment with Chinese efforts to prevent nuclear proliferation to Iran and reverse proliferation to North Korea. Therefore, it will not want to become a supplicant for mutual strategic restraint, especially if China is resistant to the concept. Instead, the United States should call to the attention of Chinese leaders that strategic vulnerability is a shared and growing problem and offer an integrated framework for tackling it cooperatively and comprehensively.

If China proves to be interested in mutual strategic restraint, the United States needs to consider and manage potential implications for deterrence, military-operational requirements, regional stability, and security of allies. These concerns are neither unmanageable nor of an order that should keep the United States from exploring with China ways to avoid catastrophic conflict in strategic domains.

Overall, the United States is not in the mindset of regarding China's rise as necessarily coming at its expense, given its stake in China's economic success and its belief that it needs Chinese cooperation to meet its most serious security challenges, notably stemming nuclear proliferation and thwarting violent extremists. It also recognizes that such problems as the insecurity of energy supplies, climate change, and financial stability cannot be solved if the United States and China are at loggerheads.

While the United States can see how its own goals can be advanced by a productive relationship with China, it is less sure of China's goals, especially in East Asia. If and as threats to U.S. interests in the Middle East and South Asia subside, the United States can devote more attention to East Asia and China. Given its uncertainty about Chinese aims, how China responds to U.S. overtures of expanded military contacts and dialogue on strategic matters will have a major effect on U.S. policy toward China. In particular, if the United States advances ideas for Sino-American strategic restraint, a positive Chinese reaction would reinforce the U.S. predisposition to find common ground with the rising power. If China rejects such ideas, a more adversarial U.S. policy could emerge.

Notes

[1] James B. Steinberg, "China's Arrival: The Long March to Global Power," keynote address at the Center for a New American Security, Washington DC, September 24, 2009, available at <www.cnas.org/node/3415>; Al Pessin, "Gates in Beijing to Discuss U.S. Concerns about China's Military," Voice of America, January 8, 2011; "China-U.S. Joint Statement," January 20, 2011, available at <www.gov.cn/misc/2011-01/20/content_1789008.htm>.

[2] William Kristol and Robert Kagan, "Toward a Neo-Reaganite Foreign Policy," *Foreign Affairs* 75, no. 4 (1996), 18–33; Charles Krauthammer, "The Unipolar Moment," *Foreign Affairs* 70, no. 1 (1990), 23–34.

[3] "President Barack Obama at Town Hall Meeting with Future Chinese Leaders, Museum of Science and Technology," White House Press Office, 2010.

[4] China started taking increasingly assertive positions on such matters as climate change, financial stability, and economic recovery in 2009.

[5] Robert B. Zoellick, interview by the National Committee on the United States and China Relations, "Whither China: From Membership to Responsibility?" September 21, 2005. The Obama administration has not endorsed the "responsible stakeholder" term, but its approach is broadly compatible.

[6] Warning issued by U.S. Secretary of State James Baker to Iraqi Foreign Minister Tariq Aziz during Gulf War, 1990.

[7] Derived from a combination of Defense Intelligence Agency, Office of the Secretary of Defense, and RAND estimates.

[8] Lest there be a perception that the U.S. military will resist defense savings, Chairman of the Joint Chiefs of Staff Admiral Mike Mullen explicitly endorsed the idea that restoring U.S. fiscal balance is a high national-security priority. See Department of Defense, *National Military Strategy* (Washington, DC: Department of Defense, 2011).

[9] Department of Defense, *Military and Security Developments Involving the People's Republic of China* (Washington, DC: Department of Defense, 2010).

[10] Ibid.

[11] The offense-dominant nature of ballistic missiles and cyber warfare is addressed elsewhere. As for antisubmarine warfare (ASW), finding and tracking of submarines remain difficult in open oceans—even for the United States—though are less difficult in restricted, shallow, or coastal waters and going into and out of port. As China's submarine fleet grows in size and operates in significant numbers farther from Chinese ports, U.S. ASW will be hard-pressed to keep pace. The United States can counter this by expanding its own submarine force; however, U.S. (nuclear) submarines are much more costly than Chinese (mostly conventional-propulsion) submarines. See Andrew S. Erickson, Lyle J. Goldstein, Andrew R. Wilson, and William S. Murray, eds., *China's Future Nuclear Submarine Force* (Annapolis, MD: Naval Institute Press, 2007).

[12] *Military and Security Developments Involving the People's Republic of China*, 43.

[13] Paul Davis et al., *Developing Resource-Informed Strategic Assessments and Recommendations* (Santa Monica, CA: RAND, 2008).

[14] Barack Obama, "Statement on the Release of the Nuclear Posture Review," White House Press Office, April 6, 2010, available at <www.whitehouse.gov/the-press-office/statement-president-barack-obama-release-nuclear-posture-review>.

[15] In this book, a declaratory doctrine of no first use of nuclear weapons against a particular country is treated as the equivalent of declaring that the "sole purpose" of nuclear weapons vis-à-vis that country is to deter its use of nuclear weapons—the latter being an expression used in the 2010 U.S. *Nuclear Posture Review*. Both terms carry the implication that nuclear weapons may be used only in retaliation for nuclear attack (against oneself or one's allies). If there is a distinction between the two formulations, it would be that "sole purpose" is not an *obligation or pledge* but instead an *intention* not to use nuclear weapons first under extraordinary circumstances—for example, preemptive attack with knowledge that the adversary intends to launch a first strike. Because we mean no first use as an unequivocal pledge, we use that expression. The authors thank Elaine Bunn for drawing their attention to this possible misunderstanding.

[16] Department of Defense, *Nuclear Posture Review* (Washington DC: Department of Defense, 2010).

[17] For a thorough and balanced treatment of U.S. global precision strike conventional programs, see Elaine Bunn and Vincent Manzo, *Conventional Prompt Global Strike: Strategic Asset or Unusable Liability?* Strategic Forum No. 263 (Washington, DC: National Defense University Press, 2011).

[18] *Nuclear Posture Review.*

[19] We do not interpret the language of the *Nuclear Posture Review* regarding China as equivalent to acceptance of mutual deterrence. If that is what was intended, the document would have said it more clearly.

[20] William J. Lynn III, "Remarks on Space Policy," U.S. Strategic Command Space Symposium, Omaha, NE, November 2010, available at <www.defense.gov/speeches/speech.aspx?speechid=1515>.

[21] Ibid.

[22] Ibid.

[23] Gregory L. Schulte, remarks, *Securing Space Assets for Peace and Future Conflict* conference, National Defense University, November 30, 2010, available at <www.defense.gov/spr/docs/20101130%20 DASD%20Remarks%20on%20Securing%20Space%20Assets%20at%20NDU.pdf>.

[24] Ibid.

[25] Barack Obama, "Remarks by the President on Securing our Nation's Cyber Infrastructure," White House Press Office, May 2009, available at <www.whitehouse.gov/the_press_office/Remarks-by-the-President-on-Securing-Our-Nations-Cyber-Infrastructure/>.

[26] William J. Lynn III, "Defending a New Domain: The Pentagon's Cyberstrategy," *Foreign Affairs* 89, no. 5 (September–October 2010).

[27] Robert M. Gates, "Remarks at the Wall Street Journal's 2010 CEO Council," November 2010, available at <www.defense.gov/transcripts/transcript.aspx?transcriptid=4720>.

[28] The National Command Authority exercises control from the President through the Secretary of Defense directly to the combatant commander. The Joint Chiefs of Staff, including the Chairman and Vice Chairman, advise the President and Secretary of Defense but are not in the operating chain of command.

Chapter Three

Chinese Views on Strategic Power, Vulnerability, and Restraint

China's attitude toward the idea of mutual strategic restraint with the United States will reflect Chinese views on the United States and Sino-American relations, on the uses of force in general, and on nuclear weapons, space, and cyberspace in particular. This chapter analyzes these views and considers the circumstances in which China might accept limits on its strategic freedom of action contingent on U.S. reciprocity. It also examines civil-military relations and whether and how tensions between military-operational and national-strategic objectives could complicate Chinese views on mutual restraint.

Chinese Views on the United States and Sino-American Relations

China's approach toward international relations in general and toward the United States in particular rests on a foundation of higher priority domestic interests and concerns.[1] Many of these concerns reflect a sense of vulnerability rooted in China's history, geography, and the political relationship between Communist Party leaders and the people they rule. The failure of the Qing dynasty (1644–1911) and the Chinese republic (1911–1949) to modernize the economy and military had disastrous consequences when Western countries and an industrialized Japan sought commercial and territorial concessions. China's inability to resist pressure from superior military forces resulted in the loss of Chinese territory (Hong Kong, Macao, Taiwan, and parts of Manchuria), forced the Qing dynasty to grant extraterritorial privileges to occupying foreign powers, and eventually led to invasion and occupation of much of China by the imperial Japanese army. Karl Marx's prescriptions for economic development and Vladimir Lenin's diagnosis of the sources of imperialism contributed greatly to Marxism's appeal to Chinese nationalists who sought a way to revive and defend their country. The lessons Chinese elites have derived from this "century of humiliation" include the importance of economic development and a strong military for national survival, summarized by the goal of a "rich country, strong army." Chinese leaders also believe that domestic weakness and instability can invite foreign intervention. The PLA role in bringing the Communist Party to power (and in maintaining its rule against challenges such as the Tiananmen protests in 1989) strengthens the connection Chinese Communist Party (CCP) leaders feel between military power and domestic stability.

This interpretation of history is reinforced by security challenges imposed by geography and China's status as the last large, multiethnic empire. The People's Republic of China (PRC) covers a large territory that borders 14 other states and contains 55 different ethnic minority groups in addition to the Han Chinese majority. Many of these minority groups are concentrated in border areas in territories added to the Chinese state in the 19th and 20th centuries, most notably Uighurs in Xinjiang and ethnic Tibetans in Tibet and Qinghai provinces. China also regards the island of Taiwan as part of its territory that must eventually be unified with the mainland. China has resolved most of its land border disputes but has a host of ongoing maritime issues including disagreements with Japan about control of the Senkaku/Diaoyu Islands and the boundaries of their respective maritime exclusive economic zones and disputes with various Southeast Asia countries over control of the Spratley and Paracel Islands in the South China Sea. The disparity between the territories China claims and those it actually controls is a significant source of regional tension. China advocates a policy of peaceful resolution of international disputes, but Chinese leaders emphasize the importance of sovereignty and territorial integrity as "core interests" where compromise is impossible.

This rhetorical emphasis reflects fears of potential domestic political challenges. Chinese leaders prioritize the objectives of maintaining political stability and ensuring continued Communist Party rule. The 1989 Tiananmen protests, the subsequent collapse of communism in Eastern Europe, and the fall of the Soviet Union challenged the ideological foundations of CCP rule, even as the party was adopting economic reforms that emphasized the role of market forces and moving further away from socialist orthodoxy. As belief in socialist ideology has waned, the CCP has tried to build new sources of political support by raising living standards through rapid economic growth and by appealing to nationalist sentiment.[2] In recent years, development goals have been expressed in terms of building "a harmonious and moderately well-off society." CCP economic policies have been successful in producing rapid and sustained economic growth that has improved living standards and supported military modernization. However, this growth has been accompanied by a dramatic rise in inequality (both between coastal and inland provinces and between winners and losers from reforms) and widespread corruption. Legitimacy based on the ability to deliver rapid economic growth and improvements in living standards requires continued performance in achieving those goals; CCP leaders fear that an economic crisis or rampant inflation could produce challenges to their rule.

Appeals to nationalism as a source of legitimacy provide Chinese nationalists with an independent basis for judging the performance of Communist leaders in advancing nationalist goals such as enhancing China's international status and reclaiming lost territories. Taiwan's status as a territory outside PRC control, the Dalai Lama's role as exiled leader of the Tibetan minority, and the existence of numerous territorial and sovereignty disputes mean that outside actors can make statements or take actions that produce significant domestic problems for CCP leaders. (The reverse is also true—Chinese nationalists can take independent actions such as attacks on Japanese businesses that turn into foreign policy incidents that the government must manage.) This makes issues involving nationalism especially sensitive and difficult for Chinese political leaders.

The cumulative result of these historical legacies, geographical challenges, and domestic governance issues is a sense of insecurity and weakness, even though in conventional terms China's external security environment arguably has never been better. These concerns are aggravated by the fact that China's rapid economic growth—the foundation of the CCP's ability to sustain itself in power—has been achieved by integrating China into the regional and global economy in order to tap foreign capital, management skills, and technology and to access overseas resources and markets. China's reforms have been remarkably successful in producing rapid and sustained growth, raising living standards, and building China's national power. But these international connections also mean that China's domestic economy (and political stability) are now much more dependent on imported supplies of energy and raw materials and are affected by global economic developments that lie outside the control of Chinese leaders. Economic success has created new vulnerabilities and dramatically expanded China's interests outside its borders.

Throughout the reform era, Chinese leaders have focused on maintaining a stable international environment that supports China's economic modernization. This requires China to avoid a hostile relationship with the United States, the dominant power in the current international system and a country positioned to facilitate or obstruct many Chinese objectives. Given the high costs of confrontation, Beijing seeks stable, cooperative relations with Washington. Yet many Chinese elites believe that the United States seeks to subvert the Chinese political system and to contain China's economic and military potential. These concerns are partly rooted in differences in ideology and values that often lead U.S. political leaders to sympathize with Chinese political dissidents, criticize Chinese governance problems, and take actions that create domestic problems for Chinese leaders, such as meeting with the Dalai Lama or selling arms to Taiwan. They also reflect the legacy of ideological confrontation during the 1950s and 1960s, when the United States fought the PLA in Korea and led Western efforts to isolate and contain China. U.S. economic and military sanctions following the Tiananmen protests persuaded many Chinese leaders that the United States sought to challenge CCP rule by Westernizing and breaking up China. These concerns were reinforced by Clinton administration efforts in 1993–1994 to use renewal of China's most-favored-nation trade status as a tool to force improvements in human rights conditions and by the deployment of two U.S. aircraft carriers in March 1996 in response to China's use of ballistic missile tests to intimidate Taiwan.

At a global level, many Chinese leaders and analysts believe that the collapse of the Soviet Union produced an unbalanced world order (defined as "one superpower and many great powers") that left the United States unconstrained and able to use its unrivaled economic and military power to intervene militarily, violate the sovereignty of other countries, and strengthen the foundations of its global dominance. China's domestic weaknesses and inferior power position placed it in an uncomfortable and vulnerable position relative to the United States.

China has sought to deal with a powerful United States through several means. One is to build its own comprehensive national power (a composite of economic, military, and soft power resources) to increase its ability to resist U.S. pressure. This requires a focus on long-term economic growth while avoiding a confrontation with the United States. Aware of the potential for a dominant power to feel threatened by a prospective challenger, Chinese leaders have articulated the theory of "peaceful development" and sought to reassure U.S. leaders that China does not intend to challenge the U.S. position or seek major changes in the current international order. China's leaders hope to take advantage of the first two decades of the 21st century to build the country's comprehensive national power and improve its international position. "Grasping the period of strategic opportunity" sometimes requires Beijing to compromise with Washington for the sake of stable relations. However, China's nuclear capability limits the U.S. ability to coerce China and force concessions on key issues, and improvements in Chinese economic and military capabilities are strengthening China's long-term position relative to the United States.

A second means involves efforts to build positive relationships with current and potential great powers to deny the United States the opportunity to construct a coalition to contain China and prevent its continued rise. Most Chinese analysts see an inexorable trend toward a multipolar world order as established and emerging great powers improve their standing relative to the United States. The chief debate lies in varying assessments of U.S. power relative to other great powers, and the projected timing and impact of U.S. relative decline. By properly managing relations with established and emerging great powers, its Asian neighbors, and developing countries, China seeks to preserve its freedom of maneuver and prevent the United States from organizing its allies and other countries into an anti-China coalition. Within Asia, this has prompted Chinese military restraint and active (if not always successful) efforts to reassure Asian countries that a stronger China will not threaten regional stability.

A third means has involved Chinese efforts to build a stable partnership with the United States. In the aftermath of the 1996 Taiwan crisis, Clinton administration officials sought to work toward a "constructive strategic partnership" with China. President Jiang Zemin supported the effort to downplay bilateral differences over issues such as Taiwan and identify a positive bilateral agenda for cooperation across a range of issues. Reciprocal summit visits in 1997 and 1998 were used to articulate and advance this cooperative agenda, but U.S. domestic support for a partnership collapsed amidst partisan accusations of Chinese nuclear espionage and mismanagement of relations with China. By the 2000 campaign, candidate George W. Bush was proclaiming that the United States and China were "strategic competitors," though this rhetoric cooled as his administration sought Chinese cooperation in the wake of the 9/11 terrorist attacks.

Chinese efforts to build a stable strategic partnership with Washington have not succeeded, but Beijing has sought to develop and expand bilateral cooperation in areas such as responding to North Korean and Iranian nuclear ambitions, nonproliferation, energy, and counterterrorism. China's position as a veto-wielding permanent member of the United Nations (UN) Security Council and special relationship with North Korea make it an important player on many international issues. The U.S. need for Chinese cooperation on a range of regional and global issues gives Beijing leverage in dealing with Washington. At the same time, Chinese leaders have insisted on respect for sovereignty as a key principle of international relations and have not endorsed proposals that might reinforce U.S. long-term dominance.

A fourth means has been the deepening economic relationship between the United States and China. Trade and investment ties between the countries have been a source of stability in the relationship because they benefit key actors in both countries. The United States is China's largest single trading partner and a major market for Chinese exports. U.S. companies are an important source of capital, management expertise, and technology for China's economic development. In recent years, China has become a large purchaser of U.S. Government securities, holding more than $900 billion. Both the U.S. and Chinese governments have periodically sought to use economic threats and incentives as leverage, but economic interdependence has been an important source of stability in bilateral relations. (This interdependence was vividly demonstrated in 2008–2009 by the impact of the U.S. financial crisis on the Chinese economy.) The fact that politically influential U.S. economic actors have important stakes in China has helped Beijing manage its potential vulnerability to U.S. pressure.

The net result is a complex, multifaceted, and ambiguous relationship where substantial and expanding areas of cooperation coexist with ongoing strategic tensions and suspicions. China's sense of its room for maneuver (and potential strategic vulnerability) with respect to the United States rests on the global balance of power, the relative military balance, China's domestic political vulnerabilities at any given moment, and the "balance of need" in terms of which country needs the other more.

During the Obama administration's first 2 years in office, these factors have produced a negative dynamic in bilateral relations. Chinese analysts saw broad trends toward multipolarity and the diffusion of power reducing U.S. international dominance; many concluded that the financial crisis and U.S. commitments in the Middle East were accelerating the U.S. decline. At the same time, many Chinese believed that China's rising economic, political, and military power allowed it to be less deferential to the concerns of the United States and other Asia-Pacific states and to push its own agenda by calling for reductions in U.S. arms sales and political support for Taiwan and by taking a tougher line on maritime sovereignty disputes. These perceptions were reinforced by expressions of nationalist sentiment in the Chinese media (including a number of articles by retired PLA officers) that criticized any signs of compromise by Chinese leaders and called on the government to punish the United States for actions such as arms sales to Taiwan.[3]

These perceptions coincided with Obama administration efforts to expand the areas of U.S.-China cooperation and encourage China to take on more responsibility in addressing global challenges such as climate change, nonproliferation, and the stability of the international economic system. Chinese leaders likely concluded that these proposals—intended to increase China's stake and role in sustaining the current international system—were a reflection of American weakness and indicative of a shift in the "balance of need" in China's favor. Improved cross-strait relations, which reduced China's need for U.S. support in reining in possible Taiwan moves toward independence, were another factor in this assessment.

China's temporary shift away from its "charm diplomacy" and military restraint toward a more assertive posture in 2009–2010 alarmed its neighbors and revived concerns about a threat to regional stability. A more assertive China and a series of provocative North Korean actions (including a second nuclear test, the sinking of the Republic of Korea Navy corvette *Cheonan*, and shelling of Yeonpyeong Island) have reinvigorated U.S. security alliances with Japan and South Korea. They have also produced a broader demand in Asia for an enhanced U.S. political and security role in the region.

China's more assertive policy interacted with independent Obama administration efforts to make a "return to Asia." Increased U.S. high-level attention to Asia, modest adjustments in the U.S. military posture, and enhanced U.S. security ties with both formal allies and informal partners such as Vietnam, Malaysia, and India led many Chinese leaders, military officers, and analysts to conclude that the United States had intensified efforts to contain and encircle China. President Hu Jintao's summit visit to Washington in January 2011 signaled China's return to a more restrained regional policy and helped restore a measure of stability to bilateral ties and highlight areas of ongoing cooperation. Nevertheless, officials on both sides increasingly acknowledge the competitive dimensions of U.S.-China relations and have mutual concerns about each other's military modernization efforts, deployments, and activities.

This is especially true in Asia, which has become the focal point of Sino-U.S. competition. China disclaims any desire to dominate the region and touts its "win-win" regional policy, but the U.S. political and military presence in the region is an inherent obstacle to the exercise of Chinese power to pursue its outstanding territorial and sovereignty claims and increase Beijing's regional influence. Absent the U.S. presence, Chinese leaders believe that issues such as Taiwan would have been solved long ago. Moreover, China fears that the United States might use alliances and its naval power projection capabilities to launch attacks on China in the event of a military conflict over Taiwan. This has prompted PLA efforts to purchase and develop advanced weapons for antiaccess and area denial missions that raise the costs and risks of U.S. forces operating close to China.

China's regional goals and development of antiaccess capabilities challenge U.S. treaty commitments to its allies in Asia, which require the ability to project military power into the region.[4] China has looked to nuclear deterrence and methods for exploiting U.S. military dependence on space and cyberspace as means of redressing the current U.S. conventional military advantage. However, favorable trends (for Beijing) in the conventional military balance and China's "home field advantage" when operating near its territory may eventually shift this thinking and give China more interest in a strategic restraint regime that limits the U.S. ability to escalate a conflict into the nuclear, space, or cyberspace domains. China's efforts to develop a stable nuclear deterrent relationship and elicit a nuclear no-first-use pledge from Washington indicate that Chinese leaders can see value in strategic restraint.

Chinese Views on the Use of Force

At a diplomatic level, China consistently opposes the use of force or military threats in international relations and calls for peaceful resolution of international disputes via dialogue. These views are codified in China's advocacy of the five principles of peaceful coexistence: mutual respect for each other's territorial integrity and sovereignty, mutual nonaggression, mutual noninterference in each other's internal affairs, equality and mutual benefit, and peaceful coexistence. China opposes military alliances and overseas bases on principle and has advocated a "new security concept" for Asia "which focuses on enhancing trust through dialogue and promoting security through cooperation." Chinese officials contrast these ideas with an alleged U.S. Cold War mentality focused on military alliances and opposing blocs.

The diplomatic principles discussed above resonate with some strands of traditional Chinese strategic culture, specifically those derived from the defensive, pacifistic line of Confucian-Mencian thought. But some scholars have identified another strand of Chinese strategic culture with a hard realpolitik view that emphasizes seizing the initiative, offensive action, and preemptive attack.[5] One China expert argues that these two strands interact to produce "the paradoxical outcome of idealist, principled, high-minded logic (the Confucian school) combined with hard realpolitik security policies and regular decisions to call out the troops (the Realpolitik school)."[6] In practice, China often contrasts its "principled positions" on international issues with the self-interested motives of other actors, even though its international behavior usually reflects pragmatic decisions firmly grounded in Chinese national interests.

These tensions are partly reconciled by the Chinese preference for avoiding the use of force when desired outcomes can be obtained by other means. Chinese strategists and policymakers are keenly aware of relative power balances between countries and the military balance in specific contingencies. Their ideal is not to fight and win military conflicts, but rather to create a favorable military balance that places an adversary in an untenable position and allows China to obtain its desired outcomes without the use of force. As Sun Tzu said, "To subdue the enemy without fighting is the acme of skill." A more powerful China and a more capable PLA are better positioned to prevail militarily, but improved capabilities can also contribute to resolutions on Chinese terms without the threat or use of force.

The empirical record reveals a PRC willingness to employ force in a variety of circumstances, even against superior adversaries in situations where the overall military balance is unfavorable. In particular, PRC leaders have been willing to use force or military threats to arrest negative security trends or to warn neighboring countries to stop actions that threaten important Chinese interests.[7] One study identifies four characteristics of China's use of force: early warning for deterrence purposes, seizure of the initiative (including by striking first), risk acceptance, and risk management "through closely supervised rules of engagement in an attempt to control escalation."[8] Other scholars conclude that "the historical record shows a pattern of using force in a conflict to achieve surprise and thus administer a strong psychological or political shock to an adversary."[9] Most cases involving significant PRC use of force date to the prereform (1950–1979) period.

This pattern reflects the enduring influence of Mao Zedong's strategic thought on the PLA. Mao's core doctrinal principle was "active defense," which emphasizes offensive operations aimed at decisive engagements within an overall defensive strategy. Active defense "places utmost emphasis on gaining and retaining the initiative" and highlights the role of deception as a key means of gaining the initiative.[10] The PLA record of employing force, coupled with operational lessons derived from studying the Gulf War, has reinforced the emphasis on seizing the initiative through offensive

operations in the opening phase of a campaign and led some PLA strategists to advocate "gaining the initiative by striking the first blow." The initiative is especially important because PLA strategists envision modern
high-tech warfare in terms of a relatively short and lethal conflict. Their
doctrinal focus is on employing joint operations and precision strike capabilities to attack a superior adversary's high-technology capabilities, particularly his C[4]ISR capabilities.[11]

PLA thinking about how to fight and win a "local war under conditions of informationization" has been shaped heavily by studying U.S.
military doctrine and observing the experience of the United States and
other modern militaries in combat.[12] The need to plan for a potential conflict with the United States over Taiwan has focused PLA attention on
attacking U.S. C[4]ISR systems, impeding the U.S. ability to deploy combat
forces into theater by attacking U.S. logistics hubs and the computer and
communications networks that support them, and on developing or
acquiring advanced high-tech weapons systems that can force U.S. aircraft
carriers and aircraft away from China's coast. Key antiaccess/area denial
systems include *Kilo*-class attack submarines, *Sovremenny* destroyers
equipped with advanced antiship cruise missiles, advanced surface-to-air
missiles, long-range ballistic and cruise missiles that can target U.S. air
bases and ships, and the development of an ASBM that can target U.S. carriers. Even with the addition of these advanced capabilities, PLA strategists
still emphasize the importance of seizing the initiative and prosecuting a
short, violent, decisive war if China is to prevail over technologically superior U.S. forces.

Chinese strategic culture, the historical record, and PLA doctrinal
writings all highlight China's willingness to use force and to fight when
necessary. Yet China's increasing economic integration with the United
States, Asia, and other major powers has greatly increased the absolute
economic costs of a major military conflict (and the potential for serious
domestic instability as a result). This needs to be kept in mind when considering the impact of improved PLA conventional and strategic capabilities (which may reduce the costs and risks of limited military conflicts).

Chinese National Security Decisionmaking

PRC decisions about whether to use force are made at the highest
levels of the CCP in the nine-member Politburo Standing Committee, on
the basis of advice and recommendations from other organs of the state
(such as the Foreign Ministry), the military, and the party (including the
CCP International Department). Although the Politburo Standing Com-

mittee stands at the apex of the Chinese system and approves decisions on the most important issues, in practice, the formulation of options, recommendations, and lower level policy decisions takes place in other parts and at other levels of the system. The CCP monitors developments and theoretically ensures compliance via a system of party committees set up at each level of government (ministries, provinces, cities, townships, and so forth) and of military command down to the unit level.

In practice, decisions on important national security matters that cross bureaucratic lines get made at the highest level or do not get made at all. Policymaking and implementation in China take place within stovepiped systems with responsibilities for a specific functional area. Information and authority flow relatively easily within a particular system, but the flow of information across systems is limited, and mechanisms for interagency coordination and decisionmaking are relatively weak. This is especially true on national security and foreign policy issues, where the PLA, the Foreign Ministry, and the CCP International Department all report to different top civilian leaders and cannot be forced to reach agreement or implement decisions by actors in a different system.

Although the Chinese political system has become somewhat more responsive in recent years, CCP control of the media (and efforts to control information and especially organizational activity on the Internet) limits the influence of public debate, especially on military and security issues. The partial exception is nationalist calls for tougher policies, which contribute to a policy environment where compromise on international issues is difficult. The National People's Congress is a relatively weak institutional actor that responds to CCP guidance and does not effectively articulate the interests of Chinese citizens or businesses (especially where those touch on sensitive political issues). Chinese businesses have a variety of formal and informal means of lobbying the government to influence policy decisions at the national and ministry levels and policy implementation at the ministry and local levels.[13] Large state-owned enterprises (whose top managers are appointed by the CCP) have disproportionate access to senior political leaders and government officials.

The Chinese political system can have great difficulty reaching decisions on contentious issues, especially when powerful interests disagree on priorities and can enlist patrons in the CCP or government to argue their positions. When decisionmakers at a particular level can reach agreement, that compromise is usually adopted (sometimes producing incoherent and incremental policymaking based on the balancing of competing interests). When compromise is not possible, decisions are raised to a higher level for more senior leaders to consider.[14] Contentious issues that involve broad questions of competing priorities or competing interests of powerful actors can remain unresolved for years before formal policies are adopted. For example, Chinese leaders recognize energy as a critical issue for long-term development, but there is no separate energy ministry because powerful interests (including the state-owned oil companies) regard a separate ministry as a threat to their bureaucratic and economic interests.

Within the national security arena, China lacks an interagency body such as the National Security Council that can assess intelligence and other information; prioritize national interests across the security, military, foreign policy, and economic domains; formulate options for senior decisionmakers; and work to ensure implementation once a decision has been made. Instead, China uses a system of "leading small groups" that typically unite the senior Politburo Standing Committee members with functional responsibilities with the relevant senior state, military, and party officials. However, heavy responsibilities for standing committee members and senior officials mean that the small groups can only address a limited number of issues, and their ability to reach decisions and track their implementation is constrained. It is also worth highlighting that China's current top civilian leaders have little military experience or expertise and more limited ties to the military than previous generations of PRC leaders.

The Chinese political system has particular difficulty with issues that cross economic and security lines and involve questions about military, intelligence, or security issues where relatively little information about Chinese capabilities is available to the public. This includes the issues this book raises about strategic vulnerability, where military-operational and national-economic interests may be in tension. For example, telecommunications policy decisions involve the economic interests of the companies and ministries that develop technologies and operate communications networks, the interests of party and security organs in monitoring communications networks to collect information, military interests with respect to standards and the security of military communications, and the interests of end-users. This process has sometimes produced decisions (such as China's initial ban on the use of foreign encryption software) that favor the interests of the PLA or the security apparatus over the interests of businesses and consumers. The opaque nature of the Chinese decisionmaking system and lack of public information and open debate make decisions about military and security issues especially problematic.

With respect to decisions involving military, nuclear, space, and cyber issues, the picture is mixed. Chinese civilian leaders at the Politburo

Standing Committee probably set and approve the broad outlines of major policies in these areas, with the general secretary/president playing an especially important role on military issues in his capacity as chairman of the Central Military Commission. Decisions about whether to use force and whether to employ nuclear weapons would be made at this highest political level, albeit with military input. In the nuclear area, civilian guidance has clearly had a significant and lasting influence on PRC nuclear capabilities and nuclear strategy and established political constraints on the development of nuclear doctrine and training. The degree to which top civilian leaders are fully aware of the details of Second Artillery (the branch of the PLA that controls China's ground-based nuclear forces) doctrine and campaign planning (and specifically whether they endorse military thinking on issues such as preemption) is unknown.

In the areas of space and cyber policy, the PRC decisionmaking system is much murkier, partly because these areas involve dual-use technologies with a wide range of military, intelligence, and commercial applications involving a host of government and nongovernment actors. The military origins of the Chinese space program (including both the manned and civil space aspects) suggest that the PLA and defense industry exert significant influence on decisions in this arena. As in other parts of the Chinese system, the interests of producers are probably favored over those of consumers (for example, users of space systems and services). Secrecy about Chinese military and civilian cyberspace programs makes it hard to render a clear judgment, but there is good reason to suspect that the interests of the PLA and Chinese intelligence apparatus probably have disproportionate weight in policy on the employment of offensive cyber operations for intelligence collection and cyber attacks. However, other government and commercial actors have significant interests in the less sensitive area of cyber security, so a wider range of views may be represented there.

Nuclear

China's initial quest for a nuclear weapons capability was motivated by recognition of their political value and by Mao Zedong's determination to remove China's vulnerability to nuclear blackmail, which had been a factor in several crises involving the United States.[15] China's senior political and military leaders have consistently emphasized that the principal utility of nuclear weapons lies in deterring a nuclear attack and countering nuclear coercion.[16] Although Chinese leaders believe that possession of nuclear weapons bestows international status, they do not believe that more warheads increase a state's power or status. Unlike U.S. and Soviet strategists who focused heavily on the potential impact of relative capabilities in nuclear warfighting scenarios, Chinese leaders appear to have concluded that one or a few nuclear weapons striking an adversary's homeland would constitute unacceptable damage, making a large arsenal unnecessary to achieve the desired strategic effects. Following its first nuclear test in 1964, Beijing announced that it would adhere to a policy of no first use of nuclear weapons and called for worldwide nuclear disarmament.

Western analysts have described China's nuclear strategy as a "minimum deterrent" that relies on a small number of nuclear weapons to deliver punitive countervalue responses to an adversary's first strike.[17] *Minimum deterrence* refers to "threatening the lowest level of damage necessary to prevent attack, with the fewest number of nuclear weapons possible."[18] China's choice of minimum deterrence was influenced by technological constraints on its nuclear arsenal and delivery systems but was also heavily shaped by the views of senior political leaders (especially Mao), which have had an enduring influence on PRC nuclear doctrine. Chinese leaders did not dictate a specific number of nuclear weapons; nuclear forces appear to have been sized based on the need for a few weapons to survive a first strike, penetrate missile defenses, and deliver a retaliatory attack destructive enough to deter a nuclear attack on China.

China's 2006 *Defense White Paper* provides a concise overview of the key elements of China's "self-defensive" nuclear strategy:

> Its fundamental goal is to deter other countries from using or threatening to use nuclear weapons against China. China remains firmly committed to the policy of no first use of nuclear weapons at any time and under any circumstances. It unconditionally undertakes not to use or threaten to use nuclear weapons against non-nuclear-weapon states or nuclear-weapon-free zones, and stands for the comprehensive prohibition and complete elimination of nuclear weapons. China upholds the principles of counterattack in self-defense and limited development of nuclear weapons, and aims at building a lean and effective nuclear force capable of meeting national security needs. It endeavors to ensure the security and reliability of its nuclear weapons and maintains a credible nuclear deterrent force. China's nuclear force is under the direct command of the Central Military Commission (CMC). China exercises great restraint in developing its nuclear force. It has never entered into and will never enter into a nuclear arms race with any other country.[19]

This description highlights key elements of China's nuclear strategy and policy, including the goals of deterrence, the prevention of nuclear coercion, and eventual elimination of nuclear weapons; a no-first-use policy; and China's explicit determination (which dates from the beginning of its nuclear weapons program) not to engage in nuclear arms races.

In terms of doctrine, a no-first-use policy implies an operational focus on retaliatory counterattack, or "striking after the enemy has struck." In terms of force structure, "limited development of nuclear weapons" and a "lean and effective nuclear force" do not translate directly into requirements for specific numbers of nuclear weapons and delivery systems. Rather, they suggest that the quantitative requirements for a "lean and effective" nuclear force will depend on the ability of Chinese nuclear forces to survive a potential adversary's nuclear first strike via some combination of mobility, dispersal, camouflage, and operational resilience and then to launch a retaliatory strike that can penetrate an adversary's missile defenses and inflict unacceptable damage. Chinese nuclear force requirements thus depend significantly on the intelligence, conventional precision strike, nuclear strike, antisubmarine warfare, and missile defense capabilities of potential adversaries. China's nuclear forces are not solely focused on the United States, but U.S. capabilities (and potential future advances) in these areas make it a key driver of Chinese force structure.

One distinctive aspect of Chinese nuclear thinking is the concept of counter–nuclear deterrence. This is described as "an operation used to demonstrate China's resolve and will to use nuclear weapons in response to efforts by adversaries to coerce China with nuclear threats."[20] Counterdeterrence operations involve efforts to communicate China's will and resolve to respond to a nuclear attack in order to signal that China cannot be coerced by nuclear threats and to reinforce deterrence.

The development of China's nuclear forces is broadly compatible with the thinking of Chinese top political leaders (especially Mao and Deng) described above. Technological limitations meant that the Chinese deterrent initially relied primarily on air-delivered weapons and then on vulnerable silo- and cave-based missiles. Chinese experts privately admitted that the credibility of China's deterrent rested on a potential adversary's uncertainty about whether a first strike could destroy all of China's long-range nuclear missiles. Ambiguity about the total size of its nuclear arsenal was therefore viewed as an important element of China's deterrent capability. Rather than build large numbers of highly vulnerable first-generation missiles, China decided in the late 1970s and early 1980s to develop a second generation of mobile land- and sea-based missiles that would be more survivable and better able to provide a credible second-strike capability. As these new systems began nearing deployment in the late 2000s, U.S. withdrawal from the Anti-Ballistic Missile Treaty and deployment of ballistic missile defenses challenged the premises behind mutually assured destruction, prompting Chinese complaints that the United States sought "absolute security" for itself while keeping others vulnerable.

China's current nuclear forces consist of a mix of first- and second-generation nuclear missiles, with new DF–31 and DF–31A solid-fueled mobile intercontinental ballistic missiles (ICBMs) gradually being deployed to augment existing DF–5A ICBMs. China has also upgraded its regional nuclear deterrent with the deployment of the DF–21 medium-range ballistic missile (MRBM) to supplement first-generation DF–3 and DF–4 intermediate-range ballistic missiles. In terms of a sea-based deterrent, China's initial *Xia*-class nuclear missile submarine (SSBN) suffered from a troubled development process and may never have constituted a truly operational system.[21] China has already built two follow-on Type-94 *Jin*-class SSBNs and may ultimately deploy five of the submarines, which will be equipped with JL–2 submarine-launched ballistic missiles (SLBMs).[22]

The interaction between evolving U.S. military capabilities and China's nuclear modernization is likely to produce a significant expansion of the number of Chinese deployed warheads that can reach the United States. However, it is difficult to speak about the numbers with confidence because China provides no official data on the current or projected size of its nuclear force, the number and capabilities of its delivery systems, or its overall modernization plans. A 2010 Pentagon report estimates that China's current ICBM arsenal consists of approximately 20 first-generation missiles and 30 solid-fueled, road-mobile second-generation missiles.[23]

Most observers expect nuclear modernization efforts to produce both a quantitative expansion in the number of Chinese ICBMs and SLBMs that can reach the United States and qualitative improvements in missile capabilities. China's future nuclear forces are likely to include additional second-generation ICBMs and possibly upgrades to allow its first-generation ICBMs to carry multiple warheads. The Pentagon report notes that China is developing:

> a range of technologies to attempt to counter U.S. and other militaries' ballistic missile defense systems, including maneuvering re-entry vehicles, MIRVs [multiple independently targetable reentry vehicles], decoys, chaff, jamming, thermal shielding, and ASAT weapons. PRC official media also cites

numerous Second Artillery Corps training exercises featuring maneuver, camouflage, and launch operations under simulated combat conditions, which are intended to increase survivability. Together with the increased mobility and survivability of the new generation of missiles, these technologies and training enhancements strengthen China's nuclear deterrent and enhance its strategic strike capabilities.[24]

China's nuclear arsenal has remained small, consistent with its nuclear strategy, even as technical constraints on building a larger, more sophisticated arsenal have eased. But are China's nuclear doctrine and the Second Artillery training consistent with the publicly articulated strategy? Although the official campaign outlines and combat regulations for China's nuclear forces are classified documents inaccessible to Western scholars, enough internal doctrinal materials have become available to permit an assessment. Broadly speaking, doctrinal materials and published reports about Second Artillery Corps training are consistent with Chinese public statements about nuclear strategy such as the white paper quoted above. The principles originally articulated by Mao and Deng have continued to guide Chinese nuclear strategy and campaign planning even as technical and resource constraints on development of advanced nuclear forces have eased.[25]

Debates within the Chinese nuclear community have periodically challenged these principles. One discussion in the early 1990s considered a shift to a limited nuclear deterrent with a broader mix of nuclear capabilities that would support nuclear warfighting, but this debate concluded by reaffirming the deterrence and countercoercion principles that had historically guided Chinese nuclear strategy.[26] A debate in 2005–2006 questioned whether a no-first-use policy was viable given U.S. advances in conventional precision strike capabilities (which might target Chinese nuclear missiles) and missile defenses (which might intercept the limited number of Chinese ICBMs that survived a conventional first strike). Although China did not modify its official description of its no-first-use policy, subsequent statements by officials and military officers created a degree of ambiguity about whether a conventional strike against Chinese nuclear assets or command and control systems constituted a "first use" that justified nuclear retaliation.[27]

We know little about what China's top civilian leaders in the Politburo Standing Committee—the actors who would decide whether China should employ nuclear weapons—think about nuclear weapons use or the role of nuclear weapons in crisis situations. The fact that these leaders have little military experience and likely have not been exposed to academic thinking about nuclear weapons (and nuclear dangers) may be grounds for additional concern.[28] At the end of the day, Chinese leaders, like other leaders in other countries, are acutely aware of China's vulnerability to nuclear attack and are likely to be cautious in situations having the potential to escalate to an exchange of nuclear weapons.

Chinese Thinking about Space

Chinese thinking about space emphasizes its importance across a wide range of economic, scientific, and military applications. The 2006 space white paper lists the aims of China's space activities as being:

> to explore outer space, and enhance understanding of the Earth and the cosmos; to utilize outer space for peaceful purposes, promote human civilization and social progress, and benefit the whole of mankind; to meet the demands of economic construction, scientific and technological development, national security and social progress; and to raise the scientific quality of the Chinese people, protect China's national interests and rights, and build up the comprehensive national strength.[29]

The principles for development of China's space industry include "maintaining and serving the country's overall development strategy, and meeting the needs of the state and reflecting its will. China considers the development of its space industry as a strategic way to enhance its economic, scientific, technological and national defense strength, as well as a cohesive force for the unity of the Chinese people, in order to rejuvenate China."[30] These statements have been backed by sustained investments to develop and improve China's space capabilities in both the commercial and military realms.

The CCP has derived considerable domestic and international prestige from Chinese accomplishments in space, including its manned space program, scientific exploration activities, and willingness to share space technology and provide launch services and satellite expertise to other developing countries. China's official policy emphasizes the peaceful use of outer space and calls for a ban on the weaponization of space and negotiation of a legally binding treaty on the prevention of an arms race in outer space.[31] China and Russia jointly submitted a draft treaty to the UN Conference on Disarmament in 2008. The text called for a ban on objects carrying weapons in orbit or on celestial bodies along with commitments "not to station such weapons in outer space in any other manner" or to "resort to the threat or use of force against outer space objects." However, the draft treaty contained no verification measures and does not apply to Earth-based weapons that can attack satellites or their terrestrial support infrastructure, making it largely irrelevant to the goal of limiting the danger of ASAT attacks.

Chinese thinking has been heavily influenced by the study of U.S. space doctrine and how the U.S. military has used space assets in modern military conflicts, beginning with the Gulf War. Although the PLA does not appear to have developed and approved a comprehensive space doctrine, one PLA textbook proposes "unified operations, key point is space dominance" as a guiding concept.[32] "'Unified operations' refers to applying all types of capabilities, terrestrial and space-based, active and passive measures, hard-kill and soft-kill, focused on assuring that the PLA can derive and exploit space at times and places of its choosing, while preventing an opponent from doing so."[33] Space dominance requires the integration of space operations with those of other services and the integration and unification of various types of offensive and defensive space operations.[34]

The Chinese military discusses the use of space assets to support joint military operations in terms of "space support operations," which corresponds to the U.S. terminology of "force enhancement."[35] Space support operations make use of space-based platforms to provide critical information to ground, air, and naval forces, including space-based ISR, communications and data relay services, navigation and positioning, early warning of missile launches, and Earth observation.[36] China has significant capabilities in most of these mission areas and is likely to develop more sophisticated capabilities in the future.

One expert described the military impact of Chinese space capabilities in these terms:

> Increasingly sophisticated space-based systems expand PLA battlespace awareness and support extended range conventional precision strike systems. Space assets enable the monitoring of naval activities in surrounding waters and the tracking of air force deployments into the region. The PLA is investing in a diverse set of increasingly sophisticated electro-optical (EO), synthetic aperture radar (SAR), and electronic reconnaissance assets. Space-based remote sensing systems also provide the imagery necessary for mission planning

functions, including automated target recognition technology that correlates preloaded optical, radar, or infrared images on a missile system's computer with real time images acquired in flight. A constellation of small electronic reconnaissance satellites, operating in tandem with SAR satellites, could provide commanders with precise and timely geo-location data on mobile targets. Satellite communications also offer a survivable means of linking sensors to strike systems, and will become particularly relevant as PLA interests expand further from PRC borders.[37]

Although China currently lacks satellites to provide early warning and tracking of ballistic missile launches, the utility of this capability is discussed in Chinese military writings. If China intends to deploy ballistic missile defense capabilities (it conducted a test intercept in January 2010), a space-based launch detection system would be a requisite capability. China also employs a range of telecommunications and data relay satellites to support both military operations and civilian applications such as satellite television, Internet, and telephony.[38] China is developing its own global positioning system as well.[39] Navigation and positioning information is critical for a range of military applications, including to provide guidance and targeting information for China's growing array of precision strike weapons.

China is also pursuing efforts to deny an adversary's use of its space assets. Chinese military writings emphasize the importance of offensive operations to deny a superior adversary the ability to use space, but these are not limited to attacking systems in orbit. They discuss:

> a range of efforts aimed at affecting the range of space-related capabilities, from orbiting satellites, through space-related terrestrial facilities, to the data, communications, and telemetry links that tie all these systems together. . . . Space offensive operations include not only applying hard-kill capabilities against satellites, but also attacking launch bases and tracking, telemetry, and control facilities. They also discuss the use of soft-kill techniques, such as jamming and dazzling, against satellites, in order to minimize the generation of debris, and the attendant physical and diplomatic consequences. And they also will likely involve the application of cyberwarfare methods against the various data and communications links that transfer information and allow satellites to maintain their orbits.[40]

China has developed a range of capabilities that can potentially be used to target space assets and support systems. In addition to the direct-ascent ASAT system China successfully tested in January 2007, a Pentagon report notes that China has "a multi-dimensional program to limit or prevent the use of space-based assets by potential adversaries during times of crisis or conflict." The report adds that:

> China's nuclear arsenal has long provided Beijing with an inherent ASAT capability, although a nuclear explosion in space would also damage China's rapidly multiplying space assets, along with those of whomever it was trying to target. Foreign and indigenous systems give China the capability to jam common satellite communications bands and GPS receivers. In addition to the direct-ascent ASAT program, China is developing other technologies and concepts for kinetic and directed-energy (e.g., lasers, high-powered microwave, and particle beam) weapons for ASAT missions. Citing the requirements of its manned and lunar space programs, China is improving its ability to track and identify satellites—a prerequisite for effective, precise counter-space operations.[41]

Although some Chinese military experts advocate preemptive attacks on space assets to take advantage of U.S. dependence on them and seize the initiative in the fight for information dominance,[42] it is not clear that this argument has been fully accepted by the PLA leadership or endorsed by Chinese civilian leaders. Another strand of thinking emphasizes the importance of China having offensive space capabilities as a deterrent measure. This is partly to exploit the inherent vulnerability of costly space assets as a means of deterring conflict in the first place. However, some PLA writings appear to envision an escalation ladder that runs from testing space weapons, to exercising space forces, to reinforcing space capabilities (especially in a crisis), and to actually employing space forces. Demonstrating the capability and will to attack an adversary's space assets is described as the most credible form of deterrence.[43]

Other relevant aspects of PLA writings on space issues highlight a preference for "soft kill" (which temporarily or permanently denies use of space assets by means such as jamming, blinding, or cyber attack) over "hard kill" (kinetic attacks with the potential to generate significant amounts of space debris that might affect China's own satellites). Soft-kill attacks are seen as potentially more deniable and having fewer diplomatic consequences than hard-kill attacks, which may generate debris or involve kinetic attacks on facilities in third countries. Some writings by PLA authors also stress the importance of centralized authorization of attacks due to diplomatic costs and the potential for escalation.

PLA strategists see the U.S. military's dependence on space as a critical vulnerability that can be exploited by use of counterspace assets. However, the PLA also intends to take full advantage of the contributions space assets can make to its military operations, emulating U.S. military efforts to improve their capacity to fight and win an "informationized war." This will necessarily increase PLA dependence on vulnerable space assets. PLA authors discuss a range of "space defensive operations" to protect space assets and defend against attacks from space. These include the use of camouflage and stealth measures to disguise a spacecraft's functions, deployment of small and microsatellite constellations rather than single large satellites, maneuverability, capability for autonomous operation, and deploying false targets and decoys to overload an adversary's tracking capability. They also envision offensive operations by both space-based and terrestrial assets to protect space assets.[44] These tactics might have some value in protecting military space assets but would probably do little to protect civilian satellites. PLA space experts write that space dominance will be a critical and contested objective throughout a military conflict, with the PLA seeking to preserve the operational use of its own space assets in the face of attacks by an adversary's ASAT capabilities and to deny an adversary's use of its space assets.[45]

The relationship of the doctrinal writings described above to broader decisions about space policy is unclear. Chinese space policy involves a wide range of actors interacting in a complex policy environment. Key features of the process include top leadership involvement, the influence of elite scientists, coordination by leading small groups, and operational control by the PLA.[46] Even within the PLA, responsibilities are divided, and different organizations are vying for control of Chinese space activities. The China Aerospace Science and Technology Corporation and the China Aerospace Science and Industry Corporation are the two key state-owned research and development and manufacturing organizations, while the State Council's China National Space Administration coordinates and executes international space cooperation agreements.[47]

The General Staff Department, Air Force, Navy, and Second Artillery Corps are primary military customers for information derived from space-based assets.[48] Central government agencies, such as the China Meteorological Administration and the China Oceanic Administration, and large state-owned enterprises, including commercial telecommunications providers, are the largest civil and commercial users of space-derived data, but local and provincial governments and smaller enterprises are becoming increasingly important. Key applications include telecommunications, mapping and surveying, natural resource management, satellite navigation, and weather forecasting. The Chinese government's emphasis on commercialization of space technology is likely to lead to a further expansion of space-related goods and services, with applications centered on navigation and positioning data and on the use of geospatial data for mining and resource management being areas for future growth.[49] This diversification of space uses and space users is broadening the number of Chinese actors with a stake in continued access to space, though not all voices are represented equally in the Chinese political system.

Chinese Thinking about Cyberspace and Information War

The CCP, the government, businesses, and individual citizens have embraced the importance of the Internet and computer networks for a wide range of government, business, and entertainment applications. The CCP and the government use the Internet and various network-enabled communications mechanisms to distribute information and propaganda, receive feedback from citizens, and manage party members and officials across China's vast territory. Chinese businesses, especially those with international operations, use the Internet to deal with foreign suppliers and customers (and increasingly to solicit bids and manage domestic supply chains). Over 450 million Chinese citizens have at least some access to the Internet for news, communications, shopping, and entertainment applications.[50]

PLA leaders and strategists are keenly aware of the many military applications of information technology and networking and have closely observed U.S. doctrine and practice in these areas.[51] Much of the PLA writing and thinking about space and cyber issues is couched in the emerging PLA doctrine of informationization and reflected in the PLA's task of preparing "to win local wars under the conditions of informationization."[52] This focus derives from study of U.S. military doctrinal writings and operations, with the Gulf War being especially influential on PLA thinking. *Informationization* is a broad concept that applies to the increasing importance of information and information networks in the civilian economy as well as military operations. The PLA seeks to take advantage of the opportunities provided by networking, but its doctrinal focus on information warfare and information dominance also seeks to exploit adversary vulnerabilities by attacking their information systems. Jiang Zemin endorsed the objective of informationizing weapons as early as 2000, and the concept subsequently has been formally studied, debated, and incorporated in PLA doctrinal materials, textbooks, operations regulations, and training guidance.[53]

A PLA textbook states that the goal of information warfare is to "cut off the enemy's observation, decisionmaking, and troop command and control capabilities at critical times, while maintaining our own command and control ability, thus allowing us to seize information superiority . . . and to create conditions to win the decisive battle."[54] The textbook adds that "the primary task of modern campaigns has become seizing information superiority and taking away the enemy's capability of acquiring information."[55] Key targets include command systems, information systems (ISR and computer networks), and logistics systems.[56] More recent writings highlight information dominance as a prerequisite for dominance in other battlespaces, including the land, sea, air, space, and electromagnetic domains.[57] PLA writings clearly suggest that integrating C[4]ISR systems to take advantage of the significant opportunities provided by informationization requires a military to become more dependent on access to these systems. The struggle for information dominance also requires an emphasis on offensive operations, especially for a military in an inferior position.[58] PLA computer network operations fit under the broader concept of "Integrated Network Electronic Warfare," which combines electronic attacks on sensors and communications links to disrupt the opponent's acquisition and transmission of information with network attacks to disrupt an adversary's processing and use of information.[59]

A Pentagon report notes that:

> China's CNO [computer network operations] concepts include computer network attack, computer network exploitation, and computer network defense. The PLA has established information warfare units to develop viruses to attack enemy computer systems and networks, and tactics and measures to protect friendly computer systems and networks. These units include elements of the militia, creating a linkage between PLA network operators and China's civilian information technology professionals.[60]

A U.S. cyber expert notes that "interviews and [PLA] classified writings reveal interest in the full spectrum of computer network attack tools, including hacking, viruses, physical attack, insider sabotage, and electromagnetic attack."[61] Among the advantages computer network attacks offer the PLA are their extended range, low cost, and potential to degrade a sophisticated adversary's most advanced C⁴ISR capabilities. One Chinese author writes that "computer network attack is one of the most effective means for a weak military to fight a strong one."[62]

Analysis of PLA writings suggests a number of characteristics that might govern PLA employment of computer network attacks in a conflict involving the United States.[63] These characteristics include:

- using computer network attacks in the opening phases of a conflict, potentially even via preemptive attacks

- targeting key nodes through which critical data passes, especially U.S. command and control and logistics networks

- employing computer network and electronic warfare attacks to temporarily paralyze enemy command and control systems, creating opportunities for attacks on command and control systems and military forces via conventional precision strikes

- identifying military and contractor communications and logistics information that travels over civilian networks as particularly vulnerable to attack. These civilian networks may be vulnerable to relatively simple cyber attacks, such as distributed denial of service attacks.

Definitive attribution to particular state actors is a challenging task, but a number of open source reports identify likely Chinese cyber espionage attacks against a range of foreign government and commercial targets based on the targets, nature of the information sought, and technical characteristics of the attacks. One journalist listed 10 major attacks on Department of Defense, State Department, Commerce Department, and Congressional computer systems that are widely attributed to China.[64]

A report on Chinese cyber capabilities concludes that:

China's development of its computer network operations capability extends beyond preparations for wartime operations. The PLA and state security organizations have begun employing this capability to mount a large scale computer network exploitation effort for intelligence gathering purposes against the U.S. and many countries around the world, according to statements by U.S. officials, accusations by targeted foreign governments, and a growing body of media reporting on these incidents.[65]

The report documents a number of specific attacks attributed to Chinese actors and includes a detailed case study based on forensic analysis of an attack on a large U.S. commercial firm that was assessed to be a state-sponsored attack that came through or originated in China. It concludes:

> China is likely using its maturing computer network exploitation capability to support intelligence collection against the U.S. Government and industry by conducting a long term, sophisticated, computer network exploitation campaign. The problem is characterized by disciplined, standardized operations, sophisticated techniques, access to high-end software development resources, a deep knowledge of the targeted networks, and an ability to sustain activities inside targeted networks, sometimes over a period of months.[66]

Similarly, a 2010 Pentagon report concludes that:

> in 2009, numerous computer systems around the world, including those owned by the U.S. Government, continued to be the target of intrusions that appear to have originated within the PRC. These intrusions focused on ex-filtrating information. . . . The accesses and skills required for these intrusions are similar to those necessary to conduct computer network attacks. It remains unclear if these intrusions were conducted by, or with the endorsement of, the PLA or other elements of the PRC government. However, developing capabilities for cyber-warfare is consistent with authoritative PLA military writings.[67]

Two additional points relevant to this study deserve attention. The first involves the use of "cyber militias" or "patriotic hackers" by the PLA and/or the Chinese intelligence service. Some analysts argue that PRC state entities can use covert relations with Chinese hackers to launch attacks against foreign targets with a high degree of deniability.[68] Although credible reports have documented PLA and Chinese intelligence contacts with Chinese hackers, there are indications that Chinese strategists are aware of the potential downsides of uncoordinated attacks by nonstate actors in the midst of a crisis or military conflict. In addition to the potential negative impact on crisis stability, such attacks (or defensive reactions prompted by them) could interfere with the PLA's ability to execute its own targeted computer network attacks. The National People's Congress passed an expansion of China's antihacking law in February 2009 that criminalizes previous legal activities, including creation and dissemination of malicious software. Passage of the law was followed by several high-profile arrests and convictions of Chinese hackers.[69]

The second point is the vulnerability of China's own networks to cyber attack. A U.S. expert notes that military writings on information operations are marked by a glaring omission: the refusal of PLA analysts to acknowledge that increasing reliance on advanced C[4]ISR systems will make China more vulnerable to cyber attack.[70] The PLA may feel that security measures such as airgapped networks (with no connection to unclassified systems) make their military networks secure. However, Chinese civilian computers and networks are highly vulnerable, partly due to widespread software piracy that inhibits the use of patches to fix security vulnerabilities. A Chinese government study noted that 480,000 Internet protocol addresses had used viruses to control computers in the Chinese mainland in 2010, and argued that threats were worsening as more attacks were made on "hardware and networks used in finance, security, communications, customs, and taxation." A Chinese computer security expert lamented that "China lacks a national means of coordinating cyber security affairs" and that the current government cyber security office did not have the bureaucratic clout to coordinate issues across government agencies.[71]

The question of the key Chinese actors on cyber issues depends on how the issues are defined. Debates about the proper emphasis in military doctrine and training take place in secrecy within the PLA, with final decisions and formal approval given by China's top civilian leader (in his capacity as chairman of the Central Military Commission). Debates about China's broader policies toward cyber defense and Internet security take place within a somewhat larger circle that includes economic ministries responsible for development of the telecommunications sector and the intelligence, public security, and propaganda apparatus responsible for monitoring China's telecommunications and Internet systems and the political content of material transmitted via those systems. Yet if the issue is framed in its broadest possible terms—how to use telecommunications and the Internet to support continued rapid Chinese economic growth in the 21st century—the circle of relevant actors enlarges even further to include telecommunications operators, commercial users of telecommunications and networks, and Chinese citizens. These actors may have a very different perspective on what policies will best serve China's national interests.

Conclusion

What does the preceding analysis suggest about Chinese receptivity to the idea of U.S.-China strategic restraint in the nuclear, space, and cyber domains? The chief conclusion is that Chinese civilian leaders are unlikely to accept that such a regime is in China's national interest in the near future. Secrecy and the structure of the Chinese political system favor the narrow interests of the military and intelligence apparatus in counterspace and offensive cyber capabilities over the broader interests of Chinese space and computer network users (especially commercial users and citizens). These factors will likely lead both civilian and military leaders to underestimate China's vulnerability and thus the potential value of a strategic restraint regime for China's stability, security, and economic development.

Over the longer term, however, a number of developments may change the Chinese calculus. First, as the PLA exploits the military advantages of space assets and cyberspace in pursuit of "informationization," it will become more dependent on the use of these vulnerable assets, and the current asymmetry between U.S. and Chinese military vulnerability in these domains will shrink. The PLA may eventually come to prefer restraint that protects space and strategic networks over an unrestrained environment where attacks on these assets may limit their ability to operate. Second, if current trends in the conventional military balance in the western Pacific continue to move in favorable directions for China over the next decade, PLA strategists may conclude that their improving capabilities will let them deal with forward-deployed U.S. military forces on more equal terms using conventional means. Under such circumstances, restricting the U.S. ability to escalate into the space and cyber assets domains would have greater appeal.

Third, the trends toward increased military and civilian use of the space and cyber domains described above will continue to grow over time, increasing China's national dependence on these vulnerable assets. As the economic costs of this vulnerability become clearer and more widely acknowledged over time, a strategic restraint regime that limits and manages this vulnerability may be viewed as more valuable. Fourth, Chinese civilian leaders already have a keen awareness of their vulnerability to nuclear attack, which has shaped their guidance for China's own nuclear force and their acceptance of deterrence as a means of managing U.S.-China mutual vulnerability. Over time, they may apply the same logic to the space and cyber domains, perhaps increasing their willingness to impose tighter political restrictions and authorization requirements on the use of counterspace systems and computer network attacks. These four trends may, over time, make Chinese civilian and military leaders more receptive to a U.S.-China strategic restraint regime.

Domestic political changes or a reorganization of China's national security decisionmaking structure could facilitate such a shift in thinking. If China's political system does a better job of responding to and representing broader interests of small and medium-sized businesses and consumers, this would likely make top Chinese leaders more sensitive to the costs of Chinese users losing access to space and cyber assets. This might be the result of incremental improvements in the responsiveness of the government rather than a broader movement toward democracy. Chinese leaders might also decide that expanding global interests require a new national security apparatus to manage the complex trade-offs between economic, diplomatic, and security interests. The United States reached such a conclusion after World War II and established the foundations of its current national security system in a short period of time (between 1947 and 1949). Such a shift would facilitate a broader reconsideration of where China's interests really lie. These changes would likely make Chinese leaders more receptive to a U.S.-China strategic restraint regime but arguably are not necessary conditions for acceptance.

Notes

[1] For assessments of China's grand strategy, see Michael D. Swaine and Ashley J. Tellis, *Interpreting China's Grand Strategy: Past, Present, and Future* (Washington, DC: RAND, 2000), and Avery Goldstein, *Rising to the Challenge: China's Grand Strategy and International Security* (Stanford: Stanford University Press, 2005).

[2] Erica Strecker Downs and Phillip C. Saunders, "Legitimacy and the Limits of Nationalism: China and the Diaoyu Islands," *International Security* 23, no. 3 (Winter 1998/1999), 114–146.

[3] David Shambaugh provides a good overview of these Chinese debates in "Coping with a Conflicted China," *Washington Quarterly* 34, no. 1 (Winter 2011), 7–27.

[4] See Michael McDevitt, "The PLA Navy Anti-Access Role in a Taiwan Contingency," in *The Chinese Navy: Expanding Capabilities, Evolving Roles,* ed. Phillip C. Saunders, Christopher Yung, Michael Swaine, and Andrew Nien-Dzu Yang (Washington, DC: National Defense University Press, 2011).

[5] Alastair Iain Johnston, *Cultural Realism: Strategic Culture and Grand Strategy in Chinese History* (Princeton: Princeton University Press, 1995); Alastair Iain Johnston, "Cultural Realism and Strategy in Maoist China," in *The Culture of National Security: Norms and Identity in World Politics,* ed. Peter J. Katzenstein (New York: Columbia University Press, 1996), 216–270. Also see Thomas J. Christensen, "Chinese Realpolitik," *Foreign Affairs* 75, no. 5 (September–October 1996), 37–52.

[6] Andrew Scobell, *China's Use of Military Force: Beyond the Great Wall and the Long March* (New York: Cambridge University Press, 2003), 9, 15–78.

[7] Thomas J. Christensen, "Windows and War: Trend Analysis and Beijing's Use of Force," in *New Directions in the Study of China's Foreign Policy,* ed. Alastair Iain Johnston and Robert Ross (Stanford: Stanford University Press, 2006), 50–85.

[8] Allen S. Whiting, "China's Use of Force, 1950–96, and Taiwan," *International Security* 26, no. 2 (Autumn 2001), 124–127.

[9] Mark Burles and Abram Shulsky, *Patterns in China's Use of Force: Evidence from History and Doctrinal Writings* (Washington, DC: RAND, 2000), vii.

[10] Paul H.B. Godwin, "Change and Continuity in Chinese Military Doctrine, 1949–1999," in *Chinese Warfighting: The PLA Experience Since 1949*, ed. Mark A. Ryan, David Finkelstein, and Michael A. McDevitt (Armonk, NY: M.E. Sharpe, 2003), 24–26.

[11] Ibid., 49–50; and Jianxiang Bi, "Joint Operations: Developing a New Paradigm," in *China's Revolution in Doctrinal Affairs: Emerging Trends in the Operational Art of the Chinese People's Liberation Army*, ed. James Mulvenon and David Finkelstein (Arlington, VA: Center for Naval Analyses [CNA], 2002), 47–55.

[12] See the forthcoming volume from the NBR and SSI October 2010 conference, *Other People's Wars: PLA Lessons from Foreign Conflicts*.

[13] Scott Kennedy, *The Business of Lobbying in China* (Cambridge: Harvard University Press, 2008).

[14] Ken Lieberthal, *Governing China: From Revolution to Reform* (New York: W.W. Norton & Company, 2003); Susan L. Shirk, *The Political Logic of Economy Reform in China* (Berkeley: University of California Press, 1993).

[15] John Wilson Lewis and Xue Litai, *China Builds the Bomb* (Stanford: Stanford University Press, 1988); Zhang Shu Guang, *Deterrence and Strategic Culture: Chinese-American Confrontation, 1949–1958* (Ithaca: Cornell University Press, 1992). On U.S. nuclear threats to China, see Gordon H. Chang, "To the Nuclear Brink: Eisenhower, Dulles, and the Quemoy-Matsu Crisis," in *Nuclear Diplomacy and Crisis Management*, ed. Sean M. Lynne-Jones, Steven E. Miller, and Stephen Van Evera (Cambridge: MIT Press, 1990), 200–227.

[16] M. Taylor Fravel and Evan S. Medeiros, "China's Search for Assured Retaliation: The Evolution of Chinese Nuclear Strategy and Force Structure," *International Security* 35, no. 2 (Fall 2010), 48–87.

[17] Avery Goldstein, *Deterrence and Security in the 21st Century: China, Britain, France, and the Enduring Legacy of the Nuclear Revolution* (Stanford: Stanford University Press, 2000); Jeffrey Lewis, *The Minimum Means of Reprisal: China's Search for Security in the Nuclear Age* (Cambridge: MIT Press, 2007); Litai Xue, "Evolution of China's Nuclear Strategy," in *Strategic Views from the Second Tier: The Nuclear Weapons Policies of France, Britain, and China*, ed. John C. Hopkins and Weixing Hu (San Diego: University of California Press, 1994), 167–190; and Phillip C. Saunders and Jing-Dong Yuan, "China's Strategic Force Modernization," in *China's Nuclear Future*, ed. Albert Willner and Paul Bolt (Boulder: Lynne Rienner, 2006), 79–118.

[18] Committee on the U.S.-Chinese Glossary of Nuclear Security Terms, *English-Chinese, Chinese-English Nuclear Security Glossary* (Washington, DC: National Academies Press, 2008), 36.

[19] Information Office of the State Council of the People's Republic of China, "China's National Defense in 2006," December 2006, Beijing, available at <www.chinadaily.com.cn/china/2006-12/29/content_771191.htm>.

[20] Michael S. Chase and Evan Medeiros, "China's Evolving Nuclear Calculus: Modernization and Doctrinal Debate," in *China's Revolution in Doctrinal Affairs: Emerging Trends in the Operational Art of the Chinese People's Liberation Army*, ed. James Mulvenon and David Finkelstein (Arlington, VA: CNA, 2002), 133.

[21] John Wilson Lewis and Xue Litai, *China's Strategic Seapower: The Politics of Force Modernization in the Nuclear Age* (Stanford: Stanford University Press, 1994).

[22] Office of the Secretary of Defense, *Annual Report to Congress: Military Power of the People's Republic of China* (Washington, DC: Department of Defense, 2010).

[23] Ibid., 34.

[24] Ibid.

[25] See the various editions of *The Science of Military Strategy* (*Zhanlue Xue*) and writings by Western scholars including Fravel and Medeiros, "China's Search for Assured Retaliation," and Michael S. Chase and Evan Medeiros, "China's Evolving Nuclear Calculus: Modernization and Doctrinal Debate," in Mulvenon and Finkelstein, eds., 119–157.

[26] Alastair Iain Johnston, "China's New 'Old Thinking': The Concept of Limited Deterrence," *International Security* 20, no. 3 (Winter 1995/1996), 5–42.

[27] Fravel and Medeiros, 79–80.

[28] The author's interviews with relevant faculty members at the Central Party School suggest that nuclear deterrence is not taught in the international relations and security lectures that senior party members receive.

[29] Information Office of the State Council of the People's Republic of China, "China's Space Activities in 2006," October 2006, Beijing.

[30] Ibid.

[31] Ibid.

[32] Dean Cheng, "Prospects for China's Military Space Efforts," in *Beyond the Strait: PLA Missions other than Taiwan,* ed. Roy Kamphausen, David Lai, and Andrew Scobell (Carlisle, PA: U.S. Army War College, Strategic Studies Institute, April 2009), 273–279.

[33] Dean Cheng, "China's Space Program," written testimony submitted to the U.S.-China Economic and Security Review Commission, May 11, 2011.

[34] Cheng, "Prospects for China's Military Space Efforts," 218.

[35] Kevin Pollpeter, "The Chinese Vision of Space Military Operations," in *China's Revolution in Doctrinal Affairs: Emerging Trends in the Operational Art of the Chinese People's Liberation Army,* ed. James Mulvenon and David Finkelstein (Alexandria, VA: CNA Corporation, 2005), 333–334.

[36] Li Dong et al., "Research on Concepts of Space Operations and Command," cited in Cheng, "Prospects for China's Military Space Efforts."

[37] Mark A. Stokes, prepared statement for U.S.-China Economic and Security Review Commission hearing on the Implications of China's Military and Civil Space Programs, May 11, 2011.

[38] DOD China Military Power Report 2010, 36.

[39] Ibid.

[40] Cheng, "China's Space Program."

[41] DOD China Military Power Report 2010, 36.

[42] See Pollpeter, "The Chinese Vision of Space Military Operations," 355–362.

[43] Cheng, "Prospects for China's Military Space Efforts," 234–240.

[44] Ibid., 231–234.

[45] Pollpeter, "The Chinese Vision of Space Military Operations," 355–362; Cheng, "Prospects for China's Military Space Efforts."

[46] Alanna Krolikowski, "China's Civil and Commercial Space Activities and Their Implications," testimony before the U.S.-China Economic and Security Review Commission Hearing on the Implications of China's Military and Civil Space Programs, May 11, 2011.

[47] Stokes.

[48] Ibid.

[49] Krolikowski.

[50] See Nigel Inkster, "China in Cyberspace," *Survival* 52, no. 4 (August–September 2010), 57.

[51] For a survey of early PLA thinking, see James Mulvenon, "The PLA and Information Warfare," in *The People's Liberation Army in the Information Age,* ed. James Mulvenon and Richard Yang (Washington, DC: RAND, 1999), 175–186.

[52] Chinese 2010 *Defense White Paper.*

[53] See Maryanne Kivlehan-Wise and Frederic Vellucci with Daniel M. Hartnett, "Preparing for Informationized Wars: China's Evolving Concept of Military Informationization," paper presented at China Maritime Studies Institute conference *China's Strategy for the Near Seas,* U.S. Naval War College, Newport, RI, May 10–11, 2011.

[54] AMS, *Science of Campaigns,* 169.

[55] Ibid., 170.

[56] Ibid., 95–96.

[57] Dictionary of Military Informationization Editors Committee, *Dictionary of Military Informationization* (Beijing: PLA Press, December 2008), 592.

[58] Kivlehan-Wise and Vellucci.

[59] Dai Qingmin, "On Integrating Network Warfare and Electronic Warfare," *China Military Science (Zhongguo junshi kexue)*, February 2002, 112–117, and analysis of Dai's writings in James Mulvenon, "PLA Computer Network Operations: Scenarios, Doctrine, Organizations, and Capability," in Kamphausen, Lai, and Scobell, 260–261.

[60] DOD China Military Power Report 2010, 37.

[61] Mulvenon, "PLA Computer Network Operations," 277.

[62] Cited in ibid., 257, fn 3.

[63] This paragraph draws on Mulvenon, "PLA Computer Network Operations: Scenarios, Doctrine, Organizations, and Capability," in Kamphausen, Lai, and Scobell, 253–286; and Bryan Krekel, "Capability of the People's Republic of China to Conduct Cyber Warfare and Computer Network Exploitation," report prepared for the U.S.-China Economic and Security Review Commission, Northrop Grumman, October 2009.

[64] Josh Rogin, "The Top 10 Chinese Cyber Attacks (That We Know Of)," *The Cable*, January 22, 2010, available at <http://thecable.foreignpolicy.com/posts/2010/01/22/the_top_10_chinese_cyber_attacks_that_we_know_of>. Also see Shane Harris, "China's Cyber-Militia," *National Journal*, May 31, 2008.

[65] Krekel, 51.

[66] Ibid., 7.

[67] DOD China Military Power Report 2010, 7.

[68] See, for example, Timothy L. Thomas, "China's Electronic Long-range Reconnaissance," *Military Review* (November–December 2008), 53.

[69] Krekel, 33–49.

[70] Mulvenon, "PLA Computer Network Operations," 280.

[71] "Net Security Proves Difficult Task," *China Daily*, March 12, 2011.

Chapter Four

Mutual Nuclear Restraint

The United States and China are among the original five nuclear weapons states recognized by the Nuclear Nonproliferation Treaty.[1] Historically, their strategic nuclear relationship—each side's concerns about the other's potential use of nuclear weapons—has not been a major aspect of their overall relations, in part because both were more concerned about the Soviet threat. Now, however, the rising power of China and growing significance of Sino-American relations for world security have put a spotlight on their nuclear relationship. In addition, the deployment of U.S. ballistic missile defense (BMD), cuts in U.S. strategic offensive forces as a result of U.S.-Russian arms control, and the increasing quality, quantity, and survivability of China's strategic offensive forces have raised questions on each side about the nuclear forces and intentions of the other.

For the United States, from the dawn of the nuclear era until recently, the number, features, and doctrine for using nuclear weapons were determined by the U.S.-Soviet rivalry, strategic arms competition, and danger of global war. The effect was to give the United States the ability to accurately deliver thousands of nuclear weapons on strategic missiles and bombers, along with a doctrine that contemplated both tactical and limited strategic use of nuclear weapons, albeit within a context of mutual assured destruction.

Though not its principal motivation, the United States developed ample capacity to destroy China's small and vulnerable nuclear forces, along with much of China. The United States has nuclear superiority over China—numerically (roughly a 30:1 ratio at present), qualitatively, operationally, offensively, and defensively.[2] Because China was weaker than the United States in conventional forces, questions of whether, why, and how the United States would use nuclear forces against China were not given much attention.

During this same period, China has not had a nuclear force with enough range, size, and survivability to give it a credible threat of retaliation against the United States and thus full confidence that it could deter a U.S. nuclear first strike on China in the event of war. Yet except during the

Korean War, the possibility of a U.S. nuclear attack on China has been extremely remote. Sino-American rapprochement in the early 1970s largely ended any reason for the United States to take advantage of its nuclear superiority. For 40 years, China's lack of a fully credible deterrent has not exposed it to significant risk of a U.S. nuclear attack—it has indeed been vulnerable, but not threatened.

Yet the Chinese are increasingly dissatisfied with the one-sidedness of the Sino-American strategic nuclear relationship and now have the economic and technological wherewithal to rectify it. While the Chinese do not aspire to have a strategic nuclear force equivalent in quantity or quality to that of the United States, they are determined to ensure that nuclear deterrence is mutual. The advent of U.S. BMD has deepened Chinese doubts about their ability to deter the United States by threat of retaliation, while also fanning their suspicions that the United States wants to deny China a nuclear deterrent.[3] These suspicions, in turn, make the Chinese skeptical about U.S. assurances that it accepts China as a great power. Far from dissuading China from improving its strategic nuclear forces, U.S. BMD has had the opposite effect.

Since acquiring nuclear weapons half a century ago, China's constant goal has been a minimum nuclear deterrent capability. An enemy should expect at least some Chinese nuclear weapons to survive a nuclear attack, penetrate defenses, and visit such devastating retaliation—say, the destruction of a large city or two—that that enemy, regardless of its nuclear preponderance, would be deterred from striking first.[4] Toward this end, the Chinese built a small number of exceptionally large (3- to 4-megaton) thermonuclear weapons and deployed them on an equally small force of land-based ICBMs. Such a weapon could largely destroy a major American city, if it could get there.[5]

In order to bolster deterrence, and perhaps because of its doubtful ability to retaliate, China has been adamant about its *will* to retaliate. China's 2008 *Defense White Paper* states:

> [I]f China comes under a nuclear threat, the nuclear missile force of the Second Artillery Force [the PLA's strategic nuclear arm] will go into a state of alert and get ready for a nuclear counterattack to deter the enemy from using nuclear weapons against China. If China comes under a nuclear attack . . . the Second Artillery Force will use nuclear missiles to launch a resolute counterattack against the enemy.[6]

China's nuclear posture was based not only on a belief that minimum deterrence was sufficient but also on the paucity of resources and technologies with which to build larger and better strategic forces. Until recently, modernization of their nuclear arsenal was a low priority for the Chinese. They have repeatedly pledged not to use nuclear weapons first, pressed other nuclear powers to make such pledges, resisted being drawn into a strategic arms race, and called for general nuclear disarmament. In a nutshell, the Chinese view nuclear weapons only as a way to prevent nuclear attack, and they do not believe that being a global power necessitates having more nuclear weapons than needed for minimum deterrence, despite the U.S. and Russian examples.

Even with China's economic success and political ambitions, there are no signs of the Chinese moving to a nuclear doctrine beyond minimum deterrence. Their recent efforts to strengthen their nuclear force are impelled by and limited to attaining and maintaining an assured deterrent, with no apparent interest in using nuclear weapons first or for warfighting.[7] Increases in the number, range, mobility, reliability, launch-readiness, and accuracy of its ICBMs[8] are intended to correct deficiencies in China's ability to ride out a U.S. (or Russian) first strike and deliver enough retaliation to deter such a strike. As Chinese President Hu Jintao recently affirmed:

> China . . . is firmly committed to a nuclear strategy of self-defense. We have adhered to the policy of no-first-use of nuclear weapons at any time and under any circumstances. . . . China does not participate in any form of nuclear arms race. We will continue to keep our nuclear capabilities at the minimum level required for national security, and [attempt] to advance the international nuclear disarmament process.[9]

With the tenor of Sino-American relations becoming increasingly crucial for both countries and the rest of the world, it is timely to ask what direction the strategic-nuclear aspect of those relations will and should take. For better or worse, strategic-nuclear matters will affect relations in general: if either side suspects the other of seeking strategic-nuclear supremacy, it is bound to erode that side's trust. Conversely, if the danger of nuclear war and distrust of nuclear intentions between the two can be eliminated, it should unburden the relationship and foster more cooperation. Recognizing this, the Chinese and U.S. governments have agreed to conduct a "strategic security dialogue" to discuss this and related issues.[10]

As this is written, the most salient strategic issue is whether China will attain and maintain an assured capability to strike the United States with nuclear weapons after suffering a U.S. nuclear attack, and whether the United States will try to deny China such a capability. The next part of this chapter explains why China can and will have such a capability, even if faced with a U.S. effort to prevent it. Thus, each country will be vulnerable to the other's nuclear weapons, and each will be able to mitigate this vulnerability by threatening retaliation.

Beyond such conditions of mutual nuclear deterrence, the opportunity and challenge facing the United States and China are to institute mutual restraint in the nuclear field, building confidence on the proposition that both countries accept mutual deterrence and seek to strengthen and institutionalize it cooperatively. In turn, the key issue for the *future* Sino-American strategic relationship is what mutual nuclear deterrence and mutual restraint will mean for Sino-American relations, U.S. interests, East Asia, and the world. The chapter will conclude by recommending how China and the United States should order and manage their nuclear relationship.

The Shifting Balance of Forces

There are two reasons to expect China to gain a credible nuclear retaliatory capability against the United States: first, because it can, and second, because it feels it must.[11] Offense dominance in the nuclear domain makes it easier and less costly for China, even as the less advanced power, to have such a capability than for the United States to prevent it. As a matter of essential national security, China is determined to have such capability—more determined than the United States is to deprive it of one.

Offense Dominance

The dominance of offense over defense in the nuclear realm has both economic and operational meanings: the former applies to arms competition, the latter to conflicts or crises. Economically, above a low threshold of offensive capability, the cost of defense needed to neutralize the next increment of offense is greater than the cost of that increment. Moreover, this disparity grows as the scale of offense does, making offense an increasingly good and defense an increasingly bad investment. To dramatize this, consider that the United States has spent over $100 billion on missile defense over 25 years and, to show for it, now expects to have an ability to knock down an attack on the order of tens of strategic missiles.[12] The cost of those enemy missiles, including their development, is a tiny fraction of what the United States has spent to intercept them. Moreover, the cost of developing technologies and techniques to penetrate defenses looks to be less than the cost of developing the means to neutralize such antidefense advances.

Figure 4–1 illuminates offense dominance in nuclear missile and intercept systems. It plots the cost of defense (based on the U.S. SM–3 interceptor) against the cost of offense (based on the U.S. Minuteman III ICBM).[13] If each interceptor and ICBM cost the same, if each ICBM carried only one reentry vehicle (RV), and if only one interceptor was needed to destroy one RV, the economic relationship of offense and defense would be as represented by the "Equal cost" line. However, each interceptor costs $3 million more than each ICBM, so the cost advantage of offense accumulates as a function of the number of ICBMs (represented by the "Interceptor vs. single warhead ICBMs" line). Additionally, this ICBM—and China's

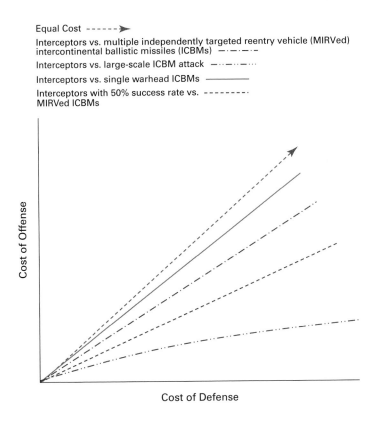

Figure 4–1. Cost of Offense Dominance in Missile and Intercept Systems

future ICBMs, if it so chooses—is capable of carrying multiple indepen-dently targetable reentry vehicles (MIRVs), making the cost gap even more favorable to offense (see "Interceptors vs. MIRVed ICBMs" line). Of course, a given interceptor is not certain of destroying a given ICBM, so the "Inter-ceptors with 50% success rate vs. MIRVed ICBMs" line represents the cost gap if an average of two interceptors is needed to destroy each incoming missile.[14]

The odds of successfully intercepting one missile decrease as the size of a missile attack increases, because missile defense systems can be over-whelmed by the complexity of trying to locate, track, target, and strike large attacks. This situation is represented by the "Interceptor vs. large-scale ICBM attack" line, which shows the offense dominance expected from a large attack from MIRVed missiles. Overall, we see sharply dimin-ishing returns for investment in defense and a reward for investing in offense and relying on the threat of retaliation to deter.

Simply put, missile defense may make sense (for those who can afford it at all) against small nuclear threats (such as North Korea) but not against large ones (for example, Russia and China). Even though the United States has the larger economy and can outspend China on strategic capabilities, for the former to commit resources to assure missile defense against the latter would be a bad investment. Indeed, it would be practically unafford-able in the context of already heavy demands on a U.S. defense budget that may have to be cut to help restore fiscal balance. China is more able to assure itself of a nuclear second-strike capability than the United States is to assure itself of a first-strike capability.

Motivations

China is also more strongly motivated to have a second-strike capa-bility than the United States is to have a first-strike capability. Given that the United States would suffer devastation from a Chinese second strike, it may seem counterintuitive that it matters more to China to have such a capability than it matters to the United States to prevent China from having it. This twist of nuclear deterrence is that China's ability to destroy Ameri-can cities is less relevant to any plausible Chinese nuclear threat to the United States than it is to the nuclear threat the United States poses to China. Even with its reduced post–Cold War nuclear offensive force, the United States can surely deter a Chinese nuclear strike. Much less certain is whether the Chinese have a sufficient retaliatory capability to deter a U.S. attack on China, which is why it is more important for China to have such a capability than it is for the United States to deny it.

Chinese strategists believe that the United States would find the loss of a city or two to be an unacceptably high cost for attacking China with nuclear weapons. Unless the United States had more to lose than the equivalent of a city or two by *not* attacking China with nuclear weapons, the Chinese are correct. It is not easy to imagine what would cause the United States to stake the destruction of, say, Los Angeles and Chicago: Chinese invasion of Taiwan? Chinese sinking of a U.S. aircraft carrier? Chinese backing of North Korea in hostilities with South Korea and the United States? If the United States had no other options but to attack China with nuclear weapons for such provocations, then perhaps it might contemplate such a course. But as the stronger military power with superior conventional capabilities, the United States could make China pay dearly for such actions without triggering a nuclear attack on itself. Moreover, because the United States is so unlikely to use nuclear weapons against China even without a Chinese retaliatory capability, American leaders may not feel that much is lost if China were to have that capability.

The Chinese believe they need a retaliatory capability not only to minimize the danger of an actual U.S. nuclear attack but also to minimize U.S. leverage from the *threat* of such an attack. While a U.S. nuclear attack on China may seem extremely far-fetched, the Chinese cannot ignore the threat, if only because it might enable the United States to coerce China in some possible future crisis, such as over Taiwan. The aversion to "nuclear blackmail" has been a consistent theme in Chinese nuclear doctrine.[15] China's interest in being able to deter a U.S. nuclear attack does not necessarily betray Chinese intent to commit hostile acts against U.S. interests without fear of nuclear war; after all, Chinese acts of war could provoke severe nonnuclear American retribution. But China is worried, justifiably or not, about being bullied by the United States. Whether or not Americans would use nuclear weapons to coerce China, it is unrealistic to expect the Chinese to be complacent in this regard, given its negative history with stronger powers.

During much of the Cold War, the Chinese were more worried about being menaced by the Soviet Union than by the United States. Even now, the Chinese are also motivated to deny Russia any ability to threaten and coerce them, which also fuels their interest in stronger retaliatory forces. Russia retains a nuclear arsenal comparable in size, though inferior in quality, to that of the United States. What is different between Russian and U.S. nuclear postures, from the Chinese perspective, is that Russia, by its own admission, is relying more on nuclear weapons, while the United States is relying less on them. Whereas the United States is stronger than China in conventional capabilities, Russia is, if anything, weaker. This creates, in theory at least, the danger that Russia would rely on the threat of nuclear weapons to gain an advantage, or to rectify a disadvantage, in a crisis or conflict with China.[16]

Their continuing concern about Russia's nuclear capabilities and doctrine notwithstanding, the Chinese are investing in nuclear force modernization mainly with the United States in mind. This is reflected in China's growing interest in very long range ICBMs and in a sea-based deterrent. Presumably, any Chinese retaliatory force adequate to deter the United States would be adequate to deter Russia. The Sino-American strategic-nuclear relationship is now driving Chinese nuclear strategy and force modernization.

On the matter of being able to deter a U.S. nuclear attack, there is no hint of disagreement or irresoluteness within China. Statements by political leaders and military commanders are clear and consistent.[17] At the same time, the Chinese would reject the notion that having the ability to retaliate for a U.S. nuclear attack is indicative of belligerence toward the United States or prejudicial to a generally cooperative Sino-American relationship. On the contrary, they view mutual deterrence as a way to inoculate the relationship against nuclear threats and coercion, to enhance stability and equity, and thus to facilitate wider cooperation. Perhaps the Chinese are more likely to cooperate internationally with the United States out of confidence than out of fear, though it is also possible that mutual nuclear deterrence will make China more assertive.

Americans do not seem overly suspicious of the Chinese determination to be able to deter a U.S. nuclear attack. U.S. official statements express no alarm about China's quest for a deterrent per se—only about the murkiness of Chinese programs and the need for greater transparency.[18] Even with limited transparency, it is clear enough from Chinese statements, forces, and investments that the goal is mutual deterrence, with China's strategic offensive force smaller than America's but still adequate.

Apart from the sheer difficulty and cost, there are two reasons why the United States should not try to retain the ability to prevent China from being able to retaliate for a U.S. attack. First, no serious American strategist would argue that launching a nuclear first strike on China is essential to safeguard security and U.S. interests in East Asia. Even with no threat of Chinese retaliation, current potential flashpoints in Sino-American relations—Taiwan, maritime rights, war between the Koreas—would not justify a U.S. nuclear attack. They pose no threat to vital American interests, the American way of life, or the American homeland.[19] Second, were the United

States to try to cling to the ability to deny China a nuclear deterrent, it would raise doubts about whether the United States wants the kind of cooperative Sino-American relationship it claims to want, as opposed to one in which the United States can exploit its nuclear leverage. It would be hard to square a U.S. insistence that it must preserve a nuclear first-strike capability against China with the sort of constructive Sino-American relationship that is favored across the U.S. political spectrum. Conversely, it would be easy for the Chinese, given their sensitivities, to interpret U.S. efforts to retain a first-strike capability as indicative of a hegemonic strategy.

It is not surprising, then, that the U.S. Government's official 2010 *Nuclear Posture Review* treats the U.S.-China nuclear relationship conceptually on the same plane as that with Russia, calling for "strategic stability" with both—a formulation that could be read as accepting Sino-U.S. mutual deterrence. This is partly in view of the difficulty and cost of denying China a second-strike capability. But it also reflects an appreciation by the U.S. Government that de facto mutual deterrence with China is compatible with U.S. security interests, including a nonconfrontational and, if possible, cooperative relationship with China. This U.S. stance is also reflected in assurances given to China (although not completely believed there) that U.S. BMD is meant to counter the likes of Iran and North Korea, not China.[20]

The U.S. Government has also shown a strong desire to reduce the prominence of nuclear weapons in world affairs, largely motivated by the belief or hope that this would help slow their proliferation. Toward this end, the administration has adopted a more restrictive policy than any of its predecessors concerning the use of nuclear weapons, stressing that their primary purpose is to deter nuclear attack. It has reserved the first use of nuclear weapons to circumscribed situations—for example, in response to a large-scale biological weapons attack—and has made clear its intent to work toward conditions that would enable it to state that the sole purpose of U.S. nuclear weapons is to deter nuclear attack.[21] This tends to confirm that the United States finds a Chinese second-strike deterrent acceptable if not inevitable.

At the same time, American strategists may still doubt the wisdom of assuring Chinese leaders that the United States would not use nuclear weapons first, as implied by explicit acceptance of mutual deterrence. These doubts include concerns about the reaction of U.S. allies in East Asia, about emboldening China to be more adventurous, and about the loss of U.S. escalation dominance in connection with a confrontation or conflict, such as over Taiwan. Nevertheless, there is little or no indication that the U.S. Government is prepared to try to deny China a nuclear deterrent vis-à-vis the United States.

A Hypothetical Sino-American Strategic Arms Race

In order to underscore the difficulty, if not futility, of a U.S. effort to deny China a nuclear deterrent, what follows is a rough approximation of the current relationship of Chinese and U.S. strategic forces followed by moves each side could take to gain or retain advantage. Because it is dissatisfied with the status quo and thus more likely to seek to change it, we start with China.

Assume that China has about 50 single-warhead ICBMs capable of reaching the United States, deployed on fixed launchers, 40 percent of them liquid-fueled (and thus slow to prepare for launch). Also assume that the United States has 1,550 nuclear warheads on deployed strategic missiles and bombers (the number allowed under the Russian-American New Strategic Arms Reduction Treaty [START]), as well as substantial long-range conventional airpower (also known as global strike), a modest BMD system, and good but not comprehensive space-based surveillance coverage of China.

Using its surveillance capabilities to locate fixed Chinese ICBMs and, say, 500 of its nuclear warheads plus conventional global strike weapons in a first strike on China, the United States could destroy most if not all of China's ICBMs (along with a lot of the country and its people). If, for the sake of analysis, five Chinese ICBMs survived the U.S. strike and were launched in retaliation, the current U.S. BMD system of sensors and interceptors could potentially destroy them all (assuming it were optimized for the trajectories of Chinese ICBMs). In the face of such odds, the Chinese would not have confidence that any of their nuclear weapons would reach the United States. Conversely, the United States would have reasonable, though not absolute, confidence in its ability to conduct a first strike on China without suffering retaliation. However improbable that the United States would actually attack China with nuclear weapons, these odds could give the United States escalation dominance, which would disfavor China in how a nonnuclear conflict between the two would be settled.[22] Such dominance provides leverage not only in hostilities but also in crises.

Deeming such a correlation of strategic forces to be both intolerable and correctable, the Chinese could in a few years take a number of remedial steps well within their current resource capacity and technological competence. They could increase the number of ICBMs from 50 to, say, 100, with the added ones all solid-fueled (enabling them to be launched faster) and deployed on mobile launchers (making them harder to target).[23] In that case, perhaps not 5 but 20 Chinese ICBMs would survive a U.S. first strike, presenting U.S. BMD with a challenge near the upper end of its capability. At that point, the United States would have much lower confidence of avoiding Chinese nuclear retaliation altogether and so could be deterred.

In order to restore its ability to deny China a nuclear deterrent, the United States could respond by planning a significantly larger first strike of perhaps 1,000 of its nuclear weapons and a larger share of its conventional strike weapons. In this desktop nuclear arms race, such a move would have very high real and opportunity costs for the United States, by requiring other strategic missions to be neglected, enlarging its conventional global strike force, and perhaps exceeding the START limit of 1,550 on deployed strategic nuclear weapons. The United States could also expand its missile BMD to counter a medium-scale nuclear attack, but also at considerable cost in sensors and interceptors and the installations on which they are deployed.

Observing this U.S. response, China could build and deploy still more mobile ICBMs and accelerate current plans to build five strategic missile–carrying submarines, which, when deployed, are even harder to locate, track, and target than mobile missile launchers. In order to reach the continental United States, the Chinese would need to extend either the patrol range of their submarines or the trajectory range of their strategic submarine-based missiles.[24] The Chinese could also develop and field decoys and other penetration aids to frustrate U.S. BMD. Finally, the Chinese could develop and arm their strategic missiles with MIRVs. All these moves are within China's expanding economic means and technological reach.

Now facing, say, 100 or more incoming weapons, plus decoys, the United States could further enhance its missile defense to counter a large-scale attack, requiring more bases for sensors and interceptors as well as more ships for seaborne missile defense. The United States could also expand its antisubmarine warfare (ASW) capabilities and operations, requiring still more surface ships and attack submarines and/or committing more of the U.S. Navy to this instead of other critical missions. The United States could also attempt to enhance its space-based capabilities for more comprehensive real-time surveillance of China in order to track and target mobile missile launchers.

Finding submarines, intercepting ballistic missiles, and tracking mobile missile launchers are difficult but not impossible tasks, especially for a country blessed with advanced sensor, computing, and communications technology. In all three cases, it requires locating an object that is moving either evasively or rapidly in the vastness of an ocean, the atmosphere, or a land mass. Once located, it must be tracked as it moves and eventually "locked on" by a long-range weapons system that can reach and destroy it. With current science, such problems can be solved. But the solutions can also be foiled, with less cost and difficulty. The target may be concealed (submarines), disguised (launchers), or accompanied by decoys (missile reentry vehicles). The sensors that seek them and communications that target them may be jammed. Meanwhile, the Chinese may increase the number of strategic targets, which would geometrically increase the technical difficulty of these problems.

During the Cold War and since, the United States has invested hundreds of billions of dollars in ASW, BMD, and space-based land surveillance. Still, it struggles to track submarines, intercept ballistic missiles, and locate missile launchers on the move, especially against large numbers of targets (or decoys). Given the physics, geometrics, and economics at play, China has the resources and know-how to assure offense dominance in the strategic domain—to "win" this hypothetical strategic arms race.

Apart from technological and operational challenges of such undertakings, the costs would either dictate a massive increase in U.S. defense spending—hardly plausible—or result in serious neglect of what are presently considered higher priorities, such as combating violent extremism and strengthening security in the energy-rich Middle East.[25] In an era of shrinking U.S. surface and submarine fleets, thanks to the climbing cost of such vessels, the investment required in naval forces alone for BMD and ASW, or the opportunity costs, would be staggering. The cost of additional satellites with more discriminating radar, optical, and other sensors to support more comprehensive U.S. surveillance of China and more robust BMD could be nearly as hefty as well.

In these major undertakings—enhanced BMD, ASW, and space-based surveillance—the United States would be faced with diminishing returns on ever-growing investments, especially if China deployed decoy weapons, mobile launchers, and underwater vehicles. Every Chinese increment of more or less proven strategic offensive capabilities would require the United States to invest disproportionately in unproven and inherently challenging strategic defenses. And the Chinese could make U.S. prospects even dimmer by adopting a launch-on-warning doctrine for their missiles forces, which they have been disinclined to do but could if and as their own space-based warning capabilities are improved. This would put an even greater burden on U.S. BMD.

As U.S. costs pile up faster than China's, the offense-dominant nature of strategic nuclear forces becomes increasingly pronounced. The Chinese would have growing confidence in their ability to ride out a U.S. first strike, launch a retaliatory barrage, and destroy American cities (along with U.S. military bases, key industrial locations, and so forth). For every increment of strategic offense capability the Chinese added, the U.S. goal of preventing retaliation would further recede.

Because of the awesome destructive power of nuclear weapons, the United States would have to prevent *every* Chinese weapon from detonating on U.S. soil, whereas the Chinese would only have to detonate *any* weapon on U.S. soil. In the course of this hypothetical strategic arms race, the chance that the United States could escape Chinese retaliation would decline. Indeed, as strategic offense-defense competition between large states spirals, the amount of offensive destructive power deliverable on the side attempting to defend itself could grow. This is the fundamental reason the United States elected not to try to defend itself against Soviet missiles during the Cold War, and it still applies today. Assuming the Chinese are determined, the United States would deplete its resources trying in vain to prevent a Chinese deterrent, only to find its cities and its people more vulnerable. In the end, China would be very heavily armed with strategic nuclear weapons. This would not only increase the potential retaliatory damage to the United States, but also would shake up U.S. allies. East Asia, a vital region, would be less stable, and hopes for a constructive Sino-American relationship would be dashed.

While this is no more than a highly simplified illustration, it is important to note that the Chinese are in reality building, developing, or at least contemplating the very strategic capabilities just described to improve the survivability, penetrability, and reliability of their offensive forces: solid-fueled missiles, mobile missile launchers, submarine-based missile forces, MIRVs, and other capabilities to overwhelm missile defenses.[26] They may even have played through multiple moves in the sort of hypothetical arms race just sketched, and as a result they know their priorities. Moreover, as the Chinese have demonstrated in the dramatic expansion of their short-range missile arsenal in recent years, they are quite capable of ramping up production of strategic missiles.

The United States has proven its ability to "pay any price" and to compete on industrial and technological grounds to confront a grave threat, such as Nazi Germany, imperial Japan, and the Soviet Union. But it is unclear how it would justify the ballooning costs of trying to deprive China of a deterrent capability. Even assuming China and the United States continue to have divergent interests and even find themselves in an occasional confrontation, the stakes would not warrant the effort required, especially in light of the futility of strategic defense against a well-resourced and committed opponent like China. Barring blatant Chinese aggression and expansionism throughout East Asia, it is hard to imagine the United States treating the denial of a Chinese deterrent as a top national security priority, given the other very real threats it faces.

In sum, the lack of a compelling national defense rationale and the technical difficulty and expected cost of countering a determined Chinese strategic-offensive build-up suggest that the United States will acquiesce in a mutual deterrent relationship with China. There are strong indications in U.S. declaratory policy that this is understood, if not unequivocally stated, in Washington. While the latest U.S. *Nuclear Posture Review* stops short of accepting a Chinese deterrent, it conveys no determination to prevent it.[27]

Implications

To say that the United States has neither the means nor the ability to deny China a credible nuclear deterrent is not to say that this is inconsequential for U.S. security interests and East Asian stability. Several potentially deleterious effects come to mind. First, Sino-American "strategic stability," based on mutual nuclear deterrence, could cause increased sub-strategic instability, especially in East Asia and the western Pacific. Second, the United States would lose escalation dominance, and thus crisis dominance, which could embolden China to become more belligerent and intransigent. Third, mutual deterrence could unsettle U.S. allies and other states in the region, making them either more susceptible to Chinese pressure or, in the case of Japan and possibly South Korea, more inclined toward unilateral capabilities—perhaps even nuclear weapons of their own.

There are two reasons why Japan and South Korea need not, should not, and probably will not become motivated to slip the moorings of their security relationship with the United States as it becomes clear that China can deter a U.S. nuclear attack. First, the United States could and no doubt would continue to extend deterrence to its regional allies against Chinese *nuclear* threats, thanks to its overwhelming retaliatory capability and China's virtual defenselessness. Second, allied and regional confidence would be shaken less by the loss of the U.S. first-strike option than by a Sino-American strategic arms race, which would result in the loss of the U.S. first-strike option and an expansion in Chinese offensive nuclear capabilities.

As for emboldening China, it is prudent to anticipate that China would become less fearful if it became clear that a confrontation with the United States would involve a fading risk of nuclear escalation. But it is uncertain what bearing this would have on the realities of East Asia. Even without the risk of nuclear escalation, the costs of a major conventional conflict with the United States would still be high. Broadly speaking, China has a strong interest in a tranquil external environment, without which its goals of economic growth and political stability could be in jeopardy. Following hostilities with India and Vietnam several decades ago, China has carefully avoided war. The Chinese are aware of the regional backlash that would result from aggression on their part. When China has shown occasional forcefulness in asserting its sovereign claims—for example, missile tests in 1995 and 1996 to dissuade Taiwanese voters from supporting independence, and recently menacing rivals over fishing and resource rights in the East and South China Seas—reactions in the region have turned sharply against China (and in favor of U.S. security ties).

While we can expect continued Chinese outward pressure, especially over maritime and resource rights, Chinese strategy appears to be to probe without galvanizing an anti-Chinese alliance among its neighbors and the United States. While unwelcome and deserving of a firm response, recent Chinese heavy-handedness is well below the threshold at which the United States would invoke a threat of intervention, much less escalation to the nuclear level.

The possible exception, of course, would be Chinese aggression against Taiwan. The improvement of Chinese antiaccess capabilities—systems such as attack submarines and antiship missiles—could erode the ability and will of the United States to come to Taiwan's defense. In time, the Chinese could wrest crisis dominance away from the United States and be better able to prevail in a showdown or conflict over Taiwan or be more able to coerce Taiwan to accept unification on China's terms without war. Might the United States enable Chinese aggression against or coercion of Taiwan by accepting mutual deterrence, especially if China-Taiwan relations take a turn for the worse?

It might, to some degree. Of course, it is most improbable that the United States would launch a nuclear attack on China in defense of Taiwan even in the absence of a credible Chinese nuclear deterrent. Keep in mind that a U.S. first strike on China would have to be very large and destructive in order to completely destroy China's retaliatory capability, with the possibility of millions of Chinese casualties. Nevertheless, because China almost certainly will have a credible nuclear deterrent, the United States must contemplate whether this could alter Chinese thinking about the use of forces against Taiwan and the possibility of war with the United States.

A Chinese attack on Taiwan cannot be excluded, given that the Chinese claim the right to unify the country by whatever means necessary and are developing and deploying capabilities to prevent or deter the United States from defending Taiwan. They might be marginally more inclined to attack Taiwan if they felt certain that doing so would not result in nuclear war. More likely, the Chinese may try to pressure Taiwan into unification without provoking U.S. intervention at all. But these are not risks that justify a massive, costly, and probably futile effort by the United States to deny China a credible nuclear retaliatory capability. Moreover, it is hard to see how Taiwan would be made more secure if the United States impelled China to expand its nuclear forces but, at the end of the day, was deterred from escalating to nuclear war in order to save Taiwan from China.

More generally, a theoretical argument could be made that East Asia could be destabilized if the United States and China were mutually deterred at the nuclear level. That argument holds that "decoupling" the danger of nuclear war from international relations, disputes, and conventional military conflicts may stimulate reckless behavior. The reasoning is that the local or regional correlation of conventional forces would matter more because the strategic nuclear domain would matter less.[28] This could be especially risky as China improves its position in the regional conventional balance.

This is a slippery argument that bits of history can either support or refute. It is generally thought that the U.S.-Soviet nuclear standoff imposed caution on the part of the superpowers and their principal allies during the Cold War, thus bolstering stability and driving down the probability of World War III. However, it must be noted that the United States explicitly coupled the possibility of nuclear war to Soviet aggression, especially in Europe, where the threat was greatest and most immediate.[29] The North Atlantic Treaty Organization's (NATO's) flexible response strategy made explicit American willingness to initiate and escalate nuclear war if need be to defend Western Europe; and this willingness helped keep NATO allies squarely in the U.S. camp.

Everywhere the United States did not threaten to use nuclear weapons first—for example, in the so-called Third World—conditions were less stable and peaceful during the Cold War, which suggests that Sino-American mutual nuclear deterrence could increase instability in East Asia. However, the Third World instability and conflicts that occurred during the Cold War were largely the result of deliberate use of proxies by one superpower or the other to gain advantage, with nuclear weapons largely irrelevant. So the analogy is far from strong.

Nuclear weapons have not played and will not play the sort of prominent role in post–Cold War East Asian security that they did in the Soviet-American standoff. First use of nuclear weapons was a credible option when the alternative could have been Soviet seizure of all of Europe. Because of the ideological context of the East-West confrontation and the observed pattern of Soviet conquest and domination in the East, the Soviet threat was seen (correctly or not) as a global and existential one. As already noted, China poses no such threat to East Asia, much less to the United States and its way of life.

Empirically, while the data are sparse, nuclear weapons have not figured in East Asian security the way they did in the U.S.-Soviet confrontation in Europe. The Korean War showed that even with a nuclear monopoly, and even when defeat looked possible, the United States would not resort to nuclear weapons in the face of a use of force by China. It also showed that China would use force if it saw its vital interests threatened even if it lacked the means to deter U.S. nuclear attack.

The deployment of thousands of battlefield nuclear weapons to Europe, the sharing of nuclear weapons with NATO allies (under dual-key arrangements), and the flat U.S. refusal to make a no-first-use pledge all reinforced the credibility of U.S. nuclear coupling with European security. With the United States making a strenuous effort to reduce the role of nuclear weapons in world politics and military affairs, it hardly seems likely that it would now embark on a comparable strategy of coupling strategic nuclear weapons to security in East Asia. If any such coupling still exists, it is very weak and far less important than the conventional Sino-U.S. military balance, stalwart U.S. allies, and wise policy in maintaining East Asian stability.

Would this relatively sanguine analysis of the regional impact of Sino-American mutual nuclear deterrence hold up if China were to gain a conventional military advantage? What if China posed such a threat to U.S. forces in the western Pacific that neither the United States nor its allies could be confident of successful defense against flagrant Chinese aggression? There is no question that such an eventuality could alter the behavior of China, the United States, and U.S. allies. Still, the assessments that China is fundamentally not an expansionist power, that its quest for greater military capabilities is motivated by deep-seated fears and self-defense, and that Chinese growth depends on a peaceful international environment would seem to transcend changes in the regional military balance in China's favor.

It is also true that PLA modernization is improving its antiaccess capabilities much faster than its ability to project and sustain combat power beyond its borders. While predictions a decade out are hazardous, an aggressive China is improbable as much for internal reasons as external ones.

Moreover, U.S. acceptance of mutual deterrence with China would be less deleterious to East Asian security and U.S. interests than a strategic arms race with China, which would swell China's nuclear arsenal and leave the United States and its allies more, not less, vulnerable. Even if the United States did not embrace mutual restraint in the nuclear domain, mutual deterrence appears unavoidable. The United States and the region must in any case prepare *together* for increased Chinese power and strategic decoupling.

While the potential deleterious implications of Sino-American mutual deterrence are likely to be manageable, there could be positive effects for U.S. interests in the Sino-American relationship. The U.S. Government has been trying to convince the Chinese that containment is not the U.S. goal. This U.S. stance is a reflection of not only the infeasibility of containing China and preventing Chinese nuclear deterrence, but also the assessment that China will find cooperation more in its interest than confrontation, especially if U.S. alliances remain strong. Indeed, China and the United States should be more able to cooperate if the United States were to accept rather than try to prevent China's nuclear deterrent. This sense that strategic stability is a natural feature of productive Sino-American relations helps account for growing U.S. acceptance of mutual deterrence. The Chinese are well advised to understand this.

Conclusion

One of the themes of this book is that objective conditions of mutual strategic deterrence in nuclear and other domains need not and should not be ends in themselves but rather a point of departure for mutual strategic restraint, which implies reciprocal acknowledgment of the acceptability of mutual deterrence and commitment to maintain it. In its most basic form, mutual deterrence requires no communication beyond making known the capability and will to attack if attacked. The only "cooperation" needed for mutual deterrence is that both sides behave rationally in the face of the threat of retaliation. Mutual restraint entails at least some communication of good faith and willingness to cooperate.

In this connection, the minimum purposes of the Sino-American strategic security dialogue that the United States has proposed and that China has cautiously accepted are to create greater transparency and to avoid costly miscalculation. In this dialogue, China could assure the United States that it seeks no more than an effective minimum deterrent, and the United States could assure China that its BMD will not be directed against China. Of course, mere assurances will not lay suspicions to rest on either side. The United States could explain in detail why its capabilities and its plans for missile defense cannot prevent a Chinese second strike yet can protect against the likes of Iran and North Korea. In turn, China could explain how its offensive force modernization programs fall well short of any nuclear aspiration beyond an assured retaliatory capability. Among the potential benefits of such exchanges is that the United States and China could spare themselves the costs of preparing to cope with strategic-offensive forces and missile defenses, respectively, that the other side does not actually intend to have.

Strategic talks could lead to even more significant results. The United States and China could agree explicitly to a mutual nuclear deterrence relationship and even enter into an explicit bilateral no-first-use agreement. This would be a bigger step for the United States than for China, which has long accepted and advocated no first use. While not a substantive concession to China, given that China will in any event possess an effective second-strike capability, the United States should approach this idea judiciously and strategically. The two most important considerations for the United States would be what to expect in return from China, and how such an accord would affect other U.S. interests, particularly in East Asia.

For the United States, the offer of a reciprocal bilateral no-first-use agreement should not be cast narrowly or only as acceptance of the inevitability, or reality, of China's ability to deter the United States, but instead as a joint commitment by the world's two strongest powers to a relationship of mutual and growing respect, trust, cooperation, and international leadership in reducing the importance of nuclear weapons in world affairs.

Ideally, the United States would also get China on record that both will conduct themselves in a way that strengthens security in and beyond East Asia under conditions of strategic nuclear stability. China would certainly not agree that such undertakings would nullify its asserted right to reunify Taiwan with China by whatever means necessary. It might, however, agree to indicate that there is no place for the use or threat of force to settle disputes. Whatever the words, the meaning is that China will not treat the end of U.S. nuclear-based escalation dominance as a license to cause crises.

In addition, the United States should expect China to be more open about its plans for further development of its strategic nuclear forces.

Perhaps most important, the United States should insist that China become a constant partner in nuclear nonproliferation in general and particularly in the toughest cases—Iran and North Korea—where Chinese assistance has been spotty. For the United States and China to exchange no-first-use pledges should bolster the international nonproliferation regime, but a more concrete dividend, in the same spirit, would be stronger Chinese support to sanction Iran and North Korea. By acceding to China's position on no first use, the United States should expect China to partner with it in preventing nuclear proliferation.

China should understand and acknowledge that allies are covered by Sino-American no first use.[30] If there is any doubt on this score, the United States should reiterate that a nuclear attack on its East Asian allies would prompt the United States to respond with means of its choosing, including nuclear weapons.

For the United States, Sino-U.S. nuclear no first use would be a further step toward reducing the importance of nuclear weapons and, as it has promised, to move toward conditions in which the only acceptable role for nuclear weapons is to deter nuclear war. Of course, this would immediately raise the question of U.S.-Russian no-first-use policy. Here, the United States must tread even more cautiously, given the doubts of its more exposed East European allies about NATO's nonnuclear ability and resolve to protect them from Russian aggression. Moreover, now that it finds itself with inferior conventional capabilities, Russia's own policy contemplates the option of nuclear first use. The United States might not find a willing partner in Russia. It is not within the scope of this study to recommend for or against a U.S.-Russia no-first-use agreement; but the pressure that a U.S.-China agreement would create could be productive.

Beyond Russia, if the United States were to begin to form no-first-use agreements with other nuclear powers, where would it lead? Presumably, the United States would not want to reward nuclear proliferation by offering no first use to all nuclear weapons states. On the contrary, only adherence to the Nuclear Nonproliferation Treaty would merit no first use, both for nuclear weapons states and non–nuclear weapons states. Thus, by pledging not to use nuclear weapons first against each other, the United States and China could demonstrate leadership in reducing the utility of nuclear weapons and thus in advancing nonproliferation.

If the United States and China were in effect to "fence off" the nuclear domain from their relationship, whether in good times or bad, why not do likewise in other strategic domains where the offensive power and vulnerability of each are growing? One possibility would be to use nuclear no first use as a model to exchange wider assurances that the two leading powers will not strike at each other's essential well-being in *any* domain. For example, nuclear no first use could be accompanied by or set the stage for reciprocal assurances that neither will attack the space assets of the other.

The United States could simply, quietly acquiesce in Chinese achievement of a second-strike nuclear capability. Or it could view and use such a development as a way to consolidate trust in Sino-American relations in general, to further its goal of reducing the salience of nuclear weapons, to advance its nonproliferation objectives, and to stabilize its strategic nuclear relationship with China.

Notes

[1] China conducted its first nuclear test in 1964. The primary motivation for this test was to deter the Soviet Union and the United States from using their weapons in a coercive manner.

[2] The United States is obligated under New START to reduce its ICBM force to 1,550, whereas China is currently estimated to possess approximately 20 first-generation fixed ICBMs and approximately 30 second-generation mobile ICBMs. Office of the Secretary of Defense, *Annual Report to Congress: Military and Security Developments Involving the People's Republic of China* (Washington, DC: Department of Defense, 2010), 34.

[3] According to the 2010 BMD review, the United States is in the process of deploying approximately 30 missile interceptors. Chinese officials have expressed concerns about the potential impact of U.S. missile defenses on China's nuclear deterrent, especially given the potential for technological breakthroughs and U.S. unwillingness to accept any binding restraints on deployment of future BMD capabilities.

[4] See Liping Xia, "China's Nuclear Policy and International Order in the 21ˢᵗ Century," *NIDS International Symposium on Security Affairs* (Tokyo: The National Institute for Defense Studies, 2009), 73–94; Information Office of the State Council of the People's Republic of China, *China's National Defense in 2006* (Beijing: State Council of the People's Republic of China, December 2006); Information Office of the State Council of the People's Republic of China, *China's National Defense in 2008* (Beijing: State Council of the People's Republic of China, January 2009); Shu Guang Zhang, "Between 'Paper' and 'Real Tigers': Mao's View of Nuclear Weapons," in *Cold War Statesmen Confront the Bomb: Nuclear Diplomacy since 1945,* ed. John Lewis Gaddis et al. (New York: Oxford University Press, 1999).

[5] According to calculations done in 2006 by Hans M. Kristensen, Robert S. Norris, and Matthew G. McKinzie, a nuclear exchange with China would cost the United States between 15 million and 40 million casualties. See "Chinese Nuclear Forces and U.S. Nuclear War Planning," Federation of American Scientists/Natural Resources Defense Council, November 2006, 10.

[6] *China's National Defense in 2008,* 29.

[7] M. Taylor Fravel and Evan Medeiros, "China's Search for Assured Retaliation: The Evolution of Chinese Nuclear Strategy and Force Structure," *International Security* 35, no. 2 (Fall 2010), 48–87.

[8] China has deployed approximately 30 DF–31 and DF–31A ICBMs. Both are road-mobile, solid propellant missiles. The DF–31A has an estimated range of 11,200 kilometers and can reach targets throughout the continental United States. Office of the Secretary of Defense, *Annual Report to Congress: Military Power of the People's Republic of China* (Washington, DC: Department of Defense, 2010).

[9] Hu Jintao, comments at the United Nations Security Council Summit on Nuclear Non-Proliferation and Nuclear Disarmament, New York, September 24, 2009.

[10] The first meeting of the Sino-American strategic security dialogue took place at the Strategic and Economic Dialogue meeting in Washington, DC, on May 9–10, 2011. The two sides agreed that a second round of the strategic security dialogue would take place prior to the next Strategic and Economic Dialogue.

[11] This chapter does not analyze whether China currently has the ability to deter a U.S. nuclear attack. If it does, it is probably marginal, and China will need to improve if not expand its offensive forces in order to ensure it has a credible deterrent in the future.

[12] "Week in Review" chart, *The New York Times,* March 3, 2011. U.S. missile defense efforts have also yielded a theater missile defense capability with value in a conventional conflict.

[13] Each interceptor costs about $3 million more than each ICBM (not including development, platforms, support costs, or sensors). It should be noted that the SM–3 is not designed for ICBM intercept, though it has that potential.

[14] A more conservative estimate is that it could require four to five interceptors, on average, to destroy a single incoming target, given current technology, making offense dominance even more pronounced.

[15] Fravel and Medeiros, 48–87.

[16] Although China and Russia signed a detargeting and no-first-use pledge in 1994, Chinese nuclear concerns persist.

[17] See Hu Jintao; *China's National Defense in 2006; China's National Defense in 2008;* Pan Zhenqiang, "China's Nuclear Strategy in a Changing World Strategic Situation," in *Unblocking the Road to Zero: Perspective of Advanced Nuclear Nations: China and India,* ed. Barry Blechman (Washington, DC: Stimson Center, March 2009), available at <www.stimson.org/nuke/pdf/UnblockingRoadZeroChina-India.pdf>; Yao Yunzhu, "Chinese Nuclear Policy and the Future of Minimum Deterrence," *Strategic Insights* 4, no. 9 (September 2005), available at <www.nps.edu/Academics/centers/ccc/publications/OnlineJournal/2005/Sep/yaoSep05.html>; Sun Xiangli, "Analysis of China's Nuclear Strategy," *China Security,* no. 1 (Autumn 2005), 23–27, available at <www.wsichina.org/back1_05.html>.

[18] James B. Steinberg, "Administration's Vision of the U.S.-China Relationship," keynote address at the Center for a New American Security, Washington, DC, September 24, 2009, available at <www.state.gov/s/d/2009/129686.htm>; *Military and Security Developments Involving the People's Republic of China,* 34–35.

[19] We define "vital" U.S. interests as those necessary to the essential well-being if not viability of the United States, its population, and its form of government. This would not necessarily include the security of U.S. allies, though the United States has indicated that an attack on allies to which the United States has a defense commitment is tantamount to an attack on the United States itself.

[20] To be clear, U.S. ballistic missile defense, at least in its theater applications, is also intended to counter Chinese conventional missile threats to U.S. forces, ships, and bases and possibly U.S. allies in the western Pacific. Whether the United States can keep pace with the expansion of Chinese short- and medium-range missiles is questionable.

[21] Department of Defense, *Nuclear Posture Review Report* (Washington, DC: Department of Defense, 2010), 15.

[22] In classic deterrence theory, the side lacking escalation dominance can be expected to retreat if convinced that the opponent will escalate; and the opponent can be expected to convince the weaker side that it has the will to escalate and will gain an expanding advantage as it does.

[23] A 2010 Pentagon report indicates that China already has deployed approximately 30 of these mobile ICBMs; *Military and Security Developments Involving the People's Republic of China,* 34.

[24] The JL–2 SLBM, originally intended to be deployed in 2010, has an operational range of around 8,000 kilometers, which leaves it unable to pose a threat to the continental United States. Additionally, the Chinese have never successfully deployed and operated a SSBN, making their ability to deploy one during a crisis highly uncertain.

[25] Department of Defense, *Quadrennial Defense Review Report* (Washington, DC: Department of Defense, 2010), 67.

[26] Robert S. Norris and Hans M. Kristensen, "Nuclear Notebook: Chinese Nuclear Forces, 2008," *Bulletin of the Atomic Scientists* 64, no. 3 (July 2008), 42–45.

[27] *Nuclear Posture Review Report,* v.

[28] For further explanation, see Christopher Achen and Duncan Snidal, "Rational Deterrence Theory and Comparative Case Studies," *World Politics* 41 (1989), 152.

[29] See North Atlantic Military Committee, "Final Decision on MC 14/3, A Report by the Military Committee on Overall Strategic Concept for the Defense of the North Atlantic Treaty Organization Area," 9–11, available at <www.nato.int/docu/stratdoc/eng/a680116a.pdf>.

[30] While Chinese acknowledgment that Sino-U.S. nuclear no first use extends to allies might be viewed as Chinese acceptance of the legitimacy of U.S. alliances in the region, Chinese interlocutors have indicated unofficially that this is not an insurmountable obstacle.

Chapter Five

Mutual Restraint in Space

Both the United States and China are increasingly invested in and dependent on space for their prosperity and security. Yet the space systems and missions of both are becoming more vulnerable to counterspace threats—notably, each other's ASAT capabilities.[1] Space is approaching the status of a strategic domain in which either global power can harm the essential well-being of the other. This chapter will begin by delving into U.S. and Chinese uses of space, including military. It will then analyze the relationship of offense to defense (for example, satellite protection) in space, as well as how space may compare to the nuclear domain in regard to both the need and the opportunity for restraint. It will conclude by examining options and suggesting an approach to Sino-U.S. mutual restraint in space.

The United States and China both use space—satellites and associated systems that position, control, communicate with, and use them—for important commercial, civilian, and security missions: public, business, and governmental communications; remote Earth sensing and imaging; weather tracking and warning; geopositioning and navigation on land, at sea, and in the air; intelligence, surveillance, and reconnaissance; military command, control, communications, and targeting; and guidance for precision weapons.[2] Increasingly, space is essential for both countries' productivity, competitiveness, normal functioning, warning, and security from natural disasters as well as human threats.[3]

In addition, the use of space supports and is supported by a more than $250 billion global industry in satellites, on-board systems, communication links, ground-based components, launch systems, and launch services, in which the United States and China are leading competitors.[4] China is expanding its technological, industrial, and operational capabilities to launch and support satellites. Its space industry is increasingly competitive in the global market, especially on price and value, whereas the U.S. space industry is struggling to hold its market share.

Because major powers prefer to build and use their own satellites, the number being launched is a reasonable indicator of national reliance on space. The data suggest that while the United States is more heavily invested in space than China, China's dependence on and role in space are expanding rapidly. The United States launches an average of about 17 satellites annually. China is now launching at a rate of about 7 annually, has the fastest growth rate in launches per year, and intends at least 10 launches annually over the next 5 years, bringing it closer to the U.S. launch rate.[5]

China's growing economy both dictates and permits greater use of space. Its integration into the global economy requires global communications, largely through space. China's voracious appetite for foreign raw materials and energy requires sensing and mapping services. Global positioning plays a growing role in everything from traffic management to navigation to Internet applications. At the same time, China's ambitions to be seen as a great power find expression in becoming a space power, strategically and commercially. China now has ample resources, know-how, and infrastructure to build, launch, operate, and use advanced satellites on a large scale. Even as access to space is becoming vital for China, it is using some of these resources to develop capabilities to deny access to others.

Of course, the United States has been active in space much longer and therefore has invested much more than China in this domain. Assuming that each launch costs $50 million and each satellite costs $100 million (which has been the average over the last 10 years), the United States has invested about $60 billion in space assets, whereas China has invested only about $10 billion. In proportion to economic scale, however, China's current investment in and growing dependence on space are comparable to America's.[6] For every satellite China currently operates, the United States operates four; but the U.S. economy is nearly four times the size of China's. As China's economic growth continues—outpacing U.S. growth—its need for and wherewithal to invest in space systems will grow as well.

Table 5–1 compares Chinese and U.S. investment in space. In addition to a comparison of the numbers of satellites in orbit and launched each year, it looks at the relationship of Chinese and U.S. space investments to their respective gross domestic products (GDPs). This better represents the economic reliance of each country on space. Because it has been investing in space much longer than China, the United States has one working satellite for approximately every $70 billion in GDP, while China has one for every $100 billion in GDP. However, China is now launching a satellite for every $700 billion in GDP, while the United States is launching one for every $800 billion in GDP. The rate of Chinese satellite launches is growing more rapidly than the Chinese economy. Broadly speaking, China is quickly becoming as dependent economically on space as the United States is. By the time China's GDP matches that of the United States, the two could be at rough parity in number of satellites being launched and in overall investment in space.

	Working Satellites in Orbit	Average Number of Satellites Launched Annually	Gross Domestic Product Per Satellite (U.S. $Billions)	Gross Domestic Product Per Launch (U.S. $Billions)
China	47	7	$106.06	$712.10
United States	201	17	$70.24	$830.53

Table 5–1. U.S. and Chinese Investment in Space

Both China and the United States depend on space capabilities not only for economic gain but also for national security and possible military advantage. Both increasingly rely on space to support military capabilities and operations, including plans for major warfighting contingencies involving the other. Space is used for wide-area intelligence gathering; focused and persistent staring; locating, tracking, and targeting enemy forces; managing and coordinating among one's own forces (jointly); assessing battlefield conditions before, during, and after hostilities; navigation of platforms; and guidance of weapons systems. Satellites are capable of observing Earth in a variety of ways, including optical, infrared discrimination, and radar, with striking resolution. The United States, with its global security interests and activities, is ahead of China in these technologies and thus its uses of space; but China is advancing on all fronts.

For both countries, space is critical for the performance of these intelligence and military functions *anywhere*. Although land and sea-bed fiber optic cables carry larger volumes of data and voice telecommunications, the more ubiquitous and flexible space-based links will remain indispensable. This is germane for how both the United States and China manage their military forces and might operate those forces in the event of conflict. The United States could not function militarily on the scale and in the way it does across the sprawling Pacific without satellites. China's reliance on satellites will increase as it extends its military reach to counter U.S. forces or to perform out-of-area missions. Similarly, observing events anywhere with potential national security implications (for example, missile launches) requires global surveillance, which the United States has and China aspires to have.

Importantly, military space assets and missions overlap with civilian-commercial ones. Most of the communications supporting the Gulf War, the Iraq War, and the Afghanistan war were and are over commercial communications satellite links.[7] The U.S. Defense Department's Global Information Grid (GIG), on which it depends for C⁴ISR, is comprised largely of commercial switching and transmission systems. Global positioning systems (GPS) support national security missions but are also available for a growing and important set of public and commercial applications. U.S. (and undoubtedly Chinese) requirements for remote Earth observation for national security are met by a flexible mix of government and commercial platforms and services. Because it has not invested as heavily as the United States in dedicated satellites for national security, China depends more on commercial services to meet this need. In sum, most U.S. and Chinese assets in space are dual-use, making a clear demarcation between military and nonmilitary capabilities hard to draw.

Both China and the United States have another interest in space: ASAT capabilities to deny an adversary's use of space. While the United States has potential, if not actual, superiority in every aspect of ASAT capability, China has conducted a successful, recognized ASAT test with at least two other reported attempts, has growing and diverse capabilities, and has the potential for an operational capability that can overcome U.S. efforts to protect most American satellites.

China is increasingly interested in soft-kill ASAT weapons, using directed energy and nonkinetic means to disable satellites or at least to impair their performance. According to the Defense Department, China is pursuing a broad range of counterspace capabilities in addition to the direct-ascent ASAT weapons. The department's most recent report to Congress on Chinese military and security developments describes China's multidimensional program to improve its capabilities to limit or prevent the use of space-based assets by potential adversaries during times of crisis or conflict.

Clearly, both the United States and China view the other as the main threat to access to space. Accordingly, both have an interest in ASAT weapons at least for purposes of deterring the other. The United States has singled out China in explaining its "comprehensive approach to deterring attack on our space systems," which includes "readiness and capability to respond in self-defense, and not necessarily in space [in order to] complicate the calculus of a government considering an attack on our space assets."[8]

At the same time, ASAT development is also motivated by a desire to have the option to attack an adversary's use of space for military contingencies. The very fact that each country considers deterrence necessary implies the interest the other one may have in using ASAT weapons for warfighting. Prospects for mutual restraint in using ASAT weapons must confront the reality that knocking out the opponent's satellites could be advantageous during combat.

Use of ASAT weapons can also have more strategic consequences, if not purposes. Commercial and other civilian satellites that enable economies and societies to function are typically more vulnerable than military and intelligence satellites (though no satellite can be invulnerable). Moreover, civilian-commercial satellites may be inviting targets for escalation aimed at breaking the enemy's will, and possibly its broader warmaking capacity. Yet because many satellites are dual-use, the line between battlefield (to hamper enemy military operations) and strategic (against civilian uses of space) ASAT weapons is blurred. There is no firebreak in space.

The interests of the United States and China, the only two current counterspace powers, in ASAT capabilities are each strongly motivated by the other's interest in space and counterspace. Clearly, neither would find it acceptable for the other to have a monopoly. Again, deterrence logic is at work: given the difficulty of defending satellites, the best way to mitigate the vulnerability of one's satellites is to be able to retaliate against the enemy's satellites. It is reasonable to expect that the origin of ASAT attacks will be identifiable, especially because few countries have such potential.[9] Because both the United States and China will almost certainly have deployed ASAT capabilities, as well as vulnerable satellites, it is likely that some degree of mutual deterrence will take effect, whether or not the two countries agree explicitly to mutual restraint.

U.S. and Chinese Military Space Dependencies and Strategies

One of the chief obstacles to mutual restraint is the potential military benefit of attacking an adversary's satellites in the event of hostilities, and the fact that this benefit grows as space becomes more critical to complex military operations over great distances—the sort of operations for which the United States and China plan and prepare. Unlike nuclear weapons, ASAT weapons may be integral to and thus hard to decouple from conventional hostilities, especially in the form that hostilities could take in the western Pacific. Simply stated, satellites can be instruments of war, critical to success or failure. So making space a sanctuary and satellites off-limits for attack will be counterintuitive to military planners.

While space is militarily important to both powers, the nature and degree of U.S. and Chinese military reliance on space vary as a function of their different positions, geographies, and strategies. The United States is an established global sea and air power that can use joint expeditionary and strike forces wherever it must to defend its interests and meet its security responsibilities. China is a rising, historically land-oriented power with growing global interests, regional ambitions, and increasing concerns about its security and maritime access.[10] Consequently, while the United States needs space as a medium through which to monitor the world and orchestrate distant military operations, China, for now at least, is using space in a limited capacity to protect itself and to extend power mainly in its immediate region and waters. While the United States relies more on space militarily—managing far-flung forces, being an ocean away from the battlefield, and having a head start in space—China's military use of space is expanding.

The military use of space by China and the United States is influenced heavily by the strategy, plans, and preparations of each for conflict with the other. The most challenging, space-intensive military contingencies either country could face are with the other—namely, a large-scale war in the western Pacific, perhaps over a Chinese assault on Taiwan, with mainly U.S. naval and air strike forces pitted against Chinese amphibious, antiaccess, naval, and air forces. The proximity of a conflict to China, the transpacific distance from the United States, and the greater U.S. prowess in and reliance on integrated warfare shape respective Chinese and American attitudes and plans about space and counterspace.

China's strategy in such a contingency is to deter, delay, or degrade U.S. intervention, contain the fighting in geographic scope, duration, targets, and weaponry, and score a sudden and irreversible victory (for example, control of Taiwan) without a full-scale and protracted Sino-U.S. war, in which the United States could bring superior power to bear. U.S. strategy, for purposes of our analysis, is to stop Chinese forces with strike forces and to expand and prolong the conflict as necessary to prevail operationally and weaken China's ability and will to fight. Space is essential to both strategies, although in different ways.

Because it is assumed that China may start a conflict over Taiwan, it is crucial for the United States to have strategic and tactical warning by conducting space-based surveillance of Chinese warfighting capabilities, readiness, and military movements. Absent such warning, the United States would be less able to concentrate enough of its forces to prevent China from succeeding with a swift seizure of Taiwan. In the event of hostilities, the United States must use space to locate, track, and target Chinese forces: amphibious ships and surface combatants, air forces, missile launchers, radars and other sensors, command and control nodes, and force concentrations, staging, and flows. The United States would then use space to guide weapons to their Chinese targets. Increasingly, U.S. precision strike weapons rely on off-board guidance, which makes each weapon more affordable and thus allows more of them. Space is therefore a critical medium for weapons performance.

The United States would also use space platforms and links to direct, coordinate, and manage U.S. forces, as well as to enable collaboration among them. This is especially important because U.S. expeditionary and strike forces are joint and operate best in an integrated way. Any unit, platform, sensor, or weapon anywhere should be able to support or be supported by those anywhere else, regardless of armed service. The United States is especially committed to fighting its forces this way in complex and intense operations against a militarily formidable enemy. Its ability to harmonize the actions of all its forces can be a huge advantage, made possible by digital communications and, when at great distance, by the use of space. At the same time, this U.S. integrated warfare makes its ability to use, secure, and control space of paramount importance—a U.S. dependence that the Chinese fully appreciate.

Because hostilities would be close to its mainland and because its forces would be relatively concentrated, China can make greater use of land, sea-bed, and other terrestrial communications links in which it has invested heavily. However, one of China's greatest challenges is that of long-range surveillance—learning where U.S. strike forces are, especially mobile forces such as ships. As Chinese antiaccess and area-denial capabilities improve, the United States is becoming more reliant on greater standoff ranges, stretching back into the Pacific. The longer the range of U.S. strike systems, the farther China must see to target them. While China is developing and fielding extended-range ground-based sensors (such as over-the-horizon radar), its ultimate solution is space-based sensors to find distant and distributed U.S. strike platforms. Once having found U.S. forces, the Chinese increasingly will rely on space to support precision strikes against these forces, chiefly by medium- and longer range missiles. As essential as space systems are now to the ability of the United

States to intervene, they will become essential to the ability of the Chinese to prevent effective U.S. intervention.

In the event of a conflict over Taiwan, Chinese strategy calls for being able to attack U.S. aircraft carriers, thus either deterring U.S. intervention by threatening loss of the carriers or, failing that, delaying and degrading their strike operations. The chief weapons China would use for this purpose are attack submarines, which it is buying and building in significant numbers, and ASBMs with maneuverable terminal trajectories, which it is vigorously developing and about to field.[11] The range of submarines and ASBMs is only helpful to China if it knows where to send them. So space is becoming essential for China's military strategy: reconnaissance and warning, space-based navigation and weapons guidance, finding and tracking carriers, and augmenting land-based communications to command, control, and coordinate air, missile, and submarine attacks. As U.S. forces begin to operate at greater ranges because of Chinese antinaval capabilities, China's military reliance on space will grow. Without the use of satellites, it will be difficult for the PLA to locate and engage U.S. forces at a distance, placing China at a disadvantage despite its improved close-in defenses.

Assuming that each side will have ASAT weapons available, Chinese and American reliance on space in a conflict presents each with a conundrum: which side stands to gain, or lose, more if the conflict includes destroying or disabling satellites? With the loss of its satellites, China would be seriously handicapped in attacking U.S. strike platforms at the distances from which they are able to strike, leaving Chinese forces, operations, and potential homeland targets vulnerable. Whether China could gain control of Taiwan under such conditions depends on the losses it is prepared to absorb. China's dilemma is that losses could mount if it either fails to deny U.S. forces the use of space or loses its own use of space.

With the partial loss of its satellites or impairment of their performance, the United States would find it more difficult to locate Chinese targets and to control its joint forces in integrated operations. The Chinese have identified space as the U.S. Achilles' heel.[12] They may even be convinced that without using ASAT weapons, they cannot defeat U.S. forces.[13] But as China attempts to extend its military—naval, antinaval, and aviation—reach, the vulnerability of its satellites will become its Achilles' heel as well. Once both countries have robust ASAT capabilities, China will face a tough choice between escalation of a conflict into space and maintaining its use of space.

It is safe to expect that the United States will have better ASAT capabilities than China for the coming decade, given its wealth of direct-ascent and directed energy technologies and options. But China also has the technological and economic wherewithal to field enough ASAT capability to degrade U.S. use of space in a conflict. Thus, for now, the United States may be more dependent on space but somewhat less vulnerable to Chinese ASAT weapons than China is to U.S. ASAT weapons, given superior U.S. ASAT-related technologies. This situation provides a powerful impulse for *both* to intensify development and deployment of ASAT capabilities— which, in deterrence theory, is called *arms race instability*. Notwithstanding the perils of ASAT warfare for both, China and the United States are poised for an ASAT race (which Chinese stated policy seeks to avoid).

The introduction of ASAT weapons into Sino-U.S. military contingencies may also create *crisis instability*—a decided advantage in attacking first and, knowing that the other side knows of that advantage, preempting. Moreover, given the low costs of attacking and the absence of casualties, one side or the other—eventually both—may elect to attack the other's access to space as an alternative to more costly and deadly military combat. Thus, a crisis or incident involving Chinese and U.S. forces could trigger attacks against satellites, which could lead to escalation in space, if not in the conflict as a whole.

To illustrate, the Chinese might decide to conduct soft-kill attacks on U.S. satellites at the outset or in expectation of a conflict, aiming to degrade the entire U.S. joint expeditionary and strike capability or, better yet, to deter U.S. intervention. They might be willing to risk the loss of their own satellites, expecting the United States to retaliate with ASAT weapons. But by then, China would have gained a critical initial advantage by knocking out the C^{4}ISR network that is indispensable to the entire U.S. concept of operations. This would be consistent with China's general strategy of gaining the initial upper hand, deterring or disrupting U.S. intervention, promptly achieving its war aims, and then presumably seeking a ceasefire with the United States. First use of ASAT weapons is also consistent with two tenets of general Chinese doctrine: using asymmetric weapons and tactics to neutralize U.S. conventional military superiority, and striking U.S. vulnerabilities, of which space is clearly one.

Of course, knowing the Chinese could see it this way, the United States might choose to preempt by launching a large-scale attack on Chinese satellites, possible ASAT launchers, and ground-based space-tracking facilities, which are on the Chinese mainland. The compounded dangers of Chinese first use and U.S. preemption could trigger a large conflict, including strikes against China itself, the moment either side calculates it would be imprudent *not* to attack the other's satellites. The crisis instability of ASAT weapons could lead to not just satellite warfare but also general warfare, which is what the Chinese especially want to avoid. Then again, the Chinese could come to believe that their only chance of prevailing in a conflict with the United States, if one looks likely, is to use ASAT weapons first.

Offense versus Defense in Space

Concern about these instabilities in Sino-U.S. counterspace rivalry stems in part from the fact that space, like the nuclear domain, favors offense (ASAT weapons) over defense (satellite protection). Satellites are exposed objects with little or no potential for self-defense. Though increasing in number, satellites are conspicuous singularities in space: easy to observe and virtually impossible to hide. They are also distinguishable and trackable based on their orbits, physical characteristics, performance, and communications signatures. Both China and the United States seek to catalogue all objects in space. China's efforts to do so are aided by U.S. openness.[14] A fair assumption is that the United States and eventually China will have all of the other's important satellites in their cross hairs.

Being inherently fragile, satellites can be physically destroyed with interceptors using high-precision tracking, targeting, and weapons guidance technologies of various types. Because they are either in predictable (low) or geostationary (high) orbit, targeting is getting easier as sensing, data processing, and communications technologies improve. The challenge of reaching satellites with direct-ascent ASAT interceptors is a function of rocket thrust and in-flight boosting for as many stages as it takes to get to and beyond the upper atmosphere. Launching ASAT interceptors is no harder than launching other strategic and space payloads. Both China and the United States have the potential capacity to reach high-orbit satellites with direct-ascent interceptors.[15] Compared to other advanced weapons systems, such as ballistic missile defense, ASAT guidance and kill systems are not especially complex or costly, assuming they are fed data from targeting and guidance systems. A variety of information technologies make it possible to place an ASAT weapon at an exact point in space when and where the target satellite is there, regardless of its orbital speed.

Satellites can also be destroyed or disabled by directed energy weapons, such as lasers, microwave, and particle beams. These can be land-, sea-, or space-based. Co-orbital ASAT weapons represent another avenue of attack. In addition, ground stations that process and relay mission data can be located and struck.

Satellites and the systems in which they function are electronically fragile and thus vulnerable to being disabled, rendering them no more than space junk. It is thus unnecessary to be able to attack satellites physically to have counterspace capabilities. Whether jamming and other interference with satellite communications links and computer-based performance are deemed ASAT or cyber war is a distinction that could matter in the event that China and the United States consider mutual restraint in either or both domains.

Commercial satellites are more vulnerable than military and intelligence ones because they are typically not hardened with antijamming devices and are not given extra fuel to maneuver. However, even dedicated military and intelligence satellites, being fragile machines hanging in regions of space within ASAT reach, are inherently hard to protect. For every measure to protect them, there looks to be a more effective countermeasure, implying diminishing returns on investment to outrace counterspace capabilities. This is especially so when recognizing that counterspace assets can target satellite missions, not just satellites.

The U.S. national space policy calls for resilience and redundancy as ways to ensure access to space. While this is surely prudent, it is important to note that ASAT interceptors are decidedly cheaper than the sort of high-performance satellites that could be targeted, especially when the cost of the satellites and of launching them is taken in account.[16] While resilience and redundancy do not depend solely on numbers of satellites, economics dictate strongly against increasing satellite numbers as a way to improve security.

Figure 5–1 shows how inexpensive it is for the offensive side to produce and launch interceptors compared to the cost of producing and launching satellites. If each satellite launched was afforded protective measures or methods, the gap between the cost of defense and the cost of offense would be even greater.

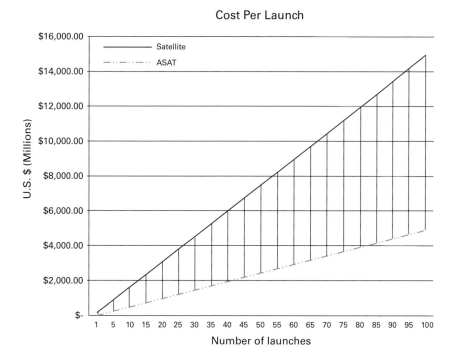

Figure 5–1. Costs of Offense and Defense in Space Domain

Nuclear and Space Domains: Similarities and Dissimilarities

Chapter four highlighted the merits of Sino-U.S. mutual restraint in the first use of nuclear weapons. Having established in this chapter that space already is or is becoming a strategic domain of importance to the economy and security of both countries, that both the United States and China will possess counterspace means to harm the other in this domain, and that offense dominates defense, an interesting hypothesis is that a similar accord regarding ASAT weapons is worth considering. Testing this hypothesis should begin with a comparison of the Sino-American strategic relationship in the two domains.

The dissimilarities are evident. In the nuclear domain, because the United States has an unchallenged lead in strategic offensive power, China would suffer far more destruction in the event of nuclear war. In contrast, because the United States currently depends more on space than China does, it potentially has more to lose in the event of ASAT warfare (assuming the two have roughly equivalent ASAT capabilities). In the nuclear domain, China is content with minimum deterrence and thus with substantially smaller offensive forces than the United States has. There is no indication that China would be content with minimum ASAT deterrence or would allow the United States significant ASAT superiority.

When taking into account military reliance on space, the United States is more dependent than China because of the criticality of space-based C⁴ISR to its ability to conduct expeditionary strike operations at transpacific distance. The Chinese may even contemplate initiating satellite warfare, despite the likelihood and effects on China of U.S. retaliation. The PLA can be counted on to resist any measures that would preclude this option. Overall, then, China may be less interested than the United States in mutual restraint in using ASAT weapons, whereas the opposite is the case in the nuclear domain. Again, this might change as informationization increases Chinese military reliance on space.

In contrast to nuclear weapons, the domain of space is integral to both U.S. and Chinese military strategies and war expectations. Moreover, unlike nuclear weapons, ASAT weapons can lead to crisis instability: while the incentive to use nuclear weapons preemptively is negligible for the United States (given its nonvital stakes) and nonexistent for China (given the huge consequences), both sides could have an incentive to use ASAT weapons first.

The stigma and lasting political condemnation associated with the use, especially first use, of nuclear weapons are not matched in space, where the only immediate casualties of war would be satellites or their performance. Other countries have frowned on ASAT tests. But in a war between China and the United States, which would be alarming enough, it is not clear that crossing the ASAT threshold would shock the world. The relative lack of moral compunction about attacking satellites cuts two ways: on the one hand, it makes the use of ASAT weapons more likely; on the other hand, it might make agreed mutual restraint all the more useful.

Nuclear weapons and the deterrence theories surrounding them have sharp firebreaks, two in particular: the nuclear threshold itself, and the break between battlefield and strategic (homeland) targeting. There are no such sharp firebreaks in counterspace. Again, while both countries have dedicated military and intelligence satellites—for example, for high-resolution, specialized, and persistent surveillance—they also rely militarily on a host of dual-use satellites—for low-resolution/broad area surveillance, GPS, and communications. The latter can be as critical as the former for supporting complex military operations. Consequently, if operational necessity motivates one or the other country to target satellites that contribute to military effectiveness, there is a strong logic in favor of attacking at least some dual-use systems along with dedicated military and intelligence ones. Moreover, even if initial attacks avoided dual-use systems, escalation could readily cross that line. Thus, the distinction between dedicated military and intelligence satellites and dual-use ones critical to military operations is at best a very weak firebreak—not one that either side would count on the other side to observe in a conflict.

Similarly, there is no clear threshold in regard to ASAT warfare as there is in nuclear warfare. An ASAT war—presumably as an extension of conventional war—could begin with jamming or computer network interference and then move to electronic disabling, directed energy attack, and physical destruction—begging the question of what the threshold is. With nuclear war, the first "event" is the detonation of a nuclear weapon. With ASAT war, the event may be some degradation of the performance of certain satellites—hardly as shocking or as certain to produce devastating retaliation.

The final dissimilarity between the nuclear and space domains is in attitudes about ASAT weapons within U.S. and Chinese civilian and military circles. The Chinese are of one mind that a U.S. nuclear attack would be catastrophic, that China must have a credible second-strike deterrent capability, and that nuclear weapons should not be used first or for warfighting. Americans are more ambivalent about nuclear weapons, recognizing that trying to deny China an effective retaliatory capability would be terribly costly and difficult, but they are also concerned that decoupling security in the western Pacific from the strategic level, by endorsing mutual nuclear deterrence, could be destabilizing.

Regarding ASAT weapons, both the Chinese and the Americans are ambivalent. U.S. strategists appreciate the advantages of being able to degrade China's ability to target U.S. aircraft carriers by knocking out Chinese satellites, but the consequences for U.S. military effectiveness of ASAT warfare are not lost on them. It is also possible to read the Chinese two ways. The first is that China must have ASAT weapons to prevent U.S. supremacy and deter U.S. use of ASAT weapons.[17] The second is that China needs ASAT weapons to neutralize U.S. expeditionary strike superiority, which clearly implies ASAT warfighting and possible first and early use.[18] The problem in knowing which of these Chinese views will prevail is that both justify a robust Chinese effort to develop ASAT weapons.

This last uncertainty matters a great deal, for the ASAT-for-deterrence view would imply possible Chinese interest in mutual restraint in space, whereas the ASAT-for-warfighting view would imply Chinese interest in first use and therefore aversion to mutual restraint. The Chinese have been coy about their positions on ASAT weapons and other space security issues. They have declined to support no first use of ASAT weapons, while advocating nuclear no first use. The Chinese campaign against the militarization of space, but this is aimed at U.S. BMD and other possible space-based weapons,[19] not at ASAT weapons (which for now are ground-based). It must be assumed that the Chinese are unconvinced that agreed mutual deterrence in space would be advantageous. This in turn means that if the United States desires mutual restraint in the use of ASAT weapons, it will have to find a way to convince the Chinese. This finding informs the recommendations that follow.

Options for Mutual Restraint

An attempt at ASAT arms control by the United States and the Soviet Union in the 1970s was unsuccessful in large part because neither side wanted to forego an undeveloped but seemingly promising warfighting capability, and neither side was so dependent on space as to give it a compelling reason to negotiate. In addition, negotiations foundered over definitional and verification difficulties.

Could traditional approaches to arms control (such as efforts to limit development, testing, and deployment of ASAT weapons through legally binding treaties) succeed with U.S. and Chinese ASAT weapons today? Almost certainly not. While both sides are dependent on space, both see sufficient military utility in ASAT weapons that they will be reluctant to forego such capabilities even if the other were willing to do so. Moreover, there are too many ways to degrade satellite and satellite mission performance, and too little possibility of effectively controlling them, to make traditional ASAT arms control promising. For instance, neither side is going to give up direct-ascent rocketry or directed energy systems of the sort that could be used as ASAT weapons but have plausible alternative uses (for example, BMD). Limitations of soft-kill capabilities would be even harder to formulate, much less achieve agreement about. Verification of compliance with limitations on capabilities is virtually impossible. Moreover, because development of ASAT weapons could not be retarded even if systems were not operationally deployed, there would be huge breakout potential in any ASAT arms control agreement. Finally, unlike in U.S.-Soviet/Russian strategic nuclear arms control, third parties—India, Japan, and Russia, for example—could not be ignored.

A more promising course is to mitigate U.S. and Chinese space-access vulnerability by reciprocal restraint in denying such access. Given that both China and the United States might want to preserve options to disable an opponent's warfighting satellites while avoiding loss of access to space for other purposes, the logical measure would be mutual restraint in attacking non-warfighting satellites. However, satellites for communications, positioning and navigation, geographic and situational awareness, and other functions are largely dual-use, making it hard if not impossible for either side to disable satellites that can support warfighting without also affecting commercial and other civilian uses and benefits. Given the cost of building and launching satellites, it is unlikely that dual-use satellites will be abandoned in favor of dedicated ones for either the United States or China. Indeed, apart from missions that are exclusively of military interest, economics will encourage both increasingly to "piggy-back" dual-use satellite systems for critical military purposes.

This lack of a firebreak brings us back to whether the two sides might agree to make *any* interference with access to space permissible only in retaliation. This would include both hard and soft kill, and it would cover dedicated, dual-use, and civilian satellites. As already suggested, the United States should have an interest in broadly defined mutual ASAT deterrence, given its reliance on space for critical C⁴ISR, the civilian and commercial importance of space, the difficulty of protecting satellites, and growing Chinese ASAT capabilities. The main drawback of mutual ASAT restraint for the United States would be forfeiture of the option of striking China's space-based assets that support its ability to find and strike U.S. carriers. However, for the United States at least, the value of access to space for military purposes arguably exceeds the value of denying China access to space for military purposes. This implies that the United States would not favor a military-civilian ASAT firebreak, even if one were possible. In terms of deterrence—the underpinning of mutual restraint—the United States would regard any type of Chinese ASAT attack on any U.S. satellite as grounds for retaliation, possibly against Chinese dual-use satellites that support operations against U.S. forces.

The Chinese might be more reserved about mutual ASAT restraint than the United States—and decidedly less enthused about it than about mutual nuclear restraint. Chinese leaders may see merit in averting attacks on satellites that serve civilian and economic purposes. Indicative of this, at their January 2010 summit, President Hu agreed with President Obama that "the two countries have common interests in promoting the peaceful use of outer space and agree to take steps to enhance security in outer space." Nevertheless, the PLA may oppose restrictions on its options to disable U.S.

C⁴ISR satellites. Again, however, a military-civilian firebreak is not easy to establish, especially since the United States would presumably resist the idea.

This raises the question of whether and how the United States could encourage the Chinese to accept mutual ASAT restraint. A necessary condition for mutual restraint in any strategic domain is some degree of mutual deterrence. It can be assumed that the United States will continue ASAT development along every promising path, which will bring home to the Chinese their vulnerability in space. The United States could also clarify that it reserves the right to retaliate for a Chinese ASAT attack by disabling any Chinese satellite that could support military operations—by implication, including satellites that may also support such civilian functions as communications, Earth observation, and GPS. In essence, the United States would be expressing the view that however ASAT war begins, it could escalate to widespread loss of access to space. This could be of great concern to the Chinese, who depend increasingly on space to support their economic growth. It would also elevate the matter of ASAT operations from a PLA warfighting concern to a Chinese national security concern.

China might try to sidestep such a U.S. deterrence policy by expanding its cooperation with other countries in civilian satellite programs. However, absent agreement on strategic restraint, ambiguity about whether such satellites would be targeted by the United States could dissuade others from cooperating with China. The Chinese might also respond to such a declaratory U.S. policy, backed up by continued U.S. ASAT weapons development, by accelerating development and proceeding with deployment of ASAT weapons. But the premise of this analysis is that China will in any case have robust ASAT capabilities, which the United States can best counter by deterrence (given offense dominance).

With the United States adopting a robust ASAT retaliatory posture, the Chinese would be faced with the possibility that ASAT deterrence would make a better strategy for them than ASAT warfighting—a matter on which they are currently of mixed minds. After all, they cannot protect all their satellites, cannot launch a disarming strike against U.S. ASAT capabilities, and cannot hope to deter the United States from launching a retaliatory attack for a China ASAT attack. Chinese refusal to accept mutual deterrence could lead the United States to redouble its ASAT development, leaving Chinese satellites of all kinds even more vulnerable.

As in the nuclear domain, there is an argument for going beyond de facto mutual deterrence. Mutual restraint in the use of ASAT weapons would signify that both countries agree on the imperative of respecting each other's access to space. More than that, an agreement on reciprocal

ASAT no first use could add confidence and demonstrate Sino-American initiative in reducing the threat to space. Given U.S. and Chinese advantages in ASAT weapons, other countries would have strong incentives to join a multilateral ASAT no-first-use regime. In this regard, the United States would want to stress that restraint in the use of ASAT weapons should apply not only against nations that possess ASAT weapons and can therefore deter their use, but also to nations that do not have ASAT capability. Indeed, in order not to stimulate proliferation of ASAT capabilities, the United States should favor ASAT no first use as a global norm.

Additionally, by working out a form of understanding on mutual restraint in space, the United States and China each would have greater assurance that the other accepts the logic of deterrence. As in the nuclear domain, mutual restraint would bolster confidence that deterrence is accepted and will be maintained, and thus that access to space is that much more assured, which is the overriding U.S. goal.

ASAT no first use begs the need to define what it is that the parties agree not to use first, given the difficulty of identifying, much less agreeing on, either a threshold or a firebreak. Would jamming of satellite signals be banned? Interference with space-linked computer networks? Electronic disabling of satellites? One definition of threshold would be *any attack on a satellite*, regardless of means and medium. By this standard, initiating directed energy and other nonphysical attacks that might damage satellite performance yet spare the satellite would be proscribed. But interfering with communications to or from a satellite would not be banned because the satellite itself could be unscathed.

The problem with restraint that covers only attacks on satellites is that there are ways, already noted, by which the performance of a satellite can be degraded without attacking the satellite itself. A satellite is part of a complex system that also includes communications links (up- and down-links) and ground stations. In this sense, because "access to space" means more than the presence of satellites, access can be lost without losing satellites. For the United States, as well as for China, the question of a narrow versus a broad definition of ASAT weapons use boils down to whether it is better off preserving soft-kill options at the cost of making its access to space vulnerable to the other side's use of such options. On balance, the United States should prefer mutual restraint in regard to any operation that could deny or impair its access to space, backed up by a threat to retaliate for any such operation.

Our expectation is that both China and the United States will have ASAT capabilities, perhaps quite robust and diverse ones. This is what creates strong incentives to restrain their first use. However, as in the nuclear domain, no first use is no more than a contingent exchange of promises. This requires consideration of whether the parties to such an agreement could be expected to align their behavior in some way that would build confidence in no first use. Traditional approaches to ASAT arms control are not promising, but a Sino-American ASAT no-first-use agreement could be reinforced by agreement not to test those weapons that may not be used first. Such a moratorium would be hard to define, verify, and enforce, however. There are too many ways to portray testing of direct-ascent or directed energy weapons, and the possibility of breakout would make an ASAT testing moratorium fragile.

Even with the United States providing strong incentives for mutual restraint, the Chinese may feel they have more to lose than to gain by fore-going first use of ASAT weapons, particularly as a way to degrade the C^4ISR that is so vital to U.S. military operations in the western Pacific. Another possibility is that Chinese political and economic leaders would see the merits but be stymied by the opposition of the PLA, where most expertise on such matters resides.

The uncertain prospect for mutual ASAT restraint raises an important question: should the United States accept nuclear no first use, which the Chinese clearly want, without obtaining Chinese acceptance of ASAT no first use? It could be counterstrategic for the United States to accept mutual nuclear restraint while facing the combination of Chinese first use of ASAT weapons and anticarrier strikes, which could improve China's chance of executing its strategy of degrading U.S. forces and winning an intense but brief and contained conflict. Moreover, if the United States is keen on mutual restraint in space but merely willing to go along with mutual nuclear restraint, whereas the Chinese are keen on mutual nuclear restraint, it stands to reason that the United States should insist on both.

Thus, a case is emerging for the United States to favor mutual strategic restraint *generally*, with the nuclear and space domains necessary components. It could argue that the power and vulnerability of the United States and China give them a shared responsibility and an opportunity to institute restraint at the strategic level. This is a natural extension of the case already put forward by the U.S. Government for Sino-American "strategic stability" and reassurance.[20] The United States has said it intends to take up the issue of space security in the Sino-U.S. Strategic and Economic Dialogue.[21]

Notes

¹ The United States and China are not the only countries with an interest in ASAT, but they are the two most capable. The Soviet Union was the first to deploy an ASAT system, in 1979; but it discontinued the program shortly later and declared a unilateral moratorium on ASAT testing. It is generally assumed that Russia has not resumed the old Soviet program and has no active ASAT development under way.

² As a measure to improve the performance and reduce the cost of precision weapons, the United States has increasingly relied on "off-board" position, navigation, and guidance technologies.

³ For an empirical demonstration of the increasing role of space, see the Union of Concerned Scientists satellite launch database, available at <www.ucsusa.org/nuclear_weapons_and_global_security/space_weapons/technical_issues/ucs-satellite-database.html>.

⁴ Space Foundation, *The Space Report 2010: The Authoritative Guide to Global Space Activity* (Colorado Springs: Space Foundation, 2010).

⁵ Eric Hagt, "China's ASAT Test: Strategic Response," *China Security* (Winter 2007), 41–42.

⁶ Ibid.

⁷ John Edwards, "Commercial Sat Market Stirs," *Aviation Week & Space Technology* 162 (January 17, 2005), 147.

⁸ Gregory Schulte, testimony to Congress, May 2010.

⁹ Soft-kill ASAT attacks are less easily attributed than hard-kill ones, which at present involve the launching of ASAT interceptors.

¹⁰ See the Chinese sources cited in Michael A. Glosny and Phillip C. Saunders, "Correspondence: Debating China's Naval Nationalism," *International Security* 35, no. 2 (Fall 2010), 161–169.

¹¹ Yoichi Kato, "China's New Missile Capability Raises Tensions," *Asahi Shimbun*, January 27, 2011, available at <www.asahi.com/english/TKY201101260340.html>; Andrew Erickson, " Take China's ASBM Potential Seriously," U.S. Naval Institute *Proceedings* 136, no. 2 (February 2010).

¹² Ashley Tellis, "China's Military Space Strategy," *Survival* 49, no. 3 (2007), 48.

¹³ Ibid.

¹⁴ Ibid., 53.

¹⁵ Ibid., 48.

¹⁶ The cost of launching a new satellite is equivalent to launching 3.75 ASAT interceptors. The cost of placing a satellite in orbit was calculated by adding the average cost of a boost rocket and the average cost of a commercial payload. In reality, the cost of launching mission-critical satellites is probably far higher. The cost of launching an ASAT missile was derived from the Pentagon's estimate of how much it cost to destroy Satellite USA 193 in 2008.

¹⁷ For further discussion, see Zhang Hui "Space Weaponization and Space Security: A Chinese Perspective," *China Security* 2 (2006); Teng Jianqun, "Trends in China's Space Program and the Prevention of Outer Space Weaponization," *China Security* 2 (2006); Bao Shixiu, "Deterrence Revisited: Outer Space," *China Security* 5 (2007).

¹⁸ For further discussion, see Dean Cheng, "Prospects for China's Military Space Efforts," in *Beyond the Strait: PLA Missions other than Taiwan,* ed. Roy Kamphausen, David Lai, and Andrew Scobell (Carlisle, PA: Strategic Studies Institute, U.S. Army War College, 2009); Kevin Pollpeter, "The Chinese View of Military Space Operations," in *China's Revolution in Doctrinal Affairs: Emerging Threats in the Operational Art of the Chinese People's Liberation Army,* ed. James Mulvenon and David Finkelstein (Arlington, VA: CNA Corporation, 2002).

¹⁹ At the 2008 Conference on Disarmament, China continued to call for the "prevention of the placement of weapons in outer space and the threat or use of force against outer space objects," and the 2008 Chinese defense white paper stated that China seeks to prevent an arms race in space.

²⁰ Deputy Secretary of State James B. Steinberg, keynote address, "China's Arrival: The Long March to Global Power," Washington, DC, September 24, 2009; Department of Defense, *Nuclear Posture Review Report* (Washington, DC: Department of Defense, 2010), 4–5.

²¹ Schulte.

Chapter Six

Mutual Restraint in Cyberspace

Cyberspace—shorthand for the capabilities and content of computer networking—meets the criteria for a domain in the Sino-American strategic relationship. Both the United States and China are heavily digitized and critically dependent on computer networking for their prosperity, knowledge, and security. At the same time, each is able to penetrate, foul, and crash networks on which the other side depends, and each is continuously improving its ability to do so. Against the sort of large and sophisticated attacks that both China and the United States are capable of conducting, network defense can be exceedingly costly and yet still be inadequate. Consequently, each nation is vulnerable to great harm from the other in and through cyberspace. Yet it is unrealistic to expect either to forego capabilities to attack computer networks, which go hand in hand with capabilities to defend them, and traditional negotiated arms control of such capabilities is plainly impractical.

Because this mutual vulnerability in cyberspace will only get worse, China and the United States should be interested in reciprocal restraint in at least the most damaging kinds of attacks on at least their most important networks. Rather than rely predominantly on defense, deterrence based on the threat of retaliation for network attacks could undergird restraint in cyber war and thereby improve cyber security. Thus, cyberspace could become another domain in which the United States and China together manage and reduce strategic vulnerability—despite, yet also because of, their respective offensive capabilities.

Notwithstanding such logic, the complexity of computer networks, their myriad uses, and the many ways of interfering with them could make reciprocal restraint in cyberspace markedly more difficult than in the nuclear and space domains. The notion of deterrence based on mutual restraint presupposes that it is possible to define and in turn agree on the kinds and scale of network intrusion that qualify as an attack and that could warrant retaliation. Lack of clarity and understanding about the threshold for retaliation may invite mischief, cause miscalculation, and weaken deterrence. Moreover, the possibility of the attacker concealing its identity could militate against retaliation, the credible threat of which is key to deterrence—the bedrock for mutual restraint. Still, because China and the United States can harm one another so much by large network attacks, and because defense against such attacks is so hard, both should have an incentive to pursue the idea of mutual restraint in cyberspace.

Unlike the nuclear and space domains, cyberspace is obviously not all strategic. For instance, a large swath of bandwidth is for entertainment; while this may bring pleasure to hundreds of millions of Chinese and Americans, neither nation would be seriously hurt by its interruption.[1] In contrast, networks that enable financial, transport, commercial, communications, industrial, utility/power, and government/administrative functions, not to mention those that support intelligence and military missions, are critical for national productivity, cohesion, progress, and security. So is the Internet itself, on which many sectors and users rely for important functions. Major attacks on these precincts of cyberspace can be considered strategic; attacks on lesser ones cannot.

Having made this distinction between strategic and other networks, one wonders why either the United States or China, as states, would attack functions in the other's nonstrategic cyberspace.[2] In any case, threats to unimportant networks need not preoccupy the U.S. and Chinese governments. The two can and should concern themselves with the need for mutual restraint in strategic cyberspace, where the potential to suffer national harm is greatest, the motivation to inflict such harm strongest, and the benefit of mutual restraint clearest.[3]

While the distinction between strategic and nonstrategic networks is reasonable conceptually and also necessary for progress toward mutual strategic restraint in cyberspace, these two subdomains cannot be completely partitioned. The interconnectivity among networks—so complex that it is not entirely understood—means that an attack on unimportant networks can infect important ones (and vice versa). But this does not argue against focusing mutual restraint on strategic networks. The notion of restraining all attacks on all networks is as impractical as it is utopian, yet to abandon the goal of restraint regarding strategic networks because they are not hermetically isolated from nonstrategic ones would be to make the utopian the enemy of the good.

Thus, although the demarcation between strategic and nonstrategic cyberspace is blurred, subjective, and porous, this need not preclude deterrence and restraint where they matter most. Defining and agreeing on a precise threshold of strategic cyber attack, akin to detonating a nuclear weapon or destroying a satellite, are neither possible nor necessary. As long as there is a *substantially* shared view of what is strategic—something a Sino-U.S. strategic dialogue could address—the lack of an exact threshold could foster more restraint, not less.

It is also important to recognize at the outset that cyberspace, unlike nuclear and space domains, is largely the realm of nonstate entities, including unfriendly ones that would attack Chinese or American strategic networks if they could. This makes determining the origin of a cyber attack and the identity of the attacker that much more difficult. Moreover, the network paths that attacks take often transit intermediate countries, especially if the attacker wishes to cover its tracks. These nonstate and transnational aspects of cyberspace make it harder to take to task countries from or through which nonstate cyber attackers may operate, compounding the difficulty of establishing deterrence and thus mutual restraint across a large family of cyber threats. Indeed, blaming attacks on rogue hackers operating from their territory is a predictable deflection for state attackers.

The presence of nonstate hackers should not and does not absolve sovereign states of responsibility to control actions originating on their soil that can harm other sovereign states.[4] A good analogy is terrorism, where a state that is recognized as sovereign over territory from which terrorists operate internationally is responsible not merely for refraining from supporting the terrorists but also for actively defusing the threat they pose. This is not to argue that it is right for governments to attempt to tightly control cyberspace and those who use it; rather, it means that governments are obligated at least to try to curb domestic activities with deleterious international effects, be they cyber or other activities. Given its authoritarian political system and intrusive state security apparatus, it should be easier for China than the United States to meet this fundamental responsibility. In any case, if either China or the United States were to claim incompetence in controlling attacks from or through their countries, the answer should be not to cede cyberspace to trans-state attackers but to cooperate against them. Rather than an insurmountable obstacle to Sino-American restraint in cyberspace, the nonstate threat could be a subject of Sino-American cooperation in cyberspace.

Even those segments of cyberspace that are strategic are fraught with complexities and ambiguities that could encumber the pursuit of mutual restraint. Keeping this in mind, this chapter looks at U.S. and Chinese vulnerabilities and capabilities in cyber war, in both civilian and military domains. It then examines the relationship between offense and defense to see if the offense dominance that characterizes the nuclear and space domains applies in cyberspace as well. Further, it considers whether and under what conditions deterrence can actually work in cyberspace, given the uncertainties in identifying the source of an attack.

If mutual deterrence in cyberspace appears at least theoretically possible, a number of questions still need to be considered before applying it in the Sino-American case: What conduct, above what threshold, can and should be deterred? Can cyber warfare be decoupled from conventional warfare? What norms, policies, and behavior are needed to support mutual restraint in strategic cyberspace? Does cyber deterrence cover allies? Can Sino-American restraint and cooperation in cyber warfare be extended to others? These issues are tackled in the pages that follow.

Vulnerability and Capability

The United States has not suffered any major damage from attacks on segments of cyberspace that are strategic, as defined here. The Internet and other critical systems have proven resilient; users are increasingly vigilant when serious viruses, worms, and other network attack agents have appeared. Computer network protection has become a government priority.[5] Leading information technology firms are working to make their products more secure. A cyber protection industry is flourishing. The most serious penetrations of sensitive U.S. national security networks, publicly attributed to be the work of Chinese intelligence services, have been essentially espionage—unwelcome, but not debilitating or, for that matter, especially hostile, given the norms of international spying.

The absence of major cyber attacks on critical U.S. networks may mean that subtle deterrence is already working. Perhaps China has chosen not to move from computer network exploitation to computer network attack out of fear of U.S. retaliation. In any case, the Chinese evidently have not found themselves in circumstances in which the advantages of disrupting or degrading U.S. strategic networks would outweigh the risks of retaliation, political condemnation, or economic sanction. China and the United States have not had a serious confrontation since President Clinton sent two aircraft carriers into the Taiwan Strait to signal U.S. willingness to defend Taiwan. One can speculate about whether a crisis of that order today would produce a Chinese cyber attack.

Although the United States has not suffered a major cyber attack, there is evidence of the mounting danger of attacks too sophisticated to defeat, too broad to isolate, and too damaging to tolerate—attacks of the sort that well-resourced and technically capable nation-states like China, Russia, and a few others can conduct. Moreover, as noted, there may be logic to conducting such an attack on strategic U.S. computer networks, especially in the context of a wider crisis or conflict. Aside from nuclear attack (unthinkable), homeland terrorism (unthinkable except by terrorists), and ASAT weapons (nascent), the United States presently has no other obvious strategic vulnerabilities. A growing chorus of high officials and credible strategists describes cyberspace as the soft underbelly of U.S. security.[6]

One of the factors contributing to growing concern about strategic cyber attack is the expectation of a death toll of zero. Of course, the harm from cyber war, and the main argument for mutual restraint, is chiefly in economic terms. Broadly speaking, the damage from cyber war could be on the same order as that from "violent" strategic attack. Government estimates of the impact of potential cyber attacks on the U.S. economy range from $70 billion to over $900 billion (see table 6–1).[7]

Sector	Estimated Cost (In U.S. $Trillions)
Electric power	0.3–0.4
Oil and gas	0.1–0.4
Telecom/Internet	0.4–0.7
Banking and finance	0.9–1.3
Water and sanitation	0.1–0.1
Chemical industries	0.3–0.6
Air transport	0.1–0.3
Ground transport	0.3–0.6
Health care	1.0–2.2
Total	**3.7–6.9**

Table 6–1. Economic Cost of Cyber Attack by Sector

An enemy, if undeterred by the threat of retaliation, might think that damage on this scale (but with no casualties) is the best way to stop U.S. intervention abroad or weaken U.S. will in a conventional conflict. Moreover, such damage can be visited at negligible cost to the attacker. Add to this the potential to disrupt U.S. military operations by attacking U.S. C[4]ISR networks, and cyber attacks loom as a tempting option, given U.S. superiority in other categories of force and the possibility that the attacker's identity can be concealed.

Thus, while attacks on U.S. networks have not yet risen to the strategic level, they could.[8] For now, however, we have to rely analytically on what is publicly known about third-party strategic cyber attacks to get a feel for motivations and effects. It is widely believed that agents of the Russian state conducted or orchestrated large-scale attacks on the computer networks of Estonia in reprisal for removal of a Soviet war memorial, and then on those of Georgia, in concert with a Russian mechanized invasion.[9] These cases serve as a reminder that although cyber threats come in all sizes and with many motivations, threats from large and technically advanced states motivated by national security interests are the most formidable, most difficult to stop, and most damaging.

While extrapolating analytically from just two cases can only be done with caution, the exercise is illuminating. Estonia is particularly advanced in its reliance on data networking; for example, banking there is done almost entirely on line. Therefore, the effects of attacks on Estonia, which were severe if temporary, provide a glimpse of the possible effects of attacks on U.S. networks. Depending on the cyber weapons used and the targets, scale, and duration of attack, critical U.S. networks and associated functions could be degraded for days or weeks. In addition to the major shock this would have on U.S. markets and production, it could shake, though not necessarily break, American resolve in a crisis. It could also have secondary and longer term economic repercussions (including on the global economy). At least a would-be attacker could reasonably expect such effects.

The alleged Russian attacks on Estonia and Georgia may be indicative in several respects. First, strategic attacks are more likely to occur in an international crisis or conflict than out of the blue. This may help to explain why the United States has not experienced its "cyber Pearl Harbor." (U.S. opponents in conflicts since the end of the Cold War—Serbia, Iraq, the Taliban—have hardly been masters of cyber war.) Also, it implies that the United States would have time to prepare itself and its networks for attack as a crisis developed, and perhaps to take preventive or preemptive action. Second, these two cases suggest that attributing an attack to a likely attacker is far from hopeless. Like counting angels on pinheads, experts point out alternative explanations for the Estonia and Georgia attacks, but the circumstantial evidence points to at least state complicity, and thus sovereign responsibility. Third, Russia was obviously not deterred, perhaps because neither Estonia nor Georgia could have inflicted very damaging retaliation. Fourth, there was no known strategic retaliation against Russian networks for the Estonia or Georgia attack, so Russia (and others) may not feel deterred from launching new attacks.

Thus, the sparse data we have on strategic cyber warfare suggest that:

- a strategic cyber attack on the United States is more likely to be in the context of an international crisis or outright conflict than a "bolt from the blue"

- the absence of an attack to date could mean only that there has been no crisis to precipitate it

- a large and sophisticated attack is most likely to come from a capable state

- circumstances, including the presumed attacker's behavior before and after an attack, could aid in identifying the source

- the attacker, though vulnerable itself, probably expected no major retaliation

- a perceived risk of U.S. retaliation could be a decisive factor in the adversary's decision to attack.

While these inferences are not definitive, they do illuminate a most likely case. A state like Russia or China with the capability to launch a strategic cyber attack against the United States is less likely to do so absent a crisis or if it expected retaliation against its strategic networks. By this reasoning, the United States should strive to present the opposite of the Estonia and Georgia circumstances to any state contemplating an attack— briefly stated, a strong prospect of retaliation more costly to the attacker than the cost of not attacking.

Closely related is the possibility of a foreign attack on networks vital to U.S. *military* preparedness and operations. Again, this would presumably be in connection with a crisis or conflict, and thus with warning. Given the overlap between military and civilian networks, such an attack could escalate to general cyber warfare involving all sorts of critical national networks. While such a path to Sino-American strategic cyber war is, by definition, no more probable than a Sino-American crisis that would precipitate it, it bears especially careful analysis because it could stand in the way of agreement on mutual restraint or else could cause such restraint to fail in a crisis.

Chinese and U.S. vulnerability in cyberspace differs because of differences in the two countries' stages of economic development, their integration into the world economy and the data networks that enable it, and their political ability to endure serious economic dislocation caused by major cyber attack. At present, China is somewhat less dependent on computer networks than the United States for critical functions and has a somewhat more self-contained and secure communications infrastructure. Consequently, the Chinese might believe they have more to gain than to lose from resorting to cyber war.

But the Chinese are becoming more reliant on cyberspace (see figure 6–1). While this depicts only Internet users—a figure skewed by China's large population—it is also the case that China's productivity, trade and investment, competitiveness, cohesion, and national security all depend increasingly on computer networking. As a result, and to the extent the Chinese fear U.S. cyber attack, China's interest in mutual restraint should grow. Moreover, when taking into account the risk that economic reversals could cause political upheaval, China may become more sensitive than the United States to the effects of strategic cyber war.

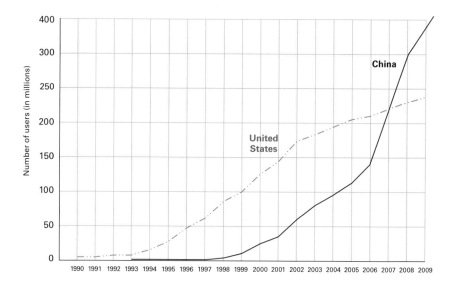

Figure 6–1. China's Internet Usage (1990–2009)

The link between Chinese economic development and dependence on computer networking is clear and strong. China's aggregate growth is tightly bound to increasingly sophisticated production of more complex goods for global markets. This has required both industrial division of labor and integration into international distribution systems in components, subassemblies, and finished goods flowing into and out of China.

Parallel payment and credit networks allow the transactions that make these markets work. This pattern, so essential for China's economic success, demands massive, rapid, uninterrupted exchange of data. Just as the expansion of Chinese affluence has spurred extraordinary growth in personal Internet use, the investment, manufacturing, trade, and financing that produce this affluence are demanding more data networking. China's growing dependence on cyberspace is both a consequence and a requirement of its economic success. With China's economy projected to overtake the U.S. economy in a decade or so, it will become at least as vulnerable to cyber war. Indeed, given the strong inhibitions against using nuclear weapons, the Chinese ought to be far more concerned about cyber security than about nuclear security.

Counterintuitively, for an authoritarian political system, Chinese use of cyberspace is at present mainly personal—80 percent of Internet use is at home—rather than industrial, commercial, or governmental.[10] This is a manifestation of rapid world-wide growth of Internet popularity and significantly rising income levels for most Chinese.[11] Data also indicate that this pattern is shifting toward a greater share of industrial and commercial use, which is to be expected given the complex production market networks that are propelling China's economic growth.[12]

The impact of even a temporary loss of critical networks on the Chinese economy could soon—if not already—be measured in percent of GDP, not unlike the U.S. impacts shown earlier. The fundamental reason for this is that the Chinese economy has grown more productive, more competitive, and larger as a result of internal and external *integration*. A highly fragmented economy has become networked, allowing vast improvements in efficiency, specialization, and optimization. In a country as large and diverse as China, economic integration is possible only with data networking. In addition, China's growing economic strength is the result of its integration in global trade and investment, the backbone of which is, again, data networking.

Although growth in Chinese industrial and commercial use has been slower than in personal use, it will accelerate as more Chinese enterprises integrate and operate throughout China, the region, and the world. Until recently, Chinese production for world markets has been largely a function of foreign direct investment and thus flowed through foreign corporate distribution systems, operations, supply chains, and financing. The data networking vital to these global business systems has been largely the responsibility of U.S., European, and Japanese multinational corporations.

This pattern has begun to change dramatically, as Chinese enterprises themselves accumulate the confidence, capital, and experience to become multinational—to globalize. This is readily seen in patterns of Chinese direct investment abroad, compared to foreign direct investment in China (see figure 6–2). As Chinese enterprises come to own, control, extend, and integrate operations, supply chains, distribution systems, market presence, and financing links, they will become more dependent on worldwide networking.[13]

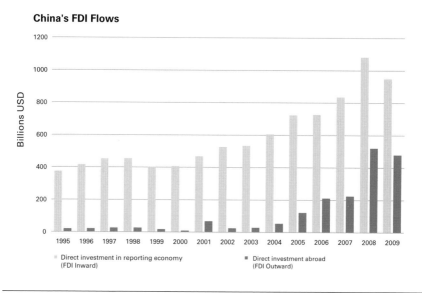

Figure 6–2. China's Foreign Direct Investment Flows

Another way to get a sense of China's reliance on data networking is to consider the importance of trade to its economy and, by extension, its political stability. China currently accounts for approximately 10 percent of total global exports, as opposed to approximately 8 percent for the United States. Trade (exports plus imports) accounts for about 40 percent of China's economy. Trade and the international commercial, financial, insurance, and logistic activities that enable it are highly communications-intensive. The implication of this is that disruption of the data that flows through business networks to and from China, even if brief, could have a large impact on Chinese trade and therefore on Chinese economic health.

China is stepping up to these dependencies by building a thick system of fiber optics and space-based communications in the region, taking a stake in the global information infrastructure. Yet far from giving China some sort of self-contained cyberspace, the connectedness of data networks, especially those that are Internet-based, makes it increasingly vulnerable to the sort of sophisticated cyber attacks that an advanced state like the United States (or Russia) may be capable of conducting.

One would almost expect the Chinese government to have become an advocate for cyber war restraint. As it is, political and economic elites have not spoken out or made any apparent effort to muzzle PLA chatter (in the form of published articles) about the warfighting advantages of attacks on U.S. C⁴ISR networks in the event of hostilities. Perhaps Chinese leaders are under the impression that China's investment in landline communications will make it invulnerable. In interviews in Beijing, the authors discovered few Chinese analysts who are aware that China's economic integration and continued growth would necessarily make it dependent on networks susceptible to attack. Progress toward Sino-American mutual restraint in cyberspace will depend on whether U.S. officials and researchers can convince Chinese counterparts that vulnerability will inevitably develop as the Chinese economy does.

As one Chinese interlocutor acknowledged, China could also suffer from secondary but sizeable damage should it attack U.S. computer networks.[14] This boomerang effect is a twist on deterrence theory (loosely akin to the self-deterring effects of the danger of jet stream–borne radioactive fallout from one's own nuclear attacks). An attacker such as China has to worry about not only the global interconnectedness of networks, but also the interdependence of the economies that depend on networks. For instance, Chinese credit card accounts are cleared through U.S. systems. The Chinese would be well advised to contemplate the effects on the Chinese economy of a strategic cyber attack on the United States even in the absence of U.S. retaliation. Of course, given the huge U.S. stake in China's economy, there is a comparable risk of substantial rebound damage from U.S. efforts to wage cyber war on China. Generally speaking, the global connectedness of cyberspace and of the economic growth it serves argues for mutual restraint—at least among major states, like China and the United States, that are both capable of and vulnerable to cyber war.

Finally, China is susceptible to political tsunamis caused by economic earthquakes. Circumstantial evidence of this comes from the regime's own strategy, which is to sustain strong per capita GDP growth to assure domestic calm. While economic damage may cause political uproar in a sturdy democracy like the United States, it does not have China's potential for instability, with a regime whose legitimacy is wedded to national economic performance and the ability to meet rising expectations. Shocking the U.S. economy could threaten current office-holders; shocking the Chinese economy could threaten the regime itself.

Cyber war appears to have a high escalatory potential, especially if the side attacked decides to strike back in kind but with a vengeance. Compounding this problem is that electrons, worms, and viruses do not necessarily conform to human plans.[15] Again, what may begin as military cyber war could spread inadvertently, if not by design, into general cyber war. A critical question for the prospect of mutual deterrence is whether it is possible to discriminate between networks supporting military functions and systems supporting civilian functions, even if such networks rely on the same infrastructure.

In sum, Chinese economic and political exposure to large-scale network attacks should provide a basis for deterrence and an incentive to explore mutual restraint with the United States in strategic cyberspace, especially when taking into account that China could suffer secondary network and economic effects of large-scale network attacks it may conduct. Given its acknowledged vulnerability, the United States should have a similar incentive. Demarcating critical national networks—"strategic cyberspace"—is hard but not impossible. Restraint in strategic cyberspace without restraint in tactical-military cyberspace may be even harder.

Cyberspace and Sino-American Military Contingencies

The previous chapter explained that the United States is critically dependent on space-based C^{4}ISR to carry out its military strategy in the western Pacific, while China is increasingly dependent on it to carry out its counterstrategy. The same can be said for computer networks, which are largely space-based over the expanses of the Pacific. In addition to China's potential to disable U.S. satellites, it has the possibility of interfering with the computer networks on which U.S. readiness and operations depend.[16] Some of these networks are dedicated, isolated, and well defended. At the same time, the global cyber infrastructure that supports the Defense Department global information grid is for the most part not dedicated, not isolated, and not entirely well defended.[17] It must be assumed that the PLA would attack not only dedicated defense and intelligence networks but also any networks that enable U.S. military operations, including dual-use and less-defended ones and the Internet itself.

From fighting forces to support services, from peacetime to hostilities, the U.S. military is thoroughly networked, especially for intense, complex, joint expeditionary and strike operations. Similarly, the intelligence systems that collect, process, analyze, and disseminate information vital to U.S. military readiness and combat could not function without the capability to ingest, process, and distribute data. The more formidable the enemy forces and their antiaccess capabilities, the more vital computer networking is to U.S. military success.

More specifically, in a military contingency involving Chinese forces in the western Pacific—again, a conflict over Taiwan is an appropriate example—the United States would depend on data links from intelligence collectors to give as much warning as possible of Chinese preparations to attack Taiwan and U.S. forces. USPACOM would need to direct combat forces and logistics tails as they prepare and deploy from far-flung bases and peacetime locations in and out of the region. A major operational advantage of U.S. forces is that they can be highly distributed yet function in an integrated way. But this is possible only through reliance on computer networks for command, control, and communications. Throughout hostilities, links between sensors and strike forces and among strike forces would permit tracking and targeting of Chinese forces, optimal use of weapons, and continuous assessments of their effects.

Because the Chinese intend to conduct sudden, rapid, and brief operations in order to seize the initiative and accomplish their mission before U.S. forces can stop them, U.S. data networks could make the difference between the success and failure of the U.S. response. In countering this Chinese strategy, targets of interest to U.S. strike forces are diverse and dispersed: Chinese air forces, airbases, air defenses, command and control nodes, sensors, missile launchers, surface and subsurface naval forces, amphibious forces and their staging areas, and logistics hubs and flows. Of growing concern to U.S. forces are Chinese ASBMs, along with the extended-range sensors and communications links that enable them to target U.S. aircraft carriers intervening against Chinese forces.

Chinese military strategy is not only to move suddenly and swiftly but also to degrade and delay U.S. forces en route to defend Taiwan. Of course, the Chinese would prefer to deter the United States from intervening, but that requires the ability to disable U.S. carriers. Knowing the importance of achieving their military objectives before U.S. forces can prevent it, the Chinese regard the nodes and links of computer networks that comprise U.S. C^{4}ISR as an inviting if not a compelling target. The same logic that attracts the Chinese to ASAT capabilities explains their interest in cyber attacks. Because they might not be confident of taking down dedicated and well-protected U.S. military and intelligence networks, they might also target the GIG's dual-use backbone. To the extent the Chinese would want to be sure of degrading and impeding U.S. forces, they would have an incentive to target broadly rather than narrowly.[18] By design or by effect, Chinese cyber war agents could infect and affect far more than U.S. C⁴ISR functions.

Of course, the United States could also launch either retaliatory or preemptive cyber attacks in such a conflict. The Chinese, owing to geographic proximity and prudent planning, have less exposed networks for supporting military operations. Theirs are largely landline and sea-bed fiber optic cables and mainland-based servers, routers, switches, and transmission systems—not entirely beyond reach of U.S. cyber attacks, but relatively inaccessible. As a consequence, even if Chinese forces are as dependent as U.S. forces on the ability to distribute data, their operations may be less susceptible to degradation than U.S. forces, even if the latter has superior cyber attack capabilities.

However, this asymmetric vulnerability will diminish as Chinese forces extend outward in peacetime and contingency operations. As Chinese networks are required to connect and direct increasingly distant and distributed Chinese forces and sensors, including spaced-based ones, the PLA will have to leave its communications fortress. The Chinese have no practical, affordable alternative to relying on existing or otherwise exposed information infrastructure in the waters and space beyond China. In sum, as PLA forces become more information-based—their stated goal—and extend into the Pacific to engage U.S. strike forces, they become more dependent on less secure computer networks. This dependence would also be manifest if dedicated military communications networks were damaged in a military conflict.

The Chinese know they must operate in more joint, integrated, and data-intensive ways, not just because U.S. forces do but also because their military strategy demands it. The Chinese have made no secret of this; indeed, they advertise their goal of informationization of warfare, which guides PLA investments and plans.[19] In a Taiwan contingency, the PLA must be able to stage and flow large land and air forces; find and target the U.S. strike fleet; target U.S. airbases in the region; attempt to gain air control over Taiwan and the Strait; operate an integrated air defense; launch short- and medium-range ballistic missiles against Taiwan and U.S. forces; place its strategic nuclear forces on alert and on the move; attack U.S. satellites and C⁴ISR networks; and support these complex operations logistically, which requires liaison with local civilian officials. Again, this involves all branches of the PLA and must occur suddenly, swiftly, and like clock-work to succeed.

The Chinese should be aware that U.S. cyber attacks on increasingly important and exposed Chinese C⁴ISR networks could derail their strategy, such as by damaging their ability to track, target, and attack U.S. carriers near, en route to, or at standoff range from China. Before long, U.S. cyber attacks could be as devastating to Chinese operations as Chinese cyber attacks could be to U.S. operations. A paradox—and potential trap—awaits Chinese military strategy: the more prepared PLA forces are to carry out informationized operations, the more vulnerable the PLA is to U.S. cyber war. In the context of Sino-U.S. conventional war, cyber war could leave China no better off and possibly worse off. Instead of complementing China's growing antiaccess capabilities, cyber war could undermine their effectiveness. While this scenario depends on a number of assumptions about the cyber war capabilities and vulnerabilities of both sides, the Chinese have to consider it.

Cyber war capabilities can contribute to crisis instability. Cyber attacks have little or no counterforce potential for either side, in the sense that the attacking side is no less vulnerable to cyber attacks for having conducted them. The advantage in striking first in cyberspace lies not in protecting oneself from retaliatory strikes but in degrading the opponent's C⁴ISR and operations before one's own are degraded. Conversely, exercising restraint with no expectation that the opponent will do likewise could be disadvantageous. In any case, if either side is inclined to use cyber war to degrade the capabilities and performance of the other's military forces, there is logic in doing so early. Because striking early could be advantageous, there is the potential that a cyber attack could be the trigger that turns a confrontation into a conflict. The United States (or China) would likely interpret Chinese (or American) cyber attack as a prelude to physical attack.

An improbable but extremely consequential danger is that an attack by either side on the other's C⁴ISR could be interpreted as intended to obstruct the ability to mobilize strategic nuclear forces. The separation of tactical and strategic C⁴ISR is not a public matter. However, in the confusion of disrupted surveillance and command networks, the possibility cannot be excluded that strategic forces would at least be placed on higher alert, creating a risk of faulty calculation with incalculable results.

The Chinese would be imprudent to think that the United States would respect firebreaks in cyberspace. Whether it acts preemptively or in retaliation, the United States would have an incentive to attack Chinese cyberspace broadly rather than narrowly on dedicated and protected Chinese military networks. Not only would this harm China's economic activity, it could also degrade the ability of the leadership to direct Chinese operations and even to communicate with the population. U.S. attacks could isolate Chinese leadership and sow confusion in the population. Chinese cyber attacks could prompt the United States to retaliate without diminishing U.S. capability to do so. The Chinese have a lot to consider before beginning cyber war.

Another feature of cyber warfare may aggravate this crisis instability: the option of subtle attacks or demonstrations. Before hostilities have begun, it might occur to one side that a mild cyber attack—a nonlethal display of one's resolve—could warn and deter the other side and demonstrate its vulnerability. Knowing this, the side attacked might well opt to escalate in cyberspace. Even more dangerous is the potential that a cyber attack intended to show resolve could be interpreted as a prelude to general hostilities, thus triggering, instead of deterring, a conflict.

It would be a gamble for either side to bet that cyber war could be controlled. Every network, whether military or dual-use, that could support military operations would likely be targeted. Networks that support intelligence collection and dissemination would be attacked, making both sides less certain about what was happening but by no means more passive in the conflict. Moreover, one side or the other might consider escalating cyber war to critical networks such as those supporting economic and financial functions, transportation, power, and state control. In sum, the existence of dual-use networks, the possibility of willful escalation, and the difficulty of controlling viruses, worms, and other infections, regardless of human plans, lead to a conclusion that limiting cyber war to the tactical military level would be hard.

Assuming neither could refrain from cyber war if the other engaged in it, U.S. and Chinese calculations of the wisdom of initiating cyber war can be summed up as linked dilemmas:

- For the United States, is it better to degrade the PLA's ability to track, target, and strike U.S. forces (especially naval) than to maintain the C^{4}ISR needed to operate U.S. forces effectively in the way they are meant to operate?

- For China, is it better to degrade U.S. strike operations by degrading U.S. C^{4}ISR than to be able to conduct Chinese strike operations against U.S. forces?

■ For both, what is the better path to military success: physically striking the other's forces, or attacking the networks that enable the other side to strike one's own forces?

While Chinese strategists may currently calculate that it is better to degrade U.S. C⁴ISR than to preserve their own, this could change over time. Conversely, it could be unrealistic for U.S. strategists to think it is possible to maintain undiminished C⁴ISR to direct U.S. operations while striking Chinese C⁴ISR capability to direct PLA operations.

Once again, these tactical military calculations have to be combined with a strong possibility that cyber war could spread from the military to other realms, with imponderable economic and political effects for both sides. It is easy to imagine how cyber war could start in a Sino-U.S. conflict but hard to see how it would end.

Offense Versus Defense

Much of the detail of U.S. and Chinese cyber warfare capabilities is secret. For our purposes, it suffices to say that the United States and China are able to break into, disrupt, and degrade each other's data networks. Those abilities range from extensive, in the case of publicly accessible and lightly protected networks, including the Internet, to challenging and limited, in the case of dedicated and heavily protected ones.

It is clear that the stronger the attack and the more capable the attacker, the harder it is to defend targeted computer networks. But is the relationship between offense and defense such that an increment of effort to defend produces no more protection, or less, relative to a comparable effort to improve offense? Is cyberspace, like the nuclear and space domains, offense dominant?

One important difference between space and cyberspace is that all satellites are inherently vulnerable, whereas not all networks are invariably so. Lone hackers can penetrate even well-protected networks, but networks can be robust (as long as the infrastructure is intact), redundant (because of automatic or readily available rerouting options), and resilient (because of the opportunity to diagnose attacks, adapt defenses, seal breaches, and restore services). These virtues can limit the scope and duration of even major disruptions.[20]

Because networks are robust, redundant, and resilient, permanent degradation and disruption are difficult, even from major cyber attacks by large and sophisticated attackers. Most experience and analysis involving disruption of services indicate network failures of days and weeks, not months or years. Another characteristic of cyberspace is that attacks can yield information that can be used to improve defenses, even in the short term. It may be possible to adapt defense at least as quickly as to adapt offense during cyber war. Because large and unmistakable attacks carry more information than small and ambiguous ones, the former could be more conducive to diagnosis and adaptive defense than the latter.[21] In any case, the combination of attack information and availability of defensive remedies means that damage, disruption, and corruption of cyberspace may decline with time, regardless of scale.

On the other hand, the *effects* of network degradation, not the degradation itself, are what really matter. This is important in three respects. First, a large, sophisticated attack can be much harder to contain and remedy in the short term, resulting in grave and lingering damage to the economic and other functions served by the degraded networks. A small attack of the same duration could have a negligible effect. Second, the greater the short-term effects, the longer they will last. To illustrate, a brief yet total disruption of air traffic control systems may leave transportation snarled and the transportation-based economy reeling for some time, whereas a brief and minor disruption could have the effect of a passing weather front. Third, extreme defensive measures that might have to be taken in the face of a large attack, such as sealing off or shutting down threatened networks, may produce nearly as much economic harm as the attack itself. Thus, it is fair to say that the potential to cause major damage to network-dependent functions grows steeply as a function of attack and attacker size.

Figure 6–3 is a representation of a method originally derived to model the investments in cyber security by private firms.[22] It demonstrates that investments in cyber security have a diminishing marginal return per dollar spent on security. Extrapolating from it, the larger the attack, the less cost-effective defense is in preventing harmful effects.

The diminishing returns on investment in defense relative to offense are especially conspicuous when considering the disparity between "hacking" and "patching" in complexity, cost, and time required. Sophisticated network defense software contains between 5 million and 10 million lines of code; malware contains an average of 170 lines of code.[23] Protection of critical government networks typically requires standard government competition and contracting, which can take years before solutions are initiated, whereas designing an attack can be accomplished in weeks. While network defense against sophisticated attackers requires advanced

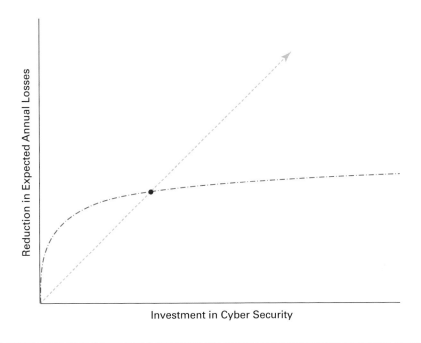

Figure 6–3. Diminishing Returns on Investment in Cyber Security

work by highly specialized firms, network attack is literally a cottage industry.

The woes of the cyber defender are compounded by the increasingly global and integrated nature of networking industries, markets, and infrastructure. Foreign components, subsystems, and whole systems (thus, hardware and software) are increasingly competitive—in price, performance, and value—and consequently are finding their way into U.S. network infrastructure. This includes formidable Chinese corporations with state connections. However difficult it may be to defend entirely made-in-America networks (an extinct species by now), the difficulty is multiplied by increasing use of foreign, notably Chinese, hardware and at least embedded software. The notion of "external" defense of networks must take into account the reality of technological integration and the attendant dangers of "internal" exploitation or disruption. At the same time, the fact of their own dependence on U.S. technology and the risks to world trade, including Chinese exports, should give Chinese political and economic leaders pause before considering or condoning an attempt to exploit for strategic purposes China's success in U.S. network systems markets—another layer of deterrence.

We do not mean to say that investment in computer network defense is pointless: it is indispensable against less sophisticated, more numerous, and hard-to-deter threats; it raises the barriers to more sophisticated threats; and in any case, it is vital to restore network functionality and service in the event of attack. Given enough time to adjust, offense may not be dominant over defense. Still, the effects of offense can dominate defenses in the short term and can increase sharply with the size of the attack and attacker. So it is crucial to consider deterrence based on fear of retaliation.

Cyber Deterrence

Whether the United States and China can agree on mutual restraint in strategic cyberspace depends heavily on whether they can be mutually deterred from making at least some classes of attacks, even in wartime. This begs the question of whether deterrence works in cyberspace—whether a would-be network attacker with something to be gained by attacking can nevertheless be persuaded not to attack because retaliation risks outweigh expected gains.[24]

History's starkest example of effective deterrence, between the United States and the Soviet Union in the nuclear domain, was elegantly simple and empirically stable: two unmistakable adversaries with tight control of their weaponry, each capable of retaliation with expected consequences that no rational leader would judge acceptable, and with no significant defense (apart from a counterforce first strike, which does not apply in cyber war). The very term *mutual assured destruction* connoted the shared cataclysmic results of general nuclear war. The result was reciprocal deterrence, self-organized though reinforced by common concepts, tight control, negotiated arms control, and transparency.

Cyber deterrence is anything but elegant. Thanks to the ubiquity and dynamics of information technology, cyber war, like cyberspace itself, would be highly complex, fluid, and unpredictable. Who has access to what networks? How is this changing? Who has what capabilities? Who is interfering with whom? Is a foreign power responsible for a given attack by a foreign adversary? Which one? With what weapons? To what end? Will defenses work? What new technology is around the corner? Moreover, the expected consequences of even large network attacks could be mild and fleeting compared to nuclear war, implying that fear of retaliation would contribute less to the strength of deterrence. The contrast between nuclear and cyber deterrence is reason not to apply wholesale the tenets of the former to the latter.

That said, the ambiguities that characterize cyberspace do not argue against exploring how deeper theories of deterrence, which transcend nuclear weapons, could be applied in some conditions—perhaps to Sino-U.S. cyber war. Most classes of cyber attackers—for example, nonstate actors and rogue states with little to lose—probably cannot be deterred by the threat of cyber retaliation. The source of lesser attacks and identity of the attackers may be difficult to determine. Consequences may be more annoying than devastating. Network defense may be adequate to contain if not prevent such attacks, reducing the importance of a threat of retaliation. Thus, deterrence is neither assured nor essential for most network attacks and attackers.

Yet the fact that deterrence does not apply against *every* network threat does not mean it does not apply to *any*. Even if adequate network protection is possible against most attackers, it might not be against all. Even if many network attackers are themselves not vitally dependent on data networking and thus unlikely to be bothered by the threat of retaliation, some might be. For our purposes, cyber deterrence need not apply generally: it need only apply to Sino-U.S. cyber war.

Beyond simple logic that some cases may not prove all cases, two factors suggest that deterrence might work under some conditions. First, states that pose the largest and most damaging network threats, for which defense is least promising, may themselves be dependent on networks and thus susceptible to threats of retaliation. Second, those posing such threats are unlikely to carry them out except in a crisis or conflict, which could help identify the attacker.

Generally speaking, deterrence is indicated when five conditions are satisfied:[25]

- adequate defense is infeasible or unaffordable
- the scale of expected harm makes it important to prevent attack
- means of powerful retaliation exist
- the enemy has more to lose from retaliation than to gain from attacking
- the attacker is identifiable *enough* to support a credible threat of retaliation.

The first two conditions make deterrence necessary; the third, fourth, and fifth make it possible.

This study finds that these conditions fit the case of Sino-American cyber war, albeit with important qualifications. The first two conditions have already been addressed. If large-scale and sustained attacks were made against strategic networks on which the United States relies—for example, those that enable financial transactions, powergrid management, telecommunications, transportation, national intelligence, or military operations—defenses are unlikely to be adequate to prevent large and lasting harm. This does not mean that efforts to defend against major network attacks are pointless; indeed, even an imperfect defense is more important against infrequent major attacks than frequent minor ones. Better defended U.S. networks may increase the adversary's costs and difficulties and reduce its prospective gains from attack. However, for at least the days and weeks following a major attack, network defense alone cannot be counted on to avoid serious national damage.

The third condition—means of powerful retaliation—has also been addressed. The United States has the means to retaliate strongly for a Chinese attack, regardless of the scale of the attack and damage done (because there is essentially no counterforce). The same could be said for Chinese retaliation for a U.S. cyberstrike. The United States and China have ways to communicate a credible threat of retaliation, which is as much a matter of will and intent as it is of capabilities.

The fourth condition—the attacker's vulnerability in cyberspace—has also been addressed, at least where China and the United States are concerned. Vital functions of each, as well as their economic stability, could be badly if temporarily disrupted, with lasting effects. In the Chinese case, this danger is compounded by uncertainty about how segments of the population would respond to the crisis to their material conditions and future. These dangers would be weighed against expected gains from launching a cyber attack or expected harm that might come from not doing so. The stakes for the United States could be high—for example, the loss of some forces (aircraft carriers) and failure to prevent China from forcibly gaining control of Taiwan. For China, the stakes could be even higher—a crushing defeat by the United States, failure to reunify the country, and a setback in China's quest to become a great power. For these reasons, cyber deterrence might not work. Yet the fact that one cannot be certain that the threat of retaliation will prevent cyber attack does not argue against a cyber deterrence strategy.

There is an important, if imperfect, correlation between the ability of states to conduct large and damaging cyber attacks and their vulnerability to harm from cyber attacks. Generally speaking, sophistication in computer networks and systems is both a byproduct of heavy reliance on cyberspace and a prerequisite for advanced cyber war capabilities. The anomalous cases are states with little use for computer networks yet advanced attack capabilities and, on the other hand, states with heavy use of computer networks but no competence in cyber warfare (the latter obviously do not matter in cyber deterrence). Figure 6–4 shows some examples of where particular states may fall on these two axes. While these are purely notional, they do illustrate that the states that may most need to be deterred, by virtue of capability, may also be susceptible to deterrence (by virtue of connectivity).

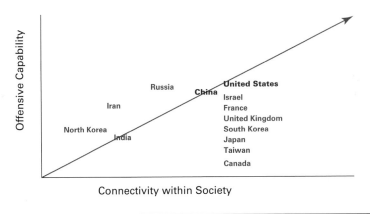

Figure 6–4. Cyber Attack: Offensive Capability Versus Vulnerability

As to the fifth condition, the credibility of the threat to inflict unacceptable retaliatory damage depends *to some extent* on knowing against whom to retaliate. Skeptics of cyber deterrence point out that network attacks can be hard to trace with enough confidence to retaliate.[26] This is true, but several factors mitigate this problem. First, the possibility of tracing an attack is greater if the attack reveals capabilities of a sort and scale possessed by only a few candidates. All else being equal, devastating attacks are more traceable than mild ones.

In this regard, only a few nation-states, including the United States and China, and no nonstates currently have the ability to overwhelm network protection and do enough harm to critical national functions to be considered strategic, as defined here. While the United States and China are obviously capable of lesser attacks, the primary aim of mutual restraint would be at the high end of the scale. The greater the scale, sophistication, and effects of attack, the fewer the possible attackers other than China (or, from China's perspective, other than the United States).

As to which of the few capable candidates is the actual attacker, it is likely that one state would have a more apparent motive than others to attack. A crisis might provide the clearest indicator of motive and thus of the attacker. Intelligence would likely reveal clues, such as military preparations. Actual hostilities would constitute a smoking gun (metaphorically and literally). In the unlikely event of a bolt-from-the-blue strategic cyber attack, the immediate aftermath would undoubtedly produce indicators of purpose. The Estonia and Georgia attacks both furnished strong if circumstantial evidence of Moscow's complicity.

In general, deterrence is more likely to work against states than nonstates because the latter have less to lose and are less vulnerable to retaliation. In cyber deterrence, there is the added challenge of identifying a nonstate attacker. Because nonstate actors could become able, as well as motivated, to conduct large attacks, this represents a potential hole in cyber deterrence: hard to defend against but also hard to deter. However, while this could in time make identification more problematic, it does not argue against trying to deter the large-state threat.

Even if identifying the attacker from the nature and context of the attack is inferential and not absolutely certain, it may be good enough. Keep in mind that the purpose of deterrence is to prevent attack, thus obviating the need for retaliation. It follows that certainty about an attacker's identity is the wrong standard by which to judge whether the United States should seek cyber deterrence. Would a state that was capable of a severe network attack on the United States but was also vulnerable in the event of retaliation want to count on the inability of the United States to identify it with certainty as the attacker, or on the United States to refrain from retaliating if less than certain as to the attacker? Would the Chinese, in the midst of a crisis with the United States, gamble that the United States would have enough doubt about the perpetrator of a large cyber attack that it could not retaliate?

Of course, deterrence *might* fail, a large attack *might* occur, and the United States *might* be unable to identify the attacker with enough confidence to retaliate. In that case, deterrence might be weakened for the future. But this is no reason for the United States to forego the advantages of deterrence against a Chinese (or other) strategic cyber attack. The same reasoning can be applied to the Chinese as they consider how to restrain the United States from such attacks on China.

Figure 6–5 depicts notionally why deterrence may work even with a lack of certainty about the identity of an attacker. As the likelihood of attri-

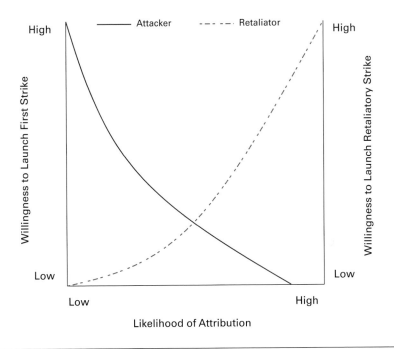

Figure 6–5. Deterrence in the Cyber Domain

bution increases, the side attacked ("retaliator") grows increasingly confident of retaliating against the actual attacker. Meanwhile, the attacker loses
confidence that it will not be identified and thus escape retaliation. The
attacker does not know for certain how likely it is to be identified or how
confident the attacked side must be before deciding to retaliate. Assuming
that retaliation would be extremely punishing—outweighing the gains of

	NO	YES
NO	■ Attacker is invulnerable to retaliation ■ Attacker is unknown ■ Defense is possible	■ Attacker is invulnerable to retaliation ■ Attacker is unknown ■ Defense is inadequate
YES	■ Attacker is vulnerable to retaliation ■ Attacker could be known ■ Defense is possible	■ Attacker is vulnerable to retaliation ■ Attacker could be known ■ Defense is inadequate

Table 6–2. Cyber Deterrence: Possible Versus Necessary

attacking—the attacker is unlikely to depend on not being identified *or* the attacked side will retaliate only if absolutely sure of the attacker's identity.

In sum, it appears that there are at least two important cases where cyber deterrence is both necessary and possible—China and the United States, vis-à-vis each other—and thus a basis for Sino-American mutual restraint in strategic cyberspace. Table 6–2 summarizes why and under what conditions cyber deterrence is both necessary and possible. The Sino-U.S. case falls into the possible-and-necessary quadrant.

Thresholds and Firebreaks

Our use of the concept of strategic cyberspace begs the question of what the threshold of that domain is. This is important if there is to be some common understanding about the field in which the United States and China expect restraint from the other.

This question does not arise in connection with the nuclear domain, where any use of a nuclear weapon crosses the well-understood nuclear threshold. The preceding chapter defined the threshold as denying the other side's access to and use of space. Such precision is impossible in cyberspace. Nevertheless, it is important to address the threshold problem if there is to be reciprocal restraint in cyberspace, for intrusions occur routinely and at very low levels. Rather than a single boundary, there are several dimensions along which strategic and nonstrategic cyberspace can be distinguished. None provides either/or indicators, but together they describe what we mean.

One dimension is the severity of an attack's effects, whether they are intended or not. Either an attack that is intended to cause grave national harm but fails or one that is not intended to cause such harm but does so could be considered strategic. This raises again the question of what is meant by national harm. The theft of information, such as what occurred to Google (allegedly at the hands of agents of the Chinese state), while colossal, did not substantially harm the United States. It is also possible to intrude into government networks, even sensitive ones, and yet not intend or cause harm. The most important example is intelligence collection. The exfiltration of secrets from government computers via the networks that link them is hardly friendly, but it is designed to be unnoticed and thus not to disrupt or damage. Although it may have national security implications, like any form of intelligence collection, it occurs often and is hard to restrain. It is, de facto, allowed by international "rules of the game." Apart from network defense, the penalty for the theft of national secrets by another sovereign state is typically to steal that state's secrets, which may be happening anyway and therefore is not retaliation.

Another dimension is to define *strategic* according to the functions of the networks that might be attacked. It is possible, though not simple, to distinguish networks according to their strategic importance, the criterion being their bearing on national well-being, such as networks often referred to as critical to the economic, physical, and societal well-being of the country and its people. Examples include weather information, air traffic control systems, stock market and interbank transactions, health information, utilities, e-commerce, and government functions. Massive disruption of email could also be critical. Nonstrategic functions include entertainment and advertising. Such distinctions are not static; for instance, social networking tools might first have been regarded as amusement but increasingly are the main media of communities of great importance to the users and to society in general.

Even if a distinction between strategic and nonstrategic cyberspace can be settled, an equally confounding and consequential matter is the boundary of cyber war as an aspect of military hostilities. The more seamless the technical link—or operational transition—from tactical-military to strategic-civilian cyber war, the harder it will be to prevent the former from leading to the latter. In the absence of an escalatory firebreak, mutual strategic restraint in the cyber domain would require a complete ban, in effect, on military cyber attacks below the strategic level. Conversely, a firebreak would permit cyber attacks by armed forces on armed forces during hostilities without undue risk of disruption of networks on which the well-being of civilian populations depends.

The concept of firebreaks figured importantly in American nuclear deterrence theory and Cold War strategy. The most salient was the distinction between battlefield use of tactical nuclear weapons—for example, in Europe—and general intercontinental exchange of strategic nuclear weapons, the former potentially engulfing U.S. troops and NATO Allies but not the U.S. (or Soviet) homeland. The implication was that it was better to confine nuclear war once begun. However, such Allies as the Germans preferred that their homeland not be thought of merely as a nuclear battlefield by the superpowers. Moreover, the United States and its Allies agreed that the Soviets should be offered no assurance that nuclear war would stop at the tactical nuclear firebreak, lest deterrence be weakened. Consequently, for most of the Cold War, the United States tried to erase rather than accentuate a nuclear firebreak. It chose to stress the possibility of escalation over the need to prevent escalation.

In cyberspace, it is not obvious that a firebreak is even theoretically possible, given how connected networks tend to be and the fact that military and civilian networks utilize a largely common infrastructure. If a firebreak is possible, it is important to ask whether it should be favored in the interest of preventing escalation or instead be avoided in the interest of strengthening deterrence by posing the danger of escalation, general cyber war, and economic catastrophe. This issue is critical because of the potential utility, if not inevitability, of military cyber attacks in the event of Sino-U.S. hostilities.

Both the PLA and the U.S. military now regard offensive and defensive network warfare as integral to regular warfare. Against a formidable opponent capable of large-scale, high-intensity combat involving joint forces, the U.S. and Chinese militaries might be considered negligent if they failed to target the C⁴ISR networks of the other and to plan for their own to be attacked. After all, military cyber warfare descends from electronic warfare, which is as old as military use of radio and radar and never considered illegitimate. To suggest that attacks on C⁴ISR should be proscribed in the same way the use of chemical and biological weapons has been or the way nuclear warfighting and space warfare could be is as unrealistic as it is impractical.

This presents a serious conundrum. As noted, military and civilian networks overlap, in the sense that they use common infrastructure. Moreover, there could be operational military rationales to attack civilian networks that can support large and far-flung combat operations.[27] To make the problem even more complex, cyber targeting is not yet so refined that the effects can be foreseen or controlled with confidence. Once networks of economic and civilian importance are disrupted by one side, retaliation by the other must be expected. Herein lies the risk that military cyber war would lead to general cyber war.

This study has been consistent in the conviction that mutual deterrence is a sine qua non of mutual restraint. Yet there is insufficient reason to think that either China or the United States will be deterred from initiating cyber attacks on military C⁴ISR networks if armed conflict were to occur. Indeed, there could be an incentive to conduct such attacks before the enemy does in order to gain tactical advantage. Considering current U.S. conventional military advantages, the PLA has all but declared its intent to exploit this U.S. vulnerability. And as Chinese military capabilities improve in general and come to rely more on C⁴ISR in particular, U.S. military interest in promptly disabling Chinese networks will likely grow. As a result, while both countries may be deterred from starting strategic national cyber war, neither may be deterred from starting tactical military cyber war.

Yet given the improbability of a bolt-from-the-blue strategic cyber attack by China or the United States on the other, the greatest danger of general cyber war is that it could be triggered by a military cyber war in an intense crisis or armed conflict. Hostilities between U.S. and Chinese armed forces may be unlikely; however, there could be strong temptations to strike preemptively in cyberspace, perhaps as the first shot in a conflict. Yet if cyber war between the United States and China is permissible—indeed, probable—during armed conflict, mutual restraint would only apply to a peacetime surprise attack, which is barely plausible. Thus, the danger of escalation from military to general cyber war provides one of the most powerful incentives for mutual restraint. Sino-U.S. agreement not to conduct cyber attacks on military networks even in the course of combat operations is not realistic and, if reached nevertheless, is unlikely to be believed or respected. Therefore, a cyber war firebreak is very desirable—for both countries.

There are at least two ways conceptually to establish a firebreak. One is to stipulate that the need for mutual restraint in strategic cyberspace extends to any military cyber operations that have the *potential* to infect and crash civilian computer networking, including civilian functions that rely on dual-use infrastructure. This approach can be derived from established norms against harm to civilians or uses of force that are disproportionate to what the opponent has committed. However, apart from the fact that such norms tend to be ignored when they may interfere with achieving victory, this approach rules out so much of military cyber war as to be nearly as unrealistic or incredible as a complete ban.

Another approach is to rely on the risk of escalation to impart prudence to military cyberspace, without proclaiming it to be governed by mutual restraint, strictly speaking. This would mean exercising exceptional caution in treating military cyber attacks as a low-risk alternative to physical force. Such caution would demand especially tight civilian control over cyber attacks even during war. In this regard, it is worth borrowing from nuclear escalation theory and practice, to which the United States and, as far as we know, China both conform: orders to release nuclear weapons must come from top political leadership. Although applying such control to cyber attacks may seem constricting to military commanders, the dangers and consequence of escalation to general cyber war suggest a need for if not chief-of-state decision authority, than at least senior political authority and strict rules of engagement.

Such an approach would treat cyber war as fundamentally indiscriminate. Because of the prevalence of dual-use network infrastructure, even if the purpose is to disrupt military networks that enable enemy forces, the effects of a cyber attack might be to disrupt networks that enable international banking, transportation, or other communications on which civilian societies rely. As noted, the United States and other governments have a way to control the use of indiscriminate weapons: they do not delegate authority to use these weapons down the military chain of command or, if they do, it is to use them only when the risks of unwanted or collateral effects, such as harm to civilians, are low. The more likely and consequential the potential effects, the higher the decisionmaking level required to authorize their use. For instance, higher authority is required to use conventional weapons on a military target that is near a civilian population, the destruction of which could do harm to civilians, than if there were little or no such danger.

This same principle could be applied to cyber war. Thus, an attack on a network that is dedicated to supporting enemy forces and completely partitioned from other networks could be authorized at a lower level than an attack on one that could also harm nonmilitary functions or noncombatants. Whereas military commanders could take small risks, political leaders would have to decide whether to take big ones, defined as presenting a nontrivial chance of affecting civilian-commercial networks. Using such delegation protocols, the danger of escalation from tactical to strategic cyber war could be managed without completely tying the hands of military commanders faced with enemy forces utilizing military computer networks.

Protocols for delegation of authority to conduct tactical cyber attacks on military networks could be designed to take into account the general state of alert in a crisis. Just as the United States has a system of graduated defense conditions that grants increasing authority to military commanders as circumstances warrant, it could adopt a system of graduated cyber conditions. For now, however, there should and will be a bias in favor of centralized political control except when the risk of unintended civilian consequences is clearly low, even—or especially—in wartime.

A technical capability to improve discrimination in cyber war could also help within such a framework. As techniques for cyber attack are refined, the key to making cyber war less indiscriminate is intelligence. With expansive and excellent knowledge of the workings of a potential adversary's computer systems—a tall order, to be sure—a state with sophisticated cyber war capabilities could target military but not civilian networks, even if they use the same infrastructure. To illustrate, a given server can support multiple networks, both military and civilian, each with its own software characteristics and identifiers. Destroying that server by, say, dropping a bomb on it would obviously disrupt all the networks being supported. However, dropping a virus into the server, with the benefit of excellent intelligence, could infect only the targeted network, perhaps a military one but not a civilian one.

With imperfect intelligence, there would be a risk that the attack would infect more than the target network. However, when combined with the procedures for delegating authority just described, such targeting would provide a way to manage risks of collateral damage and unintentional escalation. By improving discrimination and instituting appropriate decisionmaking control, it may be possible to achieve mutual restraint in attacking critical ("strategic") cyberspace without expecting a prohibition on tactical cyber war during hostilities, which is not practical, not believable, and not in the interest of the United States.

Returning, then, to the question of the boundaries of strategic cyberspace for purposes of mutual restraint, a possible Sino-U.S. approach would be to:

- agree that mutual strategic restraint applies to attacks on networks with the intent or potential of doing serious economic, civilian, or other national harm

- agree that restraint should apply to attacks on military and intelligence networks in peacetime (apart from cyber spying)

- agree that at no time should networks critical to civilian and economic well-being be subject to attacks, except in retaliation

- acknowledge jointly that the risk of escalation demands caution, discrimination, and control in wartime military cyber attacks

- apply strict delegations of decisionmaking authority regarding military cyber attacks, based on the risks of civilian and other collateral harm

- begin a dialogue, involving both civilian leaders and military commanders, to share concerns and intentions and to avert misperceptions and miscalculation.

Resting on the strength of mutual deterrence, such undertakings could reduce the dangers of Sino-American strategic cyber war.

This matter of authority to engage in cyber war is receiving attention within the U.S. Government, evidently with a view toward avoiding unwanted consequences of the sort laid out above. There recently has been some public reporting on guidelines to U.S. military commanders in connection with cyber war. In a nutshell, "the military must seek presidential approval for 1) a specific cyber assault on an enemy, and 2) the option to weave cyber capabilities into U.S. warfighting strategy." The United States can defend itself by blocking cyber intrusions and taking down servers in another country and has the right to pursue attackers via cyberspace net.[28]

Such provisions are consistent with the proposition that cyber attacks ought to be regarded as potentially indiscriminate, at least for now. Unless and until the firebreak concept developed here becomes technically and operationally reliable, the bias should be toward tight civilian control at the highest level. We expect and suggest that further thought be given to two issues: how such guidance is to be followed in the event of hostilities, once Presidential authority has been granted; and whether the principle of Presidential control can withstand pressures to engage in cyber operations as an integral aspect of 21st-century warfare, especially as potential adversaries expand their use of computer networking to support combat against U.S. forces. Broadly speaking, it seems that the United States is still in the foothills of solving the dilemma posed by the dual objectives of enabling U.S. forces to succeed while also avoiding escalation up to and including general war in cyber space.

Elements of Practical Cyber Deterrence

Cyber deterrence requires a country committed to it to address several matters: offensive capabilities, legitimacy of the threat to retaliate, declaratory policy, consistent behavior, adequate control, security of allies, and international cooperation. While these are addressed from the U.S. perspective in the pages that follow, the prescriptions apply more or less also to China on the assumption that mutual restraint in cyberspace would be symmetrical.

Any country's external use of force is constrained by international law and norms, starting with the United Nations Charter. The right of self-defense is widely understood to include deterrence and thus threats and acts of retaliatory force, within limits.[29] Less clear is the right to escalate in retaliation, which is disproportionate by design. The threat of escalation can be important for deterrence. Throughout the Cold War, the United States relied on the threat of escalation, including first use of nuclear weapons, to deter Soviet aggression in Europe; it justified this as inherent in the right of self-defense (including of allies). In cyberspace, Chinese leaders would presumably be more leery of PLA proposals to initiate cyber attacks to disrupt U.S. military operations if given reason to fear that the U.S.

response would not be limited to military forces and could damage China's own critical national networks.

Related to escalation is the issue of civilian consequences. The U.S. Government is known to have struggled with the civilian impact of cyber war, especially if waged against networks that affect a population's well-being.[30] Of course, the fact that network attacks can harm noncombatants does not call for a higher standard than for physical attacks. From the Civil War to two World Wars to Vietnam to Iraq, the United States has waged war in ways that affect civilians, while not failing to assert that industrial, infrastructure, and enemy leadership targets are legitimate because they enable enemy warmaking. Although the weaponry differs in cyber war, norms of proportionality and minimizing harm to civilians are essentially the same.

A third normative question is whether an unprovoked or initial cyber attack constitutes international aggression—an act of war. The answer must reflect the potential destructiveness of cyber warfare. It also should apply the same standard to the enemy as to oneself. If it is considered aggression, as it ought to be if the intention or effect is substantially destructive, an enemy attack would justify whatever is permissible under the right of self-defense, including both cyber and physical responses.

In this light, resorting to cyber war only in response to cyber attack would add legitimacy to the threat and act of retaliation and thus strengthen deterrence. Given its myriad other forms of power and its dependence on vulnerable networks, the United States should favor such a norm. However, networks have become so integral to military operations, for the United States and China alike, that the United States is highly unlikely to foreswear attacks on networks that enable operations of the PLA.

As an alternative, the United States could take the position that military aggression, whether physical or electronic, justifies cyber attacks. This would rule out a cyber no-first-use policy. But it would amount to a pledge not to wage cyber war unless aggression has been committed—unless hostilities have begun. If inclined toward such a pledge, the United States should make it contingent on a reciprocal one from China. Doing so would reduce the risk that China would conduct cyberstrikes preemptively or in a crisis before any shooting occurs.

In essence, U.S. policy could be as follows:

- The United States opposes aggression in the form of computer network attacks and regards such attacks as acts of war.

- It reserves the right of self-defense by responding to such attacks and will maintain the capability to retaliate in order to deter.

■ The laws of war governing the obligation not to harm civilians apply in cyberspace.

Behavior will speak at least as loudly as declaratory policy. Two behaviors that could undermine cyber deterrence vis-à-vis China are attacking Chinese networks other than in retaliation for Chinese attacks, and failing to retaliate for Chinese attacks. The greater the difference in consequences for China between attacking and not attacking the United States, the stronger the deterrence. Moreover, for the United States to attack Chinese networks absent Chinese attacks would strengthen the hands of those Chinese who argue for an aggressive cyber warfare policy and weaken those who argue that China is better off showing restraint. Conversely, U.S. failure to retaliate could undercut the credibility of deterrence insofar as the potential attacker is given reason to think that retaliation will not occur.

Such a posture is the opposite of frequent lesser network interference. It requires purposeful decisionmaking. The need for calibrated and consistent strategic behavior reinforces the need for strong civilian control, in both the United States and China. A clear distinction must be made between the technical competence to create and employ cyber weapons and the authority to determine whether, when, against whom, and for what ends to use them. Because it requires strategic behavior and is a matter of war and peace, cyber deterrence must be managed by proper authorities in the same way all other international uses of force are: politically accountable civilian officials of the executive branch and designated military commanders, with proper Congressional oversight. The United States is moving in this direction with the creation of U.S. Cyber Command (under U.S. Title 10 and the Secretary of Defense) alongside the National Security Agency (under U.S. Title 50 and the Director of National Intelligence).

The existence of security commitments to U.S. allies (and hypothetically to Chinese allies) may appear to further complicate an already difficult domain. But the cyber security of allies need not and should not be different than their physical security, at least not where destructive cyber warfare is concerned. For starters, a serious cyber attack on a NATO Ally should cause Article V of the Washington Treaty to be invoked; anything less would invite Russia to attempt again the sort of attacks it allegedly sponsored against Estonia (a NATO Ally) and Georgia. By extension, U.S. commitments to the security of Japan, South Korea, and other treaty Allies in Asia should include the option of U.S. retaliation for Chinese cyber attack. Thus, any agreement by the United States and China to show restraint toward the strategic cyberspace of the other must include at least treaty Allies.

Finally, Sino-American mutual restraint in cyberspace could be extended to cooperation against common third-party threats in that domain. Both countries have two sets of cyber security concerns: high-end state threats, and all other state and nonstate threats. For the former, deterrence is necessary and feasible; for the latter, it is less necessary and less feasible. U.S. and Chinese security against all other state and nonstate cyber threats could be improved through Sino-American cooperation, whether in bilateral or multilateral settings. At a minimum, exchanging information on potential attackers and attacks, notifying alerts, and extraordinary measures would be worthwhile, as gaining wide acceptance of mutual strategic restraint in cyberspace. While such cooperation is not essential for mutual restraint, it would be a natural and beneficial supplement.

Conclusion

China and the United States are both beginning to grasp the grave harm that could come from strategic cyber war. Their respective offensive capabilities in this domain, the difficulty of defense against large cyber threats, and thus the fear of retaliation can be the foundation for mutual deterrence. While this could be left as a de facto condition or tacit understanding, it is better to make it a matter of agreement on mutual restraint in initiating strategic cyber war, including tight political control of any military cyber attacks in the event of armed conflict. Such agreement could be bolstered by continuing discussion of thorny definitional issues and possible concrete cooperation.

The United States should be interested in pursuing an accord along these lines, though with its eyes open about the ambiguities and pitfalls. But it should do so as part of a wider approach, covering nuclear and space domains as well. As with restraint in space, the United States should not accede definitively to China's position on no first use of nuclear weapons if the Chinese reject the larger concept of mutual strategic restraint and its application to cyberspace.

These ideas might be more appealing to the United States than to the Chinese. The United States is the stronger military power, and it is more vulnerable than China to the effects of cyber war—for now. But China is becoming highly dependent on computer networks and more exposed to their disruption, and it has no more hope of complete network defense than the United States has. Perhaps Chinese leaders have the foresight to appreciate the value of mutual strategic restraint in cyberspace, and the clout to overrule objections from Chinese warfighters. In the meantime, they can be sure that the United States will not accept inferiority in offensive cyber war capabilities and that China's vulnerabilities in this domain will only get worse.

Notes

[1] An intriguing question is how important Web-based social networking might be or become for either the United States or China, given its remarkable importance in marshaling and unifying citizens on a large scale in the recent democratic revolutions in the Arab world. Of course, it is more likely that the Chinese government would interfere with social networking in China than that the U.S. Government would. For this analysis, we will not treat it as "critical."

[2] Perhaps for probing or to send a non-harmful signal. But such examples do not negate the point.

[3] Lest such a distinction between strategic and nonstrategic networks be taken as a green light to attack the latter, each country should consider its own vulnerability throughout cyberspace before conducting or condoning cyber war at any level or on any target.

[4] A basic Westphalian principle, which the Chinese above all would appreciate.

[5] For further discussion, see National Security Council, "The Comprehensive National Cybersecurity Initiative," available at <www.whitehouse.gov/cybersecurity/comprehensive-national-cybersecurity-initiative>; "Remarks by the President on Securing our Nation's Cyber Infrastructure," May 2009, available at <www.whitehouse.gov/the-press-office/remarks-president-securing-our-nations-cyber-infrastructure>; National Security Council, "The Cyberspace Policy Review," available at <www.whitehouse.gov/assets/documents/Cyberspace_Policy_Review_final.pdf>.

[6] Dennis C. Blair, "Annual Threat Assessment of the U.S. Intelligence Committee for the Senate Select Committee on Intelligence," Office of the Director of National Intelligence, 2010; Spencer Michels, interview with Michael Hayden, "Hackers Force Internet Users to Learn Self-Defense," *PBS News Hour*, August 11, 2010; Michael McConnell, "Cybersecurity: Next Steps to Protect Our Critical Infrastructure," statement before the Committee on Commerce, Science, and Transportation, Washington, DC, February 23, 2010, available at <www.fas.org/irp/congress/2010_hr/cybersec.pdf>.

[7] Scott Borg, "How Cyber Attacks Will Be Used in International Conflicts," presentation at *USENIX Security '10 Technical Symposium,* Washington, DC, 2010.

[8] The attack on Google was not strategic for two reasons. First, the purpose of the attack was to exfiltrate data, not to degrade the systems. Second, the network that was attacked was not of national importance.

[9] "Marching Off to Cyberwar," *The Economist,* December 4, 2008, available at <www.economist.com/node/12673385>; Mark Landler and John Markoff, "Digital Fears Emerge After Data Siege in Estonia," *The New York Times,* May 29, 2007, available at <www.nytimes.com/2007/05/29/technology/29estonia.html>.

[10] China Internet Network Information Center, "Statistical Report on Internet Development in China," 2009.

[11] Before assuming that personal Internet use in China will subvert the state, note that much of it is nationalistic—questioning the government not for being too strong at home but for being too weak abroad. So far, at least, the threat of cyber dissent has not caused the government to shut down Internet use, only to block any political excesses.

[12] Investment in WiFi is shifting from telecom and end-users to institutions. See Analysys International, *The Market for Wi-Fi® in China: Opportunities, Enablers and Challenges* (Beijing: Analysys International, June 2006), 24.

[13] "Being Eaten by the Dragon: Chinese Takeovers," *The Economist,* November 13, 2010, 81.

[14] Interview with Chinese expert, Beijing, December 2010.

[15] It appears to be the case that while Stuxnet was meant to target Iranian nuclear facilities, it infected the SCADA systems in several different countries.

[16] Electronic attacks on the data networks connected to space-based sensors and space-based communications could be considered either counter-space or cyber war. Because we are defining counter-space as attacks on satellites themselves, we will consider such electronic attacks as cyber war.

[17] The alternative, a cluster of U.S. defense and intelligence networks that are totally, globally isolated, would be prohibitively expensive and virtually impractical.

[18] One U.S. cyber expert makes the point that crude (and relatively indiscriminant) methods such as distributed denial-of-service attacks against U.S. military logistics networks could be an effective tool. Mulvenon, "PLA Computer Network Operations."

[19] Information Office of the State Council of the People's Republic of China, *China's National Defense in 2008* (Beijing: Information Office of the State Council of the People's Republic of China, January 2009), 11.

[20] Martin C. Libicki, *Cyberdeterrence and Cyberwar* (Santa Monica, CA: RAND, 2009), 57–59.

[21] This might be especially true in a military conflict, where the imperative to prevail might result in the use of all availability capabilities, including ones previously reserved or used sparingly to avoid compromising their effectiveness.

[22] L.A. Gordon and M.P. Loeb, "The Economics of Information Security Investment," *ACM Transactions on Information and System Security* 5, no. 4 (November 2002), 438–457.

[23] William Lynn, "Defending a New Domain: The Pentagon's Cyberstrategy," *Foreign Affairs* (September–October 2010).

[24] Deterring cyber attack by other means, such as physical attack, is possible. However, that possibility does not negate the possible merits of mutual cyber deterrence, at least as an option.

[25] For purposes of this book, we concentrate on deterrence by the threat of retaliation and not "deterrence by denial," that is, by better defense. The latter presents the attacker with only the risk of failure, whereas we are interested here in the question of presenting risks worse than failure.

[26] Some examples include Libicki; Richard Harknett, John Callaghan, and Rudi Kauffman, "Leaving Deterrence Behind: War-Fighting and National Cybersecurity," *Journal of Homeland Security and Emergency Management* 7, no. 1 (2010); Richard Harknett, "Information Warfare and Deterrence," *Parameters* 26, no. 3 (Autumn 1996); and Stephen Blank, "Can Information Warfare be Deterred?" in *Information Age Anthology,* Volume III: *The Information Age Military,* ed. David S. Alberts and Daniel S. Papp (Washington, DC: Command and Control Research Program, 2001), 125–157, available at <www.dodccrp.org/files/Alberts_Anthology_III.pdf>.

[27] A good analogy might be bombing interdiction campaigns that target dual-use transportation nodes (bridges, highways, rail switching stations) to prevent military forces and supplies from moving to the front.

[28] Lolita C. Baldor, Associated Press, June 24, 2010.

[29] There is a somewhat metaphysical debate about whether mutual assured destruction is consistent with the rules of law, given the civilian cataclysm implied. But this has never had any real impact on nuclear doctrine.

[30] For more discussion on the Kosovo controversy, see Tonia Voon, "Pointing the Finger: Civilian Casualties of NATO Bombing in the Kosovo Conflict," Washington College of Law, American University, 2001, available at <www.wcl.american.edu/journal/ilr/16/voon.pdf?rd=1>.

Chapter Seven

Integration and Implications

From this analysis of the nuclear, space, and cyberspace domains of Sino-American strategic relations, possible terms for mutual restraint have emerged:

- U.S. acceptance of mutual nuclear deterrence with China, consummated by Sino-American bilateral pledges not to use nuclear weapons first against the other
- bilateral pledges not to be the first to interfere with the other's access to space
- bilateral agreement not to be the first to attack the other's strategic cyberspace, jointly defined to include critical national networks, supported by agreement that attacks against military networks entail a serious risk of escalation and civilian damage, and therefore must be carefully targeted and under tight political control
- inclusion of allies in all terms of mutual restraint and in the underlying system of deterrence.

Analysis of general U.S. and Chinese attitudes concerning national security, strategy, and Sino-U.S. relations indicates that both countries could be favorably predisposed toward some aspects of mutual restraint but skeptical about others. The Chinese would be warmer to such restraint in the nuclear domain, while the United States would see greater advantages in restraint in space and cyberspace. Overall, the United States may be more inclined to establish a comprehensive regime of mutual strategic restraint, while it could take China more time—and greater appreciation of growing vulnerabilities and the emerging reality of deterrence—to reach the same conclusion.

Against this backdrop, this chapter will analyze how the two powers might view the particular terms of strategic restraint stated above and, from that analysis, how the terms should be packaged. It will then examine the implications of mutual restraint along these lines for military contingencies, regional stability, reactions of other states, and Sino-American relations in general. It will conclude with a look at how best to organize the Sino-American strategic relationship to reduce vulnerabilities with high confidence and low risk of unwanted effects, taking both countries' views into account.

American Perspectives

Explicit U.S. acceptance of Sino-American mutual nuclear deterrence would be a formal concession to China. Although the United States will in any case not be able, and will not try, to deny China a survivable and effective retaliatory capability, stated U.S. acceptance of such a capability would serve Chinese interests on several levels. Strategically, to the extent credible, it would mitigate China's vulnerability to a U.S. nuclear first strike and—of more concern to the Chinese—to nuclear blackmail. Militarily, it would provide relief from whatever fear the Chinese have that hostilities with U.S. forces could lead to nuclear war. Economically, it would largely obviate the need for huge additional investments to improve the survivability of Chinese strategic offensive forces, including their large-scale expansion. Politically, it would be another sign that the reigning global power acknowledges the new one, and it would vindicate China's 50-year advocacy of no first use. Although such Chinese gains can largely be won by objective conditions of mutual deterrence, Beijing would place some value on their confirmation in U.S. declaratory policy or in an explicit bilateral agreement.

Being far more capable and less vulnerable in the nuclear domain, the United States would benefit less than China from an affirmation of mutual nuclear deterrence. Yet it would advance American aims of reducing the role of nuclear weapons in international relations and warfare and at least marginally support U.S. nonproliferation policy. To the extent U.S. acceptance of mutual deterrence curbed Chinese modernization of offensive nuclear forces, it would ease pressure on the United States to respond with additional modernization efforts. Finally, it could be a constructive step in Sino-American relations with potential benefits for U.S. interests in increased Chinese willingness to cooperate on other international issues— an unverifiable but nevertheless fair prospect.[1]

At the same time, U.S. acceptance of mutual nuclear restraint has at least a theoretical potential to weaken deterrence of Chinese aggression in the western Pacific; to place more of a burden on the United States to counter China's conventional force buildup (including finding other escalation options); to stimulate competition, instability, and even hostilities in other strategic domains (space and cyberspace), unless mutual restraint is extended to them; and to raise questions about U.S. security commitments among allies in the region. To mitigate these possible drawbacks, U.S. interest in mutual nuclear restraint should be made contingent on Chinese acceptance of a broad and integrated framework of strategic restraint.

In contrast to the nuclear domain, Sino-American mutual restraint in space and cyberspace would redress increasingly acute U.S. vulnerabilities, owing to heavy economic and military reliance on both domains and to the cost and limits of satellite and network defenses against a large, capable, and determined opponent like China. If the United States can seize on China's growing reliance on and vulnerability in space and cyberspace to achieve a regime of mutual restraint in those domains, it would be a major American success.

Given that the United States will in any case possess potent ASAT and offensive cyber war capabilities, the Chinese should have an incentive to consider mutual restraint in these domains. Chinese military and political leaders should be disabused of any illusion that a preemptive, demonstrative, probing, or narrow strike on U.S. satellites or computer networks would end there: all Chinese satellites and networks would become potential targets for retaliation. In space and cyberspace, as in the nuclear domain, the underpinnings of restraint are the cold realities of national vulnerability, offense dominance, and danger of retaliation. China may resist mutual restraint in these domains and nevertheless find itself deterred.

Although it is possible to agree on mutual restraint in either space or cyberspace but not in the other domain, the interdependence of the space and cyber domains argues for dealing with strategic vulnerability in both. The importance of space stems largely from its use as a medium for the movement of data, and space sensors provide essential data for certain critical networks.[2] Being vulnerable in both domains, the United States should pursue mutual restraint in both. Moreover, given the overlap of space and cyberspace, it would not be difficult for either power to circumvent mutual restraint in one of these domains by threatening in the other.[3]

The difficulty of establishing deterrence and mutual restraint in cyberspace has already been explained. For the United States as well as for China, the chief potential drawback of agreeing on offensive restraint in cyberspace would be any restrictions on interfering with computer networks that enable the other side's military forces to conduct combat operations. Therefore, it is unrealistic to expect mutual restraint in strategic cyberspace to prohibit or prevent attacks on dedicated military networks in wartime.

At the same time, the risk of escalation from military to civilian cyber attacks (that is, tactical to strategic attacks) is inherent in the dual nature of much of cyberspace—and quite substantial given the porosity and instability of network boundaries. The question, then, is whether U.S. and Chinese pledges of mutual restraint in strategic cyberspace would reduce or aggravate this escalatory risk. On one hand, pledges of restraint at the strategic level could create the mirage of a firebreak, reducing inhibitions against attacking military networks and thereby increasing the danger of escalation to strategic cyber warfare. On the other hand, Sino-American recognition of mutual vulnerability in cyberspace, including the risk of escalation, could and should instill caution on both sides in conducting military cyber attacks.

With this in mind, in agreeing not to attack strategic cyberspace except in retaliation, both sides should also undertake to exercise caution, discrimination, precision, and control in cyberspace should conflict occur. Because cyber war at *any* level runs the risk of cyber war at *every* level, the United States will want to adapt and apply established protocols for delegation of authority to combatant commands to the cyber domain, with a focus on ensuring that any actions that could produce serious civilian commercial disruptions are approved at appropriately high levels. Of course, the United States would expect Chinese political authorities to be equally vigilant in how the PLA may conduct cyber war against U.S. forces during armed conflict. With this important condition governing attacks on military networks in times of war, the United States should favor mutual restraint in strategic cyberspace.

Thus, from the U.S. perspective, a preferred package of mutual restraint understandings becomes clear. Given U.S. vulnerabilities in space and cyberspace, it would be inadvisable for the United States to agree to no first use of nuclear weapons against China while leaving China free to attack U.S. satellites and critical networks, even if the United States was likewise free. Moreover, to the extent the Chinese might be emboldened to use conventional force because of reduced fear of nuclear escalation, it could make matters even worse if they also thought they could exploit U.S. reluctance to intervene due to fear of Chinese attacks using space and cyber warfare. The United States should insist on the principle that stability in one domain should not endanger stability in others.

Despite all the advantages of a broad approach to mutual restraint, it could imply strategic decoupling in that the United States would, in effect, be declaring that it would not escalate to hostilities in these strategic domains even if its conventional military capabilities prove insufficient to deter or defeat Chinese aggression. The United States resisted strategic decoupling during the Cold War by warning that it was prepared to use nuclear weapons, up to and including strategic nuclear weapons, if NATO's conventional defense against Soviet aggression failed. If the United States would not decouple strategic forces from conventional war with the Soviet Union, why would it do so vis-à-vis China? Put differently, if the United States was willing to risk strategic conflict to deter aggression against its European Allies in the last century, why would it not risk strategic conflict to deter aggression against its Asian allies in this one?

One reason is that the United States presently has conventional military superiority over China, whereas the Warsaw Pact was thought to have conventional military superiority over NATO well into the 1980s. Another is that China does not pose the sort of blatant, direct, and massive threat to East Asia that the Soviet Union posed to Western Europe. Serious limitations on the Chinese military's ability to project and sustain a large combat force outside its borders mean that China has no real capability to commit region-wide military aggression; nor does it geographically abut any U.S. treaty ally other than Thailand. Moreover, in contrast to the Soviet Union, whose designs on all of Europe were implied by its seizure of half of it and the offensive orientation of the Soviet and Warsaw Pact militaries, China has betrayed no interest in large-scale territorial conquest in East Asia, and it would incur untold material and political costs if it tried. If China's goal is to be a stable, prosperous, secure, and respected power, military expansionism is much more likely to jeopardize that goal than further it. The discrepancy between the territories and maritime areas China claims but does not control encompasses Taiwan, minor land border disputes with India and Nepal, and disputes over islands and maritime areas in the East and South China Seas. This discrepancy is a source of regional instability, especially as China improves its capabilities to assert its claims, but it is vastly different in nature and scope from the threat of Soviet invasion of Western Europe. The most likely threats China will pose in the region are low-grade ones over specific territorial disputes that do not affect vital U.S. interests.

Because both the dangers and the stakes in East Asia today are lower than those of the Cold War, a U.S. threat to initiate nuclear war against China—suspect even in the prior case—is not credible in any circumstances other than in retaliation for a nuclear attack on the United States or its allies. Therefore, U.S. acceptance of China's nuclear retaliatory capability should not affect Chinese calculations about the use of force. Indeed, if the Chinese really thought the United States would launch a first strike in the event of the failure of conventional defense, presumably they would not count on some U.S. promise not to do so. It follows that the risks associated with strategic decoupling are much lower in East Asia today than they were in Europe during the Cold War. Nevertheless, given East Asia's importance, the United States must preserve the stability of the region and the security of its allies in any accords with China.

In sum, broadly defined American objectives in Sino-U.S. strategic restraint should be to mitigate national vulnerabilities, deemphasize the role of nuclear weapons, curb threats to satellites and computer networks, discourage Chinese use of force, encourage Chinese cooperation, maintain regional stability, and reassure allies. These objectives are best served by an integrated and sturdy approach to Sino-U.S. mutual strategic restraint, covering all three domains, discouraging the use of force at any level, and providing for the security of U.S. allies and the region as a whole.

Chinese Perspectives

It is doubtful that China would readily accept wholesale the integrated approach to strategic restraint that the United States would favor. Yet its growing vulnerabilities and improving conventional military capabilities give China increasing incentive to avoid escalation to the strategic level. This is particularly the case in the nuclear domain, where China is most overmatched. Moreover, the Chinese would not relish a costly nuclear arms race, building more offensive capabilities to stay ahead of U.S. defense potential and possibly causing the United States to enhance its strategic offensive capabilities vis-à-vis China. Chinese policy statements consistently emphasize the imperative of avoiding costly and destabilizing arms races.

The Chinese would be more ambivalent about mutual restraint in space and cyberspace. Chinese military strategists view these domains as potential weaknesses in an otherwise commanding current U.S. conventional military edge. Operationally, the Chinese see vulnerable U.S. satellites and networks as opportunities to disrupt the C⁴ISR system on which the U.S. military depends for conducting integrated expeditionary and strike operations. The PLA might well try to block any limitations on attacking U.S. forces in those domains.

The key to the possibility of broader strategic restraint, along the lines preferred by the United States, lies in whether Chinese political leaders grasp the sweep, scale, and implications of China's national vulnerabilities and have the political will to overrule their generals. China will be vitally dependent on space and cyberspace within a matter of years, as an inescapable result of the Chinese economic integration at home and abroad. China's ability to sustain strong economic growth and perhaps to maintain political order could be dashed by conflict in these new domains.[4] Party and government leaders will recognize this from their vantage points, and increasingly influential business executives (many of whom are also senior party members) will recognize it from theirs. If the regime's leaders defer to the PLA, there may be no agreement to reduce vulnerability in space and cyberspace. In turn, because the United States may insist on an approach to strategic restraint that encompasses all three domains, there might be no agreement on mutual nuclear restraint, either.

Thus, hopes for the United States and China to address their growing strategic vulnerability to each other may hinge on Chinese civil-military relations. The PLA follows political guidance issued by top civilian leaders but increasingly expects to be able to apply its professional military judgment on matters such as military doctrine and strategy, force planning, resource priorities, war plans, target selection, and operational command and control.[5] This does not mean that decisions governing actual uses of force—starting hostilities, attacking U.S. forces, and initiating war in space and cyberspace—would be taken by the PLA without civilian consent. Consistent with the history of China's civil-military relations since Mao Zedong, only political leaders may make war-and-peace decisions. However, current Chinese political leaders, unlike their predecessors, have no personal military experience. Options presented to them by the PLA could be limited to or tilted toward PLA preferences, perhaps presenting strikes on U.S. satellites and networks as operational necessities.

A "rational actor" analysis of Chinese decisionmaking would indicate that China could accept a broad approach to mutual strategic restraint along the lines and for the reasons suggested here.[6] But a "bureaucratic decisionmaking" analysis, in which the PLA has to be brought along, suggests lower expectations. Still, one expects that China's positions on mutual restraint will rest ultimately on the views of its political leaders about national goals and vulnerabilities, China's role in the region and the world, Sino-American relations, and their own responsibilities and legacies. If those leaders see great power antagonism as the primary dynamic or are overly deferential to the military (perhaps to bolster their political positions), they will be disinclined to embrace the concept and general application of strategic restraint and be more likely to seek unilateral advantage. If they believe China's future success depends on international security, cooperation with the United States, and undisturbed growth and political stability at home, Chinese leaders may elect to pursue broad and fair mutual restraint despite military objections. In any case, the Chinese will face the reality of U.S. retaliatory capabilities in all three domains, for which the PLA has no feasible solution or persuasive answers.

Even if China's political leaders are sympathetic in principle to mutual strategic restraint, it could take years for Chinese positions to form on such complex and momentous questions. Nothing in our analysis of Chinese general predispositions and likely reactions to specific terms of mutual restraint suggests that U.S. proposals would be met by uniform enthusiasm or lead to early agreements. The exception, again, is a bilateral nuclear no-first-use deal, which we would caution the United States not to accept unless China is prepared to seriously discuss comparable restraint in space and cyberspace.

Military Competition and Strategic Restraint

The preceding sections have discussed perceptions about the costs, benefits, and preferred forms of strategic restraint in the nuclear, space, and cyber domains from the separate perspectives of the United States and China. However, there is also an interactive element to Sino-U.S. relations that will shape attitudes in both countries toward strategic restraint. This involves three key factors: the strategic military balance in the nuclear, space, and cyber domains; the conventional military balance (and how it varies with geography); and the role played by military competition and preparations for possible conflict in overall Sino-U.S. relations. In the preceding chapters, we have laid out the argument that the relative balance in the strategic domains matters much less than the absolute capability of each side to impose major damage in the nuclear, space, and cyber domains. On the other hand, the salience of the U.S.-China conventional military balance varies considerably depending on the extent to which serious conflicts of interest exist that could produce military conflict and how important these interests are compared to other aspects of the bilateral relationship, which often will have a more positive and cooperative nature.

U.S. analysts describe ongoing PLA efforts to raise the costs and risks of U.S. military forces operating close to China as an antiaccess/area denial strategy. China is developing and deploying a number of systems that fit under this umbrella, including advanced conventional submarines, an antiship ballistic missile that can target U.S. carriers, antiship cruise missiles on air and naval platforms, extended-range surface-to-air missiles, and ballistic and cruise missiles with sufficient precision and range to strike U.S. air bases throughout the region.[7] If these systems work as intended, the closer U.S. aircraft and naval vessels operate to China, the greater their risk of being shot down or sunk. The cumulative effect would be to shift the local military balance in China's favor as U.S. aircraft and ships operate closer to China, making U.S. intervention in a conflict over Taiwan more costly, less successful, and less likely.

At the same time, China has significant limitations on its ability to deploy and sustain air and naval power outside its borders, especially in a combat environment. China has no overseas air bases and only a rudimentary air refueling capability (via a small fleet of tankers and a limited number of fighters capable of being refueled). The PLA navy is gradually expanding its ability to conduct out-of-area operations, but its deployments to date have been of small numbers of ships, of limited duration, and in permissive environments.[8] After two decades of debate, China is only now preparing to deploy its first aircraft carrier (a remodeled carrier purchased from Ukraine). Despite significant improvements in PLA capabilities, a fundamental asymmetry in the U.S. and Chinese ability to project power will persist for decades. PLA antiaccess/area denial capabilities are increasing the risks for U.S. forces close to China, but the farther away the PLA gets from China, the more U.S. forces will have an advantage. The U.S. military is pursuing a variety of technical and operational efforts to respond to the general spread of antiaccess/area denial capabilities, including a new joint AirSea Battle doctrine.

If U.S.-China interests are viewed as fundamentally opposed and the risk of military conflict is viewed as high, negotiating a strategic restraint agreement would be much more difficult (even though an agreement could still have high value for both sides in limiting and regulating military competition). Under such circumstances, both sides would be highly attentive to the conventional military balance, inclined to look to counterspace and cyber attack capabilities to compensate for weaknesses in specific conventional capabilities, and highly suspicious about the other side's willingness to abide by any agreements. Competition for military advantage would be the dominant feature of the relationship. However, we believe that U.S. and Chinese interests are not fundamentally opposed and that prospects for major Sino-U.S. military conflict are low if the two sides can continue to manage the Taiwan issue prudently. Military competition will be part of the Sino-U.S. bilateral relationship, but not so central a part that restraint in the strategic realm becomes impossible when it is in the interests of both sides.

Implications of Strategic Restraint for Deterring or Waging War

Notwithstanding this relatively sanguine assessment of Sino-American relations, the prospects and effects of mutual strategic restraint must be examined in the light of possible conflict. Because the use of force by China to settle outstanding territorial disputes cannot be excluded, neither can Sino-U.S. military contingencies, given U.S. interests and commitments in this important region. Therefore, even if the relationship is not defined by military competition under the shadow of great power conflict, the effects of strategic restraint on the probability of conflict must be considered.

Decoupling the threat of strategic escalation could make conventional warfare seem less risky to the nations involved, at least in theory. In essence, it means that conflict and its costs, risks, and casualties can be confined to the military forces involved—clearly a Chinese objective in the event of conflict. If the side starting a conflict has already accounted for expected military losses, strategic decoupling can weaken deterrence by excluding other, larger losses. In the context of Sino-U.S. mutual strategic restraint, the concern is that China would be more likely to risk conflict and therefore more likely to commit hostile acts if escalation to strategic domains was believed to be unlikely. After all, China's current military strategy is designed to avoid a protracted conflict and strategic escalation, which would allow the United States to bring more forces to bear and increase the danger of Chinese defeat and serious losses.

While Sino-U.S. military conflict in the western Pacific conceivably could occur over Taiwan, Korea, or some territorial dispute involving U.S. treaty allies, the Taiwan case involves vital Chinese interests and is examined here to get a clearer sense for the risk of decoupling. China would like to achieve reunification with Taiwan without resorting to force, which would entail high military costs and risks, stoke regional fears of an aggressive China, produce painful economic sanctions, and severely damage U.S.-China relations regardless of the outcome. Nevertheless, U.S. military capabilities and the prospect of U.S. intervention are major parts of the Chinese calculus on whether to use force to gain control of Taiwan. The threat of U.S. intervention poses two specters for China: failure to achieve its war aims vis-à-vis Taiwan, and escalation to a costly general war with (and likely defeat by) the United States. Accordingly, Chinese military strategy and the operational concepts and force modernization efforts predicated on it are designed to deter, delay, degrade, and otherwise limit U.S. military intervention so that PLA operations against Taiwan can succeed swiftly and general war with the United States can be averted.[9] China's investment in antiaccess/area denial capabilities is primarily focused on raising the costs and risks of U.S. intervention in a Taiwan conflict.

How would mutual strategic restraint, as suggested here, affect the calculations about Chinese attack and U.S. intervention? In general, as the local military balance becomes less favorable and the western Pacific becomes more dangerous for U.S. ships and other forces, the United States could feel pressure to soften its commitment to defend Taiwan. The United States could also take measures to beef up Taiwan's self-defense capabilities, though there are major practical and political limits to this, especially the damage to Sino-U.S. relations of increased U.S. arms sales to Taiwan. Alternatively, the United States could rely increasingly on deterrence by threatening escalation and thus planting doubts in Chinese leaders' minds about PLA assurances of a brief, predictable, confined, and low-cost conflict. U.S. escalation might take the form of waging a longer campaign that allows the United States to bring more forces to bear or broadening the conflict into other geographic areas to exploit the U.S. military's edge in power projection. It could also involve escalating to strategic attacks—an option that would be foreclosed by a strategic restraint agreement.

Mutual restraint and strategic decoupling could contradict the U.S. threat of escalation and thus weaken deterrence even as the local military equilibrium shifts in China's favor. Yet on closer look, a more nuanced picture appears. In regard to nuclear weapons, a no-first-use pledge, if believed, could ease whatever fear the Chinese might have that war over Taiwan could end in a U.S. nuclear attack on China. But recall that the bedrock beneath any nuclear no-first-use understanding is the objective reality of mutual deterrence, which is based on a Chinese ability to have a survivable retaliatory force and a U.S. inability to prevent it. Whether or not the United States admits that it is deterred from escalating to nuclear war with China, in the end it is Chinese confidence in the credibility of the threat to retaliate that determines whether China fears U.S. nuclear escalation.

Conversely, if the Chinese were not satisfied that they had a convincing second-strike threat, they might not trust the United States to abide by a no-first-use pledge, especially if U.S. forces were about to be defeated and Taiwan was about to be seized. The Chinese would assume that whether the United States would escalate to nuclear war in the course of a military conflict would depend on American calculations at that time of the costs of doing so versus the costs of not doing so, rather than on a prior promise of restraint. While mutual restraint may be desirable, the ultimate Chinese insurance against U.S. nuclear attack is not a pledge but rather the fact that Chinese retaliation cannot be totally prevented by a U.S. nuclear first strike and missile defense. It follows that strategic decoupling is a byproduct not of mutual nuclear restraint but rather of objective, seemingly inevitable conditions of mutual deterrence, and thus a concern that the United States will have to address in any case.

Such conditions of deterrence imply that the costs of nuclear war to the United States would outweigh the costs of refraining from nuclear escalation and that it would therefore not resort to nuclear weapons over Taiwan, even if military operations were going poorly. Barring U.S. abandonment of Taiwan, the combination of a less favorable local military balance and a less credible nuclear threat would leave the United States in need of other escalatory options.

Space and cyberspace are candidates for U.S. escalation or the threat of escalation to strengthen deterrence of China, keeping in mind the expectation of minimal casualties. Experience with nuclear deterrence does not provide a simple template for judging how effective either escalatory threat could be in deterring the use of force by China. The nuclear threshold is clear.[10] Moreover, the consequences of nuclear war, while devastating, are fairly calculable. While attacking satellites is a reasonably clear threshold, the difficulty of identifying a threshold for cyber war has already been explained. Moreover, the course and consequences of escalation, especially in cyberspace, are hugely unpredictable.

These ambiguities do not mean that the threat of counterspace and cyber attacks cannot help deter the use of conventional force. Rather, ambiguity about escalation thresholds and uncertainties about effects of conflict in these domains can foster caution rather than recklessness. It follows that the threat of space and cyber attacks could contribute to deterrence, should the United States threaten such escalation. In turn, this means that deterrence of Chinese conventional aggression might be weakened were the United States to agree on mutual restraint in these domains.

At the same time, given Chinese ASAT and cyber war capabilities, U.S. interest in threatening retaliation in these domains to offset declining local military superiority must be tempered by the prospect of very damaging Chinese retaliation. Therefore, we caution against looking to such escalation as the solution to the problem of deterring Chinese use of force.

Both of these new domains are complicated by the possibility that China itself could be tempted to initiate attacks on satellites or networks. The United States might regard the extension of hostilities into space and cyberspace as dangerous and disadvantageous; therefore, it would want to be able to deter China from launching such attacks. The best U.S. deterrent of such attacks would be the threat of severe retaliation against Chinese satellites and computer networks, with the effect of delivering such a shock to China's economy that the Chinese would refrain from attacks in space or cyberspace. The prospect of Chinese retaliation against U.S. satellites and/ or computer networks is all the more reason for the United States to adopt a second-strike posture in these domains.

While the United States may be able to deter Chinese attacks in space and cyberspace, it could still be left with the problem of strategic decoupling because of *mutual* deterrence, and thus at least some erosion of its ability to deter China from using conventional force against Taiwan. This is all the more reason why the United States must consider other ways of deterring China from using its improving military capabilities, including those that can strike U.S. intervention forces. U.S. efforts to develop a new AirSea Battle doctrine focusing on effective joint employment of naval and air strike capabilities in the face of an adversary's sophisticated antiaccess/ area denial capabilities represent one potential response.[11]

While this study does not assess every U.S. escalatory option systematically, these options could include conventional strikes on Chinese forces outside the immediate initial area of hostilities, conventional strikes on war support installations on the Chinese mainland, or a naval blockade to interdict China's sea lines of communication and energy supply. The United States has an abundance of deployable and global range strike capabilities, and the longer a conflict with China lasts, the more of these it can bring to bear. Apart from attacking Chinese satellites and critical national computer networks, much less using nuclear weapons, the United States has what China does not: the ability to target and strike enemy forces and other targets anywhere, including the homeland. The United States has escalatory options that would not violate an exchange of pledges to exercise restraint in the strategic domains. (Moreover, Chinese escalation to counterspace and cyber attacks would not necessarily preclude the U.S. ability to execute these options, especially those that exploit the U.S. advantage in power projection.)

Of course, even U.S. conventional escalation could be viewed as strategic by China, especially if it involved attacks on the mainland or threatened Chinese nuclear deterrent capabilities, such as warning systems and national command and control. The Chinese are especially sensitive about U.S. global strike options, such as long-range conventional ballistic missiles and long-range bombers, even though these capabilities are not receiving substantial funding.[12] They might either insist that these be included in any assurances of mutual restraint or else make clear unilaterally that Chinese strategic restraint will be contingent on U.S. restraint in the use of such systems. The United States must be prepared to insist that PLA forces cannot expect to operate against U.S. forces from a mainland sanctuary. If China launched attacks on U.S. satellites, it could expect U.S. retaliatory attacks on its ASAT launchers and related support facilities. In any case, the United States would certainly exercise care in conventional escalation, especially in choice of targets, lest it elicit a Chinese conclusion that its ability to launch its strategic retaliatory forces was under threat, which could trigger nuclear war.

Even without conventional global strike capabilities, the United States does have conventional options to maintain deterrence of Chinese use of force under conditions of mutual strategic restraint even if China succeeds in tilting the conventional military balance in the western Pacific in its favor in the coming decade or so. With or without Sino-American accord on mutual restraint, it is imperative for the United States to be sensitive to shifts in the balance and to adapt its military strategy as needed to ensure that the Chinese remain mindful of the severe consequences of using force.

The potential problems mutual strategic restraint could pose for averting Chinese use of force and Sino-American hostilities in the western Pacific prompt three additional observations. First, apart from the dangers of combat with U.S. forces and ensuing escalation, the Chinese have many reasons not to use force, at least not on a large scale: uncertainty of success, expected high losses (even in the event of success), regional and global outrage and sanctions, the possibility of derailing China's economic growth, the long-term damage to relations with the world's superpower, and unpredictable domestic political repercussions.

Second, it is all the more important for the United States to play whatever helpful role it can in producing a fair, principled, and sustainable outcome of the Taiwan problem—the most obvious flashpoint for major war between the United States and China.[13] And third, the United States should be clear that it is concerned with not only compliance with the specific terms of mutual strategic restraint but also the overall *effects*. If the Chinese become militarily aggressive despite—or perhaps because of—arrangements of strategic restraint, the United States would obviously reassess all aspects of its relations with China, including understandings concerning restraint.

Implications for Regional Stability

A Sino-American strategic restraint agreement would affect the general stability of the western Pacific and East Asia. The United States and most of the states in the region believe that stability depends on U.S. power, in various forms, to balance the reality and perception of an increasingly potent and assertive China. Ironically, past Chinese leaders held the view that U.S. power was essential for checking the Soviet East Asian threat and for averting Japanese unilateralism and remilitarization.[14] While there is no current or prospective Russian threat, the question of Japanese intentions has not vanished. Nevertheless, Beijing now views American military power in the region as an obstacle to the stature (if not dominance) to which it aspires, as well as a potential threat to itself and to its access to the world.

The issue here is whether mutual strategic restraint would diminish U.S. ability to keep the region stable. If there is the potential for such a result, it seems faint. The extent to which the United States can check any Chinese ambitions to dominate the western Pacific and East Asia depends on a variety of factors:

- whether the United States is too preoccupied elsewhere (for example, with violent Islamist insurgencies or a nuclear-armed Iran) to give adequate attention to East Asia

- whether U.S. forces maintain robust regional basing and operating patterns

- how the United States responds to crises in the region, especially those involving Chinese muscle-flexing, such as over Taiwan and in the South and East China Seas

- U.S. steadfastness in its alliances, especially with Japan and South Korea

- whether the United States shows a tendency to address regional problems and solutions with China "over the heads" of other states of the region.

If these variables were to point toward declining U.S. interest in East Asia and growing U.S. inclination to defer to China, and if trends in regional military capabilities favored China, the mutual strategic restraint proposed here could be read by U.S. allies and others as indicative of a U.S. reduction of its responsibilities to maintain stability in East Asia. Yet given that East Asia and its stability will remain of crucial importance to the United States, if only on economic grounds, it is not easy to imagine the United States shedding its responsibilities, reducing its presence, and becoming inattentive to developments there.[15] Moreover, the United States is mindful of the danger that key regional states, primarily Japan, might embark on policies inimical to U.S. interests if the United States appeared untrustworthy. U.S. interests in the region mandate active involvement with or without mutual strategic restraint with China.

It must also be understood that Sino-American mutual strategic restraint would tend to make the United States a more, not less, reliable ally in the region. A premise of this study is that the United States is becoming increasingly vulnerable in strategic domains. Just as mutual restraint would limit U.S. escalation options, so would it limit Chinese escalation options. If growing strategic vulnerabilities could make the United States more cautious in intervening to protect allies from Chinese threats, it follows that mitigating those vulnerabilities would give the United States greater freedom of action. The United States could act more confidently in East Asia if it were less fearful that conflict would escalate to space and strategic cyberspace.

For these reasons, China should not expect agreement on strategic restraint to mean that the United States will reduce its role, presence, and willingness to act in East Asia. It would be unwise and potentially hazardous for China to think that mutual vulnerability and mutual restraint will expand its freedom of action and constrict U.S. freedom of action. Nor should it expect the United States to dismantle its alliances or close its bases in the region, regardless of any Sino-American arrangements. In view of their misgivings about Chinese intentions, states in the region are unlikely to feel that China's improving conventional capabilities and a Sino-U.S. mutual restraint agreement would require them to accept Chinese domination, provided the United States remains committed to security ties in place for over half a century.

Recent developments in Northeast and Southeast Asia suggest that China's own behavior—its failure to curb North Korea's belligerence and efforts to reinforce its expansive territorial claims in the South China Sea— is a powerful factor in the decidedly pro-U.S. tilt of regional states, including such nonallies as Vietnam. In contrast, China's willingness to improve relations with Taiwan has paid dividends. Perhaps these regional developments suggest to the Chinese the advantages of a cooperative and restrained role in the region, regardless of understandings with the United States about strategic restraint.[16] A path for China to achieve its legitimate ambitions using peaceful means will make a resort to force and intimidation much less likely.[17]

What would be certain to destabilize East Asia is Sino-American conflict in space and cyberspace. A growing number of East Asian states are as dependent on computer networking and satellites as the United States and China. This is a consequence both of their own advancement and their economic cooperation with China and the United States, which together account for 34, 29, 33, and 25 percent, respectively, of the trade of Japan, Korea, Taiwan, and the Association of Southeast Asian Nations. Because a war in space or in cyberspace would harm these states, they should welcome Sino-U.S. initiatives to reduce the dangers.

Similarly, East Asian stability would not be helped by a nuclear arms race between China and the United States, propelled by Chinese perceptions that the Americans were determined to deny them a nuclear deterrent. Such competition likely would result in a large buildup in China's offensive capabilities, opposed but not neutralized by costly U.S.-led missile defense investments. Although mutual strategic deterrence might be preserved, the region would potentially be more menaced by a larger and more rapid Chinese nuclear buildup.

Implications for the Policies of U.S. Allies and Partners

Despite this reasoning, key U.S. allies and partners in East Asia might respond ambivalently to Sino-American mutual nuclear deterrence. On one level, they have no alternative than to adjust to the reality of China's capability to deter a U.S. nuclear attack, and they would not want a nuclear arms race. Presumably, sophisticated civilian and military leaders in Japan, South Korea, and Taiwan realize that the United States has already effectively acquiesced in a Chinese second-strike capability. The U.S. nod toward mutual deterrence in the *Nuclear Posture Review* did not exacerbate regional concerns about the credibility of U.S. extended deterrence.

Nevertheless, the question is whether key states would think that an explicit Sino-American no-first-use pledge as suggested here would increase Chinese freedom of action to their disadvantage. On this question, it is necessary to address individually Japan, South Korea, and Taiwan, which have the greatest potential to be affected.

Japan's bilateral security relationship with the United States has proven extraordinarily resilient. Sequentially, it has transcended Sino-American rapprochement, the disappearance of the Soviet threat, the expansion of Chinese power, and the preoccupation of the United States with challenges in other regions in this century. Because of that relationship, Japan is able to keep defense expenditures low without sacrificing its security or its interests abroad (Japan spends less than 1 percent of GDP on defense, compared to nearly 5 percent for the United States and 2.5 percent for China). Japan presently sees its alliance with the United States as its best insurance against both China's rise and North Korea's recklessness.[18] As Japan improves its own military capabilities in select areas and exhibits somewhat greater willingness to operate its forces far from home, it does so strictly within the context of its security relationship with the United States. There seems little likelihood that Japan would jettison this relationship and either remilitarize on its own or seek a position equidistant between the United States and China. In this regard, it now appears that the initial Democratic Party of Japan government's flirtation with the idea of being closer to China and less close to the United States was an anomaly that is unlikely to be repeated.

Nonetheless, there is no point in taking chances that Japan could misinterpret Sino-American mutual strategic restraint, especially in the nuclear domain. Because of the extreme sensitivity of nuclear weapons in Japan, both the Japanese and U.S. governments are circumspect about conditions in which the latter might use such weapons. While there is an acknowledged U.S. nuclear umbrella over Japan, obviating the need for Japan to have nuclear weapons, its nature is vague. Clearly, it means that the United States could retaliate with nuclear weapons if China used nuclear weapons against Japan. Much less clear, if not doubtful, is whether Japanese leaders count on the United States to respond with nuclear weapons if China were to use conventional force against Japan or its military forces.

The Japanese would be unsettled, to the point of considering their own nuclear options, if they perceived that the U.S. nuclear deterrent no longer applied to the case of a Chinese nuclear threat against them. Although China has already adopted a universal nuclear no-first-use policy, the Japanese would be alarmed if they thought the United States had agreed not to use nuclear weapons unless China used nuclear weapons against the United States itself. Therefore, any Sino-American no-first-use pledge would have to clarify that *both* parties, not just the United States, understood this also to cover "allies," a term that plainly applies to Japan. This means that the United States would reserve the right to launch nuclear retaliation in the event that China, notwithstanding its national no-first-use policy, attacked Japan with nuclear weapons. While a Chinese nuclear attack on Japan is far-fetched, this clarification could ease Japanese concerns about Chinese nuclear blackmail while also averting a Japanese reconsideration of its own nonnuclear status.

The same clarification is no less important in regard to South Korea, where the matter of nuclear weapons is complicated by several factors: North Korea's possession of nuclear explosives, the declining health of Kim Il-Sung and the growing belligerence of his regime, and the prospect of

Korean unification. Neither China nor the United States wants to see South Korea or, in the event of unification, a Korean successor state with nuclear weapons. The former is very improbable. The latter could occur if the Korean successor state takes control of, and then drags its heels in dismantling, North Korea's nuclear arsenal. Such an eventuality might be more likely if the Koreans perceived the United States as having foresworn the option of nuclear retaliation in the event of a Chinese nuclear attack on Korea. Clarification that mutual nuclear restraint covers allies is also important for Korea.

The case of Taiwan is complicated by several factors: the fact that it is not a formal U.S. ally, the lengthening shadow of a Chinese conventional military threat, and the increasing vulnerability of U.S. conventional forces available nearby to aid in the defense of Taiwan. Although cross-strait relations have been good of late, owing to pragmatism and flexibility on both sides, there is no assurance that this will continue if a new government comes to power. Meanwhile, China is improving both its capabilities to threaten the island (including many more short-range ballistic missiles than missile defense systems can possibly intercept) and its antiaccess/area denial capabilities.

The United States has not threatened to use nuclear weapons if China attacks Taiwan. Therefore, a U.S. exchange of no-first-use pledges with China should not in and of itself weaken deterrence or damage Taiwan's confidence. Again, Taiwan's leaders and strategists understand that China will have a credible nuclear retaliatory capability if it does not already. Moreover, China has never hinted at the possibility of using nuclear weapons against Taiwan, which is, after all, claimed as part of China.

At the same time, if the United States and China entered into a broad agreement to refrain from attacks in any strategic domain—nuclear, space, or cyberspace—both China and Taiwan could interpret this as limiting options for U.S. escalation. Even if the probability of a Chinese attack on Taiwan remains low, the perception of the United States retreating from escalation, even as trends in the local military balance favor China, could have two effects. First, China would be more confident and thus less flexible in negotiations and arrangements with Taiwan, including terms of reunification. Second, rather than choosing a unilateral military buildup and possibly acquiring nuclear weapons, Taiwan is more likely to become pliable in its relationship with China, perhaps even to the point of accepting unfavorable terms for reunification.

While these risks are less easily managed by the United States than the Japanese and Korean concerns mentioned earlier, they are not sufficient to derail pursuit of broad strategic restraint with China. Again, the alternative scenario of China and the United States in a nuclear arms race and threatening each other's satellites and computer networks is hardly a promising one for Taiwan. But the United States will need to tailor if not the content, then at least the presentation, of mutual restraint with China to avoid compromising Taiwan's confidence.

Implications for Sino-U.S. Relations

China has long held the position that nuclear weapons should be marginalized from world politics, bilateral affairs, and, of course, military conflict.[19] Being weaker in this domain than the United States, as well as Russia, and adhering to a minimum deterrence policy, it is natural for the Chinese to downplay the importance of nuclear weapons in their foreign relations. From the Chinese perspective, mutual deterrence with the United States would not be seen as much as an emblem of a trustful new relationship than as rectification of a discrepancy in the existing relationship. Moreover, because China has not treated U.S. reluctance to endorse mutual deterrence as an obstacle to cooperation on other matters, it is unlikely that a change in U.S. nuclear policy will cause China to show a burst of cooperation.

Still, at this formative moment in the development of the world's most important relationship, it would do no harm and potentially some good to marginalize nuclear weapons from the Sino-American agenda, in contrast to the way they dominated the U.S.-Soviet agenda. This may be the Chinese view, but it would also be advantageous for the United States. After all, the United States benefits from China's policies that it will not be drawn into a nuclear arms race and is satisfied with an effective minimum deterrent. If China takes the view that nuclear weapons are neither an instrument nor a yardstick of power, the United States should agree. Such an understanding goes hand in hand with the mutual restraint proposed here, as well as with the American desire to marginalize the role of nuclear weapons in world affairs generally.

If mutual restraint extends to space and strategic cyberspace as well, there is an opportunity for China and the United States to develop a long-term relationship in which the vulnerability of each to the other will have been mitigated cooperatively and at least partially removed as a source of mistrust, misunderstanding, and possible miscalculation. A premise of this study is that Sino-American relations in the broadest sense will be shaped by both convergent and divergent interests. In and of itself, mutual strategic restraint in the domains examined here will not determine whether the world's two leading powers have a harmonious or confrontational relationship or guarantee cooperation on other specific issues. Yet for the established world power and the rising world power to agree to foreclose strategic warfare against each other would herald a joint commitment to a constructive and prudent relationship.

The United States should regard the mitigation of strategic vulnerabilities not only as an important end in itself, but also as part of the foundation for a durable, constructive relationship between it and the world's other leading power, which could benefit generations of Americans to come. Without setting preconditions on strategic restraint, the United States should lay out a vision in which such restraint becomes the basis for prudent behavior by the two powers toward each other, each other's partners and allies, and all responsible states. The idea animating such a vision is that with exceptional destructive power comes exceptional responsibility. This idea, more often trashed than honored by great powers historically, is increasingly important as the world becomes more integrated and states, weak and strong, become more vulnerable. Mutual Sino-American strategic deterrence is important but insufficient, and it must not create conditions in which temptations to use force grow along with China's power.

The antithesis of this idea would be that strategic restraint liberates great powers from the danger of escalation and enlarges their freedom to use force or coercion below the strategic level. We do not mean to suggest that the Chinese would take such a retrogressive view. But there will be factions in China and opportunities for China to take advantage of a situation in which the strategic threat from the superior power has been neutralized. Therefore, it is important for the United States to articulate its larger vision, if only to go on the record that the United States will monitor compliance with not only the terms but also the effects of mutual restraint. In the long run, the American commitment to mutual restraint will and should be related to the entirety of Chinese behavior. The implication should be clear: if China were to threaten Taiwan, Japan, South Korea, or the Southeast Asian states with which it has territorial disputes, the United States would naturally review its assumption that strategic restraint would strengthen stability.

Whether in striving to achieve understanding regarding mutual restraint in strategic realms or in respecting the letter and spirit of those understandings, the problem is less of a monolithic antipathy than of civil-military disagreement that China's political leaders have neither the power nor the process to settle. China does not have a fully effective policymaking system for making coherent national security policy decisions in which political leaders take seriously but do not necessarily defer to the advice of the military and intelligence services. It is worth noting that the United States had no such system until being thrust into a leading global role with the end of World War II. Now that China is becoming a more active and important global power, its lack of a system to integrate national security policy is becoming conspicuous, both in regard to reactions to unforeseen problems abroad and in coherent long-term policy.[20] The possibility of entering into, abiding by, and building on understandings with the United States on mutual strategic restraint will certainly tax China's policymaking ability.

In sum, provided the Chinese neither reject mutual restraint nor, at the other extreme, pursue it to gain unilateral advantage and greater freedom of action in East Asia, the ability of the world's strongest power and its fastest rising power to agree not to attack each other strategically should have a salutary effect on the world's most important and potentially most dangerous relationship. All else being equal, it could dispose both states to cooperate on a host of common global security concerns.

Confidence-building and Consultation

Taking into account possible Chinese ambivalence, as well as the PLA's grip on military strategy, plans, and operations, the United States will want to institutionalize mutual restraint in order to monitor results, strengthen trust in compliance, and promote a larger vision of responsible conduct by the world's strongest powers. This could take two forms:

- confidence-building measures (CBMs) that demonstrate that the two sides are living up to the terms and purposes of mutual strategic restraint

- a process of regular high-level review of concepts, issues, misperceptions, notification, transparency, and ways to improve mutual strategic restraint.

The United States has considerable experience with CBMs and an even larger body of analysis about them.[21] China also has a fair amount of experience in negotiating and implementing CBMs.[22] As the term suggests, CBMs can help assure parties that agreements are being kept, intentions are known, behavior and capabilities are not misconstrued, and provocative actions are avoided. When well designed and implemented, the openness they provide can obviate the need for worst-case assessments and planning. Given that the understandings about Sino-American mutual restraint suggested here concern intentions, CBMs could help enable and sustain such understandings.

A way to think about CBMs in this context is to pose the question: how could one party know if the other intended not to honor the terms and purposes of strategic restraint? The answer should inform which CBMs are adopted. In the nuclear domain, for instance, if the United States accepted mutual deterrence but was actively pursuing a capability to launch a disarming first strike against China, it would keep alive the option of a very large-scale national BMD system. Accordingly, China would be interested in a CBM that would expose any such U.S. intent.

This study does not analyze in depth the details, feasibility, and pros and cons of all possible CBMs bearing on restraint in the nuclear, space, and cyberspace domains. But several promising ones can be derived from the proposed terms of mutual restraint.

In the nuclear domain, the Chinese will worry that the United States will continue to develop and deploy capabilities that could threaten the survivability of China's second-strike force: ASW technologies and forces, ballistic missile defense, offensive nuclear forces that could disarm China's retaliatory force, surveillance systems to track and target China's strategic forces (for example, mobile ICBMs), and long-range conventional strike systems. The problem is that the United States will, for many reasons, be active in all these areas, irrespective of its intent toward China's deterrent. ASW is needed to protect U.S. surface ships and strategic submarines; BMD is needed to defend against rogue states and to protect U.S. expeditionary forces; U.S. offensive nuclear forces must be modernized; improved surveillance of Chinese capabilities of all sorts is only prudent; and long-range conventional strike forces have many missions. How, then, could Chinese suspicions be allayed?

For its part, the United States could become concerned that China will continue to develop and deploy strategic offensive forces beyond those required for a minimum deterrent.[23] Meanwhile, China will not cease its efforts to ensure an effective and survivable retaliatory force regardless of U.S. endorsement of mutual deterrence. Of the two, Chinese concerns could be considered more warranted, for the United States has little reason for concern that China could be building more than a second-strike capability, whereas the Chinese are unconvinced that the United States is truly prepared to abandon the option of a first-strike capability against China. Nevertheless, the United States will be as insistent on CBMs to allay its concerns as it should be receptive to CBMs to assuage China's fears.

Against this background, three types of CBMs bear consideration. The first, already favored by the United States, is reciprocal openness about nuclear doctrines, capabilities, and programs.[24] Chinese resistance to this is ironic, since China has greater concerns about U.S. nuclear capabilities and plans than the United States does about Chinese nuclear capabilities and plans. The Chinese defend their secretiveness about nuclear capabilities as a requirement of their minimum deterrence posture, which leaves little cushion.[25] If the Chinese think the United States will not relinquish the option of a disabling first strike against China, why would they make information available about the size, capabilities, and whereabouts of their retaliatory forces, or about their modernization programs? It follows that such Chinese secretiveness could be eased if the United States explicitly accepted China's deterrent. China's ongoing shift to a second-generation nuclear deterrent with mobile ICBMs and a sea-based deterrent could also reduce perceived costs of greater transparency. Moreover, Chinese political leaders should see merit in greater transparency measures if those measures addressed Chinese concerns about U.S. programs—BMD above all—and facilitated U.S. acceptance of mutual nuclear deterrence.

The second type of CBM would address concerns about nuclear attack, particularly a no-warning attack necessary for successful first strike. In particular, each side's offensive nuclear forces could be placed on lower alert status. One difficulty with this is that the readiness of U.S. deterrent forces is not predicated on the possibility of Chinese attack but instead on the possibility of Russian attack, for which lower readiness would be considered imprudent. As for China, while doctrine calls for being able to ride out a first strike before retaliating, China regards increased alert status of its nuclear forces as a key means of signaling resolve in a crisis and may be reluctant to foreclose this option.

The third type of CBM is at once the most intriguing and most problematic: to involve the Chinese in BMD cooperation, along the lines of U.S. offers to involve the Russians. This could allay, though not eradicate, Chinese fears that U.S. BMD could be developed and someday used to intercept a Chinese retaliatory force. The problem is that U.S. BMD efforts, although primarily directed against the likes of Iran and North Korea, are not irrelevant to the Chinese conventional missile threat. In particular, the United States would not want to share with China any data that could reduce the efficacy of U.S. missile defense of its own forces, ships, and bases against China's growing arsenal of precise conventional ballistic missiles. Under present conditions, the United States would also be concerned about leakage of sensitive BMD information from China to hostile states such as North Korea or Iran.

On balance, it would be best to concentrate on openness—something the United States has sought and that China should, for its own reasons, welcome. In time, each side should see that the other is not investing in significantly more capabilities than those required to sustain mutual deterrence. This, in turn, could take the "worst" out of worst-case planning and perhaps obviate the need for investments in new capabilities. Meanwhile, exchange of information could add to the trust needed for and implied by mutual restraint.

Confidence in a Sino-American agreement not to be the first to interfere with the other's access to space could be reinforced by a moratorium on ASAT testing. However, such a moratorium would require dealing with ambiguities over the purpose of space-capable rocket tests, directed energy tests, and other operations that could interfere with satellite performance. The difficulty of specifying which type of testing is not permitted would aggravate breakout risks. Moreover, China would undoubtedly try to exploit an ASAT test moratorium to prohibit U.S. testing of ballistic missile interceptors. Finally, an ASAT test moratorium could have the perverse effect of weakening deterrence. Testing is needed for better ASAT performance, which makes the threat of retaliation on which deterrence depends more credible. In sum, while an ASAT test moratorium could be explored as a possible CBM, the drawbacks might exceed the benefits.

What could be more promising is Sino-U.S. agreement to notify each other of space launches, with explanation and perhaps within specified parameters.[26] The United States is currently more capable than China of detecting such launches using its own national means, yet neither side would have to reveal sensitive information. Generally speaking, space-launch notification would seem to be a reasonable practice to increase transparency and trust. Moreover, it could be a modest step toward a more cooperative approach to space, which current U.S. space policy professes in general to favor.

Confidence-building measures to bolster restraint in strategic cyberspace are more problematic than those for the nuclear and space domains. Each side will continue to develop offensive options because of a wide range of needs and potential adversaries, and because the line between offense and defense can be blurry. At a minimum, any state that wants to improve computer network protection must have the ability to try to defeat its own best defenses. Moreover, the terms of Sino-American mutual restraint in cyberspace suggested here would cover only attacks on strategic computer networks, such as those critical to national well-being. The sides might not refrain from other intrusions. Thus, both parties will presumably have and use offensive cyber war capabilities in some fashion.

Nevertheless, there are two CBMs that could complement Sino-American mutual restraint in strategic cyberspace. First, the parties could set up a mechanism for consultations on suspicious events, such as probes of networks that could be considered strategic, attacks on less important networks, concerns about attacks coming from platforms within one or the other country but not necessarily with state complicity, and complaints from enterprises about attacks. Second, the parties could consult and cooperate on third-party threats, including but not necessarily limited to non-state threats.

The United States and China could go so far as to share intelligence and cooperate on defense. However, any cooperation on third-party threats and defenses could run afoul of the extreme caution of both countries with regard to intelligence and network protection. Any CBMs of this sort will have to start modestly and intensify cautiously as the two countries build trust in each other's intentions in cyberspace. At present, that trust is low.

In addition to specific CBMs, the United States and China should maintain a regular high-level dialogue on strategic restraint, which could deal with nuclear, space, and cyberspace together or separately. The dialogue should include both political and military leaders, with the former in charge. While modalities can be left to government ministries, the purposes of strategic dialogue should be to:

- reach and refine understandings concerning mutual strategic restraint
- raise and resolve compliance issues regarding restraint as well as CBMs
- exchange information on concepts, capabilities, plans, and doctrine
- explore ideas for expanded restraint, cooperation, and transparency
- air concerns about conduct that contradicts the purpose and effectiveness of mutual restraint, broadly defined
- discuss the participation of others in strategic restraint terms and measures.

A Sino-American strategic security dialogue has in fact begun, with the first meeting occurring in the context of the May 2011 U.S.-China Strategic and Economy Dialogue. It is unrealistic to think that the United States, having sought such a process, would set preconditions on the direction it should take. At the same time, strategic dialogue is more likely to be fruitful if the sides could agree early on some of the basic purposes and principles of restraint:

- the need for restraint in light of growing vulnerabilities
- the responsibilities that attach to strategic power
- the intent to address nuclear, space, and cyberspace domains
- the need for political control of use of capabilities that can cause strategic harm
- the need for concrete measures to build trust and confidence.

Perhaps some of the ideas offered here can energize and serve as grist for this dialogue.

Conclusion

The United States could now explicitly accept China's second-strike nuclear deterrent, paving the way for a bilateral no-first-use agreement. Such a step would recognize the reality of Chinese offensive capabilities, the futility of defending against them, and the wastefulness of a Sino-U.S. offense-defense arms competition. It would also advance U.S. interests in reducing the role of nuclear weapons in world politics and warfare and in relieving Chinese distrust in U.S. willingness to acknowledge China as a world power. However, recognizing that this step would be a concession to China and would leave the United States with more serious vulnerabilities in space and cyberspace, it should be taken only as part of an integrated U.S. approach to mutual strategic restraint.

Such a U.S. approach would be guided by certain principles:

- China and the United States should exercise restraint in those strategic domains where both are highly and increasingly vulnerable. In addition to the nuclear domain, this must include space and strategic cyberspace.

- Such restraint must not empower either country to use force or coercion below the strategic level. Rather, it should foster prudent behavior in general toward one another and others, on the premise that power brings responsibilities.

- The United States is interested in not only compliance with the specific terms of a strategic restraint agreement but also the effects on broader strategic restraint. Its commitment to them would inevitably be affected if China seeks advantage by the threat or use of force.

- Strategic restraint must also apply to allies (provided they themselves respect the terms and do not acquire nuclear weapons, threaten satellites, or attack computer networks).

■ Recognizing that states in the region may interpret these understandings as U.S. strategic decoupling, aggravated by local military trends that favor China, the United States should make clear through actions and presence that East Asia is vital to U.S. interests and that it will continue its presence to assure a regional balance of power.

Again, the Chinese may prefer a narrow nuclear no-first-use understanding, believing that this would neutralize a U.S. strategic advantage, relieve the danger of U.S. nuclear blackmail, give China more freedom of action, and leave open Chinese options in space and cyberspace. They might feel that as their power grows, their vulnerabilities will decline. If they do, they are mistaken. The paradox of power in the 21st century is that vulnerability comes with power. In particular, China is becoming so reliant on cyberspace and space that hostilities in those domains would do great harm to its economy and possibly its political stability. Accordingly, the Chinese should be receptive to mutual restraint in space and strategic cyberspace not just because the United States would not otherwise accept China's nuclear deterrent, but also because China will find itself at least as vulnerable as and less powerful than the United States in these domains.

However, the Chinese might not be so agreeable, particularly if the PLA persuades the political leadership that mutual restraint in cyberspace would ruin China's chances of neutralizing the U.S. advantage should a conflict come. It is not clear that China's political leaders can ignore the argument that Taiwan cannot be taken by force if the PLA is prohibited from striking U.S. vulnerabilities: the satellites and computer networks that enable U.S. forces to respond and defeat Chinese forces before they can accomplish their mission of unifying China.

The United States should not abandon the idea of broad-based Sino-American strategic restraint if China is unwilling or, because of divided Chinese views, unable to engage seriously on this agenda. Even if the United States fails to get a definitive strategic restraint agreement, engaging Chinese civilian leaders may sensitize them to China's growing vulnerabilities in the space and cyber domains and to the importance of close civilian control of military contingency plans and activities in the space and cyber domains. Such a realization may heighten Chinese awareness of the high costs and risks of military conflict with the United States, thus reinforcing deterrence.

Moreover, the passage of time may work to the advantage of the United States for two related reasons. First, Chinese political and economic elites will become increasingly aware of China's vulnerabilities in space and cyberspace as its use of these domains grows. Second, as offense dominance and the threat of U.S. ASAT and cyber war capabilities become more apparent, the Chinese will find themselves increasingly deterred from striking first in these domains.

The prospect of a lengthy but ultimately promising strategic dialogue on mutual restraint argues for U.S. persistence. This, in turn, argues for building a bipartisan consensus in favor of Sino-American strategic restraint. This may not be easy, given the controversy surrounding China mainly because of economic issues. On the other hand, the mainstreams of both parties fundamentally accept the goal of a constructive relationship with China as long as U.S. interests and friends are protected along the way.

Assuming the Chinese are not prepared to embrace broad mutual restraint at once, the United States would be wise at least to offer a joint framework for discussing and eventually agreeing on concepts and terms. The next chapter sums up what that framework might include, assesses what difference it would make for the United States and Sino-American relations if the framework is eventually agreed or not, and offers several recommendations.

Notes

[1] Consider the contribution of a ratified New Strategic Arms Reduction Treaty agreement to the positive "reset" of U.S.-Russian relations.

[2] Long-haul communications links, remote Earth sensing, global positioning systems and navigation, weather forecasting, and so forth.

[3] The aims of a network attack could be at least partly achieved by disabling a network-supporting satellite, and the value of a satellite could be destroyed by attacking the networks it serves.

[4] Any war with the United States would be damaging to China. The extent of direct damage other than denial of space and network service would depend largely on whether the United States opted to strike targets on the mainland. If it did so, it might restrict strikes to military targets and spare industry and infrastructure. Thus, war with the United States that escalated into space and cyberspace could cause more civilian and economic harm than if there were no such escalation.

[5] For recent writings on civil-military relations, see Nan Li, ed., *Chinese Civil-Military Relations: The Transformation of the People's Liberation Army* (New York: Routledge, 2006); David M. Finkelstein and Kristen Gunness, eds., *Civil-Military Relations in Today's China: Swimming in a New Sea* (Armonk, NY: East Gate, 2007); and Michael Kiselycznyk and Phillip C. Saunders, *Civil-Military Relations in China: Assessing the PLA's Role in Elite Politics,* China Strategic Perspectives 2 (Washington, DC: National Defense University Press, August 2010).

[6] Graham Allison, *Essence of Decision: Explaining the Cuban Missile Crisis,* 1st ed. (New York: Little, Brown and Co., 1971).

[7] Department of Defense, *Military and Security Developments Involving the People's Republic of China* (Washington, DC: Department of Defense, 2010).

[8] Christopher D. Yung and Ross Rustici with Isaac Kardon and Joshua Wiseman, *China's Out of Area Naval Operations: Case Studies, Trajectories, Obstacles, and Potential Solutions,* China Strategic Perspectives 3 (Washington, DC: National Defense University Press, December 2010).

⁹ Department of Defense, *Military and Security Developments Involving the People's Republic of China* (Washington, DC: Department of Defense, 2010).

¹⁰ Apart from theories about "demonstration shots" that were developed by the North Atlantic Treaty Organization in the late 1960s, the demonstration use of tactical nuclear weapons would be designed to exhibit alliance determination to resist an attack and to warn the enemy that his actions inexorably increase the likelihood of a more general nuclear response.

¹¹ The 2010 QDR called for development of an AirSea Battle concept to "[Defeat] adversaries across the range of military operations, including adversaries equipped with sophisticated anti-access and area denial capabilities. The concept will address how air and naval forces will integrate capabilities across all operational domains—air, sea, land, space, and cyberspace—to counter growing challenges to U.S. freedom of action." Department of Defense, *Quadrennial Defense Review Report* (Washington, DC: Department of Defense, 2010), 55. Also see Andrew Krepinevich, *Why AirSea Battle?* (Washington, DC: Center for Strategic and Budgetary Assessments, 2010); and Jan Van Tol et al., *AirSea Battle: A Point-of-Departure Operational Concept* (Washington, DC: Center for Strategic and Budgetary Assessments, 2010).

¹² M. Elaine Bunn and Vincent Manzo, *Conventional Prompt Global Strike: Strategic Asset or Unusable Liability?* Strategic Forum 263 (Washington, DC: National Defense University Press, February 2011).

¹³ Phillip C. Saunders and Scott L. Kastner, "Bridge over Troubled Water? Envisioning a China-Taiwan Peace Agreement," *International Security* 33, no. 4 (2009), 87–114; Alan Romberg, "Managing the Cross Strait Issue," paper prepared for the National Committee on American Foreign Policy–Tsinghua University conference, New York, 2010.

¹⁴ For discussions of Japanese remilitarization, see Kenneth Pyle, *Japan Rising* (New York: PublicAffairs, 2007); Lee Hudson Teslik, "Japan and Its Military: Backgrounder," Council on Foreign Relations, April 2006, available at <www.cfr.org/japan/japan-its-military/p10439#p10>; Jong-Heon Lee, "The Rising Prospect of Japan Remilitarization," *Space Daily*, March 5, 2004, available at <www.spacedaily.com/news/milspace-04f.html>.

¹⁵ In 2009, the United States accounted for these percentages of total trade of East Asian countries: 13.5 (Japan), 11.4 (Taiwan), 15.4 (Philippines), 8.4 (Indonesia), 6.5 (Singapore), 10.4 (Malaysia), and 8.8 (Thailand).

¹⁶ There are some subtle public indications that the Chinese Ministry of Foreign Affairs is more convinced than PLA hard-liners or conservative political leaders of the drawbacks of Chinese heavy-handedness in the region.

¹⁷ Of course, this begs the question of what China's ambitions are and whether others, including the United States, regard them as legitimate. See James J. Przystup and Phillip C. Saunders, *Visions of Order: Japan and China in U.S. Strategy*, Strategic Forum 220 (Washington, DC: National Defense University Press, June 2006).

¹⁸ Despite the initial stance of the Democratic Party of Japan, in May 2010 the Tokyo government endorsed a plan very similar to the original 2006 agreement on the relocation of U.S. forces on Okinawa. For further discussion, see Mark Thompson, "Why Japan and the U.S. Can't Live Without Okinawa," *Time*, June 8, 2010, available at <www.time.com/time/nation/article/0,8599,1994798,00.html>.

¹⁹ Information Office of the State Council of the People's Republic of China, *China's National Defense in 2008* (Beijing: Information Office of the State Council of the People's Republic of China, January 2009), 29 (confirmed by the authors in conversations with Chinese counterparts, Beijing, December 2010).

²⁰ Recent examples such as the J–20 test flights during Defense Secretary Robert Gates's visit and the 2007 ASAT test demonstrate a lack of coordination between the military and other organs of government.

²¹ For more discussion, see "South Asia Confidence Building Measures (CBM) Timeline," Henry L. Stimson Center, August 27, 2003, available at <www.stimson.org/essays/nuclear-crisis-escalation-control-and-deterrence-in-south-asia/>; Department of State, "New Strategic Arms Reduction Treaty (New START)," April 8, 2010, available at <www.state.gov/documents/organization/140035.

pdf>; Garold N. Lawson, "U.S. Mission to the United Nations," in the First Committee of the Sixty-fourth Session of the United Nations General Assembly, New York, October 19, 2009, available at <http://usun.state.gov/briefing/statements/2009/130701.htm>.

[22] See Bonnie Glaser, "China's Approach to CBMs with Taiwan: Lessons from China's CBMs with Neighboring Countries," in *New Opportunities and Challenges for Taiwan's Security,* ed. Roger Cliff, Phillip C. Saunders, and Scott Harold (Arlington, VA: RAND, 2011), 17–24.

[23] A forthcoming RAND study by French strategic analyst Therese Delpeche posits that as China's overall power grows, its strategic force goal will shift from minimum deterrence to at least parity with the United States.

[24] Robert Gates and Liang Guanglie, joint press conference, Beijing, January 10, 2011, available at <www.defense.gov/transcripts/transcript.aspx?transcriptid=4750>; Donna Miles, "Gates: U.S. Hopes for More Openness, Transparency from China," American Forces Press Services, May 31, 2008, available at <www.defense.gov/News/NewsArticle.aspx?ID=50055>.

[25] Comment offered by Chinese interlocutor, Beijing, 2010.

[26] The United States and the Soviet Union had a series of ballistic missile and space launch notification agreements dating back to 1971. China participated in negotiations for the Hague Code of Conduct Against Ballistic Missile Proliferation, which included launch notification requirements, but ultimately declined to sign the agreement (possibly out of concern to protect their kinetic ASAT test launches). China did sign a bilateral ballistic missile launch notification agreement with Russia in October 2009. Luke Champlin, "China, Russia Agree on Launch Notification," *Arms Control Today,* November 2009, available at <www.armscontrol.org/act/2009_11/ChinaRussia>.

Chapter Eight

Conclusions and Recommendations

This study of Sino-American strategic relations finds that the United States and China each have the ability to cause the other grave harm not only by nuclear attack but also, and much more likely, by attacks on satellites and computer networks. While nuclear vulnerability is familiar, vulnerabilities in space and cyberspace are mounting as both countries increase their dependence on these domains for their prosperity and security. Technology is creating options for "nonviolent" and relatively low-cost strategic warfare, which could reduce inhibitions against attacks despite dangers of catastrophic results. Strategic defenses offer diminishing returns against large and advanced offensive capabilities, like those of the United States and China. Yet negotiated arms control of such capabilities is unpromising if not infeasible.

The United States cannot deny China a nuclear deterrent, and neither country can defend its satellites or networks well enough to prevent extensive economic damage if attacked by the other. Unlike nuclear weapons, attacking satellites and computer networks that support military operations could be of interest to both Chinese and U.S. militaries. Yet because neither space nor cyberspace is well separated into military and civilian sectors, escalation from tactical to strategic war in these two domains is a serious danger.

Conditions of *mutual strategic deterrence*, based on the futility of defense and credible threat of retaliation, either exist or are forming in all three domains, mainly because of technological and economic trends. In distinction from this, *mutual strategic restraint* signifies that the highest authorities of both states accept the imperative of mitigating national vulnerabilities cooperatively. It requires but improves on mutual deterrence: affirming Sino-American agreement not to initiate warfare in these domains and institutionalizing such agreement with CBMs, regular high-level dialogue, and continuous contact through agreed channels to avoid miscalculation. By easing U.S. and Chinese concerns about the harm they might do to one another, mutual restraint can reduce fear, antagonism, and distrust in the larger relationship, further lowering the risks of conflict and strategic escalation.

In this spirit, the United States should propose an integrated approach to mutual restraint covering all three domains. While it can accept Chinese nuclear deterrence and bilateral nuclear no first use, it should do so contingent on Chinese agreement to extend the principle of mutual restraint to space and cyberspace. The framework the United States should adopt is summarized in table 8–1.

The Chinese may not yet appreciate how greatly China's vulnerability will grow as its economy, integration, and power do. The PLA may also believe that attacking the satellites and computer networks on which U.S. forces depend is the only way to avoid defeat should war with the United States occur. Consequently, the Chinese might balk at mutual restraint in space and cyberspace, preferring agreed restraint only in first use of nuclear weapons. While this study develops the idea of mutual strategic restraint from an American vantage point, it concludes that China would be short-sighted to reject limits on attacking satellites and critical computer networks. Chinese leaders should realize that the United States possesses sufficient retaliatory capabilities to deter Chinese attack in these domains (a concept they know well from the nuclear field). Perhaps they will see enough strategic and political merit in broad-based restraint to surprise us by agreeing early on to explore it in earnest. In any case, it is in the U.S. interest to lay out its framework and pursue it with patience and persistence.

U.S. allies in East Asia could be ambivalent about Sino-U.S. attempts to limit their strategic vulnerabilities. On the one hand, they do not want Sino-U.S. tension, arms races, or hostilities at the strategic level, because they too have vulnerabilities. On the other hand, they would not want to relieve Chinese fears that using military force could escalate into these strategic hostilities. The United States can allay regional concerns about such strategic decoupling by renewing its security commitments, maintaining its presence, and insisting that Sino-American strategic restraint also apply to allies. U.S. extended nuclear deterrence of Chinese nuclear threats to U.S. allies would be unaffected but nevertheless should be reaffirmed unequivocally. In addition, by establishing that mutual restraint in all domains covers allies, the United States would in effect be extending deterrence in space and cyberspace as well, in the sense that China could face U.S. retaliation.

	Nuclear	Space	Cyberspace
Dialogue	Regular high-level contact to reinforce confidence-building measures, increase mutual understanding of these domains, and address new developments, concerns, and the participation of third parties		
Confidence-building measures	Transparency about nuclear doctrine, capabilities, and programs	Launch notification	▪ Consultation and cooperation on third-party threats ▪ Mechanism for consultation on suspicious activities
Mutual restraint	No first use of nuclear weapons against the other	No first interference with access to space	▪ No first use against strategic cyber targets ▪ Agreement to exercise political control over military cyber operations
Mutual deterrence	Because both China and the United States are vulnerable AND both have extensive offensive capabilities, this creates a situation of tacit mutual deterrence		
Mutual vulnerability	Due to the infeasibility of defense, there is no way for either country to reasonably believe that an attack can be stopped		

Table 8–1. Levels of Mutual Trust and Cooperation in Strategic Domains

The United States should be able to deter China from attacking Taiwan by conventional military escalatory options other than space and cyber escalation, much less nuclear weapons. U.S. escalation to strategic warfare would have dire consequences, including Chinese retaliation, and is not the right solution to the problem of improving Chinese conventional capabilities. In general, the United States should state its expectation that mutual strategic restraint should strengthen overall stability and security in the region—in effect, putting down a marker that Chinese conventional aggression in the region would prompt the United States to rethink mutual strategic restraint.

A Future without Sino-U.S. Mutual Strategic Restraint

This is an ambitious proposal for a Sino-American relationship that is already loaded with weighty issues, and for a region that is already unnerved by China's growing power. Moreover, though it is possible that Chinese leaders would see the virtues of mitigating national vulnerabilities by mutual restraint, it is as likely that they will be hesitant because of the sheer scope and significance of the framework and the PLA's aversion to foreclosing military options in space and cyberspace. Therefore, the U.S. administration that offers this framework may not be the one that sees it bear fruit. Moreover, current political and economic conditions in the United States are not auspicious for a major initiative premised on the idea that China can be trusted. If there is a reason for the U.S. Government to take this step, it is strategic, not political. Therefore, it is only fair for U.S. policymakers to ask why it is important to propose this *now* and what harm would come if they do not.

The failure to pursue and achieve some form of agreement on mutual strategic restraint could have several adverse results in the years to come, ranging from the unlikely but traumatic to the likely but subtle. The first is that China could unleash major attacks on U.S. satellites or computer networks in the context of or as a prelude to a confrontation over, say, Taiwan or Korea—perhaps in hopes of deterring the United States from armed intervention or out of fear that the United States might launch such strikes on China preemptively. Instead of giving the United States pause, such attacks would likely trigger U.S. retaliation, leading to a spiral of attacks and counterattacks, sending strong shock waves through the Chinese, U.S., East Asian, and world economies.

Even in the absence of armed conflict, China might mount a disruptive attack—beyond intelligence collection—on one or more critical U.S. computer networks, perhaps in response to some U.S. action perceived as highly provocative (such as the sale of advanced weaponry to Taiwan or support for Tibetan independence). In that event, the United States might well retaliate in kind, since failing to do so would leave deterrence in ruins and expose the United States to further attacks. While not necessarily leading to general war in cyberspace, this scenario suggests that both countries could suffer large-scale economic and societal damage unless mutual restraint was agreed and observed.

Short of actual hostilities in space and cyberspace, the absence of agreed mutual restraint and the corresponding growth in both countries' vulnerabilities in these domains would erode U.S., as well as Chinese, security. Both countries might feel compelled to invest more in both strategic offensive and strategic defensive capabilities, even though the former would increase vulnerabilities while the latter would fail to mitigate them. Absent mutual restraint, neither country would feel it could afford to allow the other to gain advantages.

Faced with unchecked Chinese strategic threats, it is not difficult to imagine the United States spending a growing portion of its defense budget on missile defense, satellite defense or redundancy, and computer network defense or redundancy. To illustrate, were the United States to double spending on missile defense (now about $10 billion annually), double the number of working satellites to achieve space security through redundancy, and triple the budget of U.S. Cyber Command (at least $3 billion per year), it could add about $200 billion to the defense budget over the next decade.[1] As this is written, the U.S. Government is being forced by its fiscal crisis to consider options to reduce defense spending by $400 billion to $800 billion in the coming decade. Adding new requirements for strategic capabilities would preclude such reductions or require cutting into the muscle and readiness of U.S. conventional military forces. Even if increased U.S. investments to address strategic vulnerabilities were lower than this illustration, fiscal conditions could hardly be worse for any such expenditures.

Given offense dominance, a U.S. commitment to "sufficient" strategic defense would be inherently open ended and potentially self defeating: it would induce China to invest more in strategic offensive capabilities to frustrate improvements in U.S. defenses. China faces a similar calculus: while it is increasing defense spending at double-digit annual rates, it could be pressured to commit more of these resources to competition with the United States in both strategic offensive and defensive capabilities.

Meanwhile, the increase in U.S. national vulnerabilities would accelerate. The growing precariousness of assured access to space and cyberspace could sap confidence in these domains and in the economic opportunities and benefits they afford. Awareness of the potential for large-scale disruption would weigh at least psychologically on markets and on the U.S., Chinese, and world economies. In parallel, as each country becomes more reliant on space and cyberspace for national security, both would experience sagging confidence in the ability of their forces to operate. Although each power might take some comfort in the other's military doubts, U.S. use of space and cyberspace for national security is becoming too vital to trade it for denying Chinese use of those domains.

Of course, it is possible, even probable, that conditions of mutual deterrence will emerge in all three offense-dominant domains even in the absence of cooperative, institutionalized restraint, making such strategic warfare less likely for both countries. This begs the question of what harm could come from having *mutual deterrence* without an agreed framework of *mutual restraint* recommended by this study. One danger is that unless both sides acknowledge deterrence and accept restraint, the risks of miscalculation and breakdown could be high at moments of stress. Another is that the United States could waste resources on strategic defenses in the absence of Chinese agreement not to attack first and the concrete CBMs and attendant notifications and consultations that could buttress such agreement.

Relying exclusively on fear-based deterrence without agreed cooperative restraint could also affect Sino-U.S. relations. This study began with the observation that Sino-American interests are sufficiently divergent to make mutual restraint important but also sufficiently compatible to make mutual restraint possible. The Soviet-American model was of two powers whose threats and fears of destruction caused them to set limits on their otherwise antagonistic relationship—threats and fears that occupied the core of their relationship, and limits that did little to reduce antagonism. Mutual deterrence permitted the United States and Soviet Union to carry on their struggle with less danger of it getting out of hand. For the United States and China, mutual strategic restraint is a way to replace or at least assuage fear with trust and to create more space at the relationship's core for cooperation.

Mutual strategic restraint does not guarantee that Sino-American relations will be free of friction and deliver results that invariably serve U.S. interests. However, if the United States does not offer a framework for agreed and broad-based restraint, especially as Chinese attitudes about these issues have yet to solidify, it will lose an opportunity not only to mitigate vulnerabilities but also to set conditions for the sort of relationship it claims to want. Though these concerns may not seem urgent, it is better to commence the pursuit of mutual restraint than to wait for national vulnerabilities to grow, to hope that Chinese views will not toughen, and to count on the illusion of affordable strategic defense.

In essence, mutual restraint is about the ability of humankind to foresee and manage the effects of its inventions. The advent of nuclear weapons last century was accompanied by warnings—from none other than their inventors—that that technology would require unprecedented international openness and creativity to avert destruction.[2] Humankind's discoveries and use of space and cyberspace are defining features of this century's global economy and society. Whether their promises and potential will be fulfilled or instead turned to destructive ends depends above all on whether the world's leading power and its fastest rising power can find common ground and lead. Although these proposals do not require supranational authority, as early proposals to contain nuclear risks did, they do require these two powers to accept limits on their strategic freedom of action.

The Longer Term

Although the timeframe of this study is the coming decade or so, its prescriptions could apply beyond that, assuming that offense dominance will persist and that the United States and China remain world powers, vitally dependent on and vulnerable in space and cyberspace, with both convergent and divergent interests. Take away either of these basic conditions, and the logic of mutual strategic restraint will fracture. On the other hand, Sino-American strategic restraint can perpetuate the conditions that produce this logic. By mitigating the dangers of strategic conflict, mutual restraint should help the United States and China fully exploit space and cyberspace despite their vulnerability. Moreover, it can free up the two countries to develop a more cooperative relationship. The framework offered here, if actively managed by the United States and China, can contribute to their mutual prosperity and security even as conditions evolve.

Still, given accelerating changes in technology, predictions beyond this study's timeframe of a decade or so are more art than science. Although current offense dominance in strategic domains results from discernable trends in information sensing, processing, and sharing (thereby enabling effective targeting), it is possible, if improbable, that these technologies will come to favor defense more than they have to date. Offense is not destined by laws of either physics or economics to prevail.

For example, missile defense could become easier and cheaper even against large and sophisticated attacks. Space-based sensors, directed energy, and especially breakthroughs in data processing (for example, quantum computing) could vastly improve target tracking and interception, even against large and complex attacks. If it is relatively easy to intercept a satellite with a predictable orbit, it could also become easier eventually to intercept an object in an unexpected trajectory with little warning. Still, the prospect that a single warhead would penetrate and do unacceptable damage will perpetuate offense dominance in nuclear warfare despite improvements in defense technology.

Offense dominance in space could be eroded by the placement of numerous cheap decoys, though they would have to have signatures resembling real satellites and would likely be revealed as decoys given enough time to observe them. Maneuverable or stealthy satellites would obviously increase the difficulty of targeting, at some cost in dollars and performance. Resiliency could be gained by distributing missions and functions among a large number of satellites instead of concentrating them among small numbers of high-value/high-cost platforms, as has been the general practice. Meanwhile, it can be assumed that hard- and soft-kill technologies will also progress, leaving access to space a serious vulnerability.

Information technologies are especially unstable and unpredictable, which raises questions about the persistence of offense dominance in cyberspace. Just as useful computer networks tend to be open and accessible, they can also become more self-aware, sensitive to intrusion, adaptable, and thus resilient. Even large and sophisticated attackers could find it increasingly hard to cause widespread and lasting disruption. Moreover, the concept of "dynamic defense" implies that attackers can be detected and neutralized the instant they gain unauthorized network access. Defenses could become sufficiently cost effective that even advanced attackers could be deterred not only by the fear of retaliation but also by the prospect of failure.

Such speculation about a shift toward defense dominance runs against what may be enduring features of the digital age: steadily increasing abilities to pinpoint objects on and near the Earth, to share that information, and to guide other objects to those same points—in a word, targeting. Current inventive and price performance trends in sensing, global positioning, processing, and transmission technologies suggest that targeting will, if anything, improve. By the same token, exceedingly strong market forces that favor access and collaboration will likely confront network defenses with a growing challenge.

While this study has found that neither the United States nor China can buy its way out of vulnerability through investment in strategic defense, it goes without saying that both will at least continue exploratory, competitive research for ways to overcome offense dominance. At the same time, if Sino-U.S. mutual strategic deterrence works, if mutual restraint is institutionalized in both countries and between them, and if trust grows, the urge to "break out" could decline, even if science makes it more possible. Moreover, while deterrence is static and potentially fragile under technological stress, mutual restraint can be adapted cooperatively to preserve stability despite technological stress. While technology more than a decade out is unpredictable, the safe bet—and a prudent assumption—is that the world's leading states will still be grappling with the vulnerabilities produced by their own power and global integration.

Recommendations

Beyond the core recommendation for the United States to offer a framework of concepts and terms for integrated mutual restraint, several concrete suggestions for U.S. policymakers come to mind. Initial diplomacy on actual measures of restraint would not be with China but with allies, who must be given the opportunity to contemplate and comment on U.S. views of vulnerabilities in these strategic domains, of their significance for the region, and of negotiating with China. In this regard, it is important to impress upon allies that strategic restraint is part of a larger U.S. strategy to maintain stability and eliminate the danger of destructive war in this vital region.

It would also be good early on to share with Chinese counterparts U.S. analysis of vulnerabilities in space and cyberspace, especially between large and sophisticated potential adversaries. It is not clear that Chinese leaders understand how China's growing and irreversible reliance on satellites and computer networking exposes it to possible economic harm. Dialogue could help educate them about this reality, while stressing that the United States also faces vulnerabilities and is not seeking advantage at China's expense. The United States should share with Chinese political and economic elites an alternative to the PLA view of strategic reality, including the risks and consequences of escalation in space and cyberspace. Unofficial dialogues on space and cyber security might be a good means of engaging a broad range of Chinese civilian and military actors and making them more aware of how their interests might be affected. It would also be timely to tell the Chinese that the United States is willing to consider a bilateral nuclear no-first-use pledge *provided* China is willing concurrently to discuss similar ideas about space and strategic cyberspace.

Regardless of progress on terms of mutual restraint, it is important that operational decisions that could lead to hostilities in any strategic domain have strong political oversight. In regard to the use of ASAT and offensive cyber capabilities, the United States should review its protocols for such oversight and delegation of authority to military commands under peacetime and wartime conditions and should urge Chinese civilian leaders to do likewise. Finally, the need for the United States to speak with one voice on these matters argues for intense civilian-military, executive-congressional, and bipartisan discussions.

Such steps should be taken not with undue urgency but with care, composure, and conviction that a regime of mutual strategic restraint is right for the United States, for the security of a vital region, and for putting Sino-American relations on a stable long-term strategic footing. At this formative stage in what will be the world's most important relationship for generations to come, the United States cannot afford to be passive and reactive. Because the relationship is so complex and fluid, and because vulnerabilities are growing, a better time may not come for an American initiative to offer a framework for strategic stability.

In the backdrop of such deliberations and diplomacy, the United States should be increasingly vocal and clear on the matter of strategic deterrence. Just in the past year, the U.S. Government has indicated that it will strengthen deterrence against attacks on satellites and on computer networks. This is a two-edged message: the United States will not be the first to launch strategic attacks in these domains, yet it can and will retaliate if others strike first. Even as the United States becomes comfortable with the ability of China to deter U.S. nuclear attack, it should make the Chinese uncomfortable about the consequences of satellite or cyber attacks.

This study is not meant to be the final word on the paradox of power and the need for mutual strategic restraint. We urge more debate on the strategic concepts illuminated here, not only in the United States and in China but also between Americans and Chinese. In addition, a number of questions merit further examination:

What missile defense capabilities would afford assured protection against small, hostile nuclear weapons states or unauthorized missile launches without raising doubts about the acceptance of mutual deterrence between the United States and China?

How can computer networks used for military C^{4}ISR be partitioned from those that enable civilian and commercial information-sharing so that escalation firebreaks can prevent unwanted and potentially cataclysmic general war in cyberspace in the event of crises or hostilities?

What concrete CBMs beyond those proposed here could buttress trust in Chinese and American acceptance of mutual restraint in the use of offensive capabilities?

What specific methods of Sino-American notification of third-party or ambiguous attacks in space and cyberspace could increase assurance against mistakes and miscalculation?

Under what conditions could other states with offensive strategic capabilities, such as Russia, subscribe to the principles and terms of mutual restraint?

Perhaps mutual strategic restraint will prove to be more of a process than a set of definitive obligations—a process in which political leaders and military commanders come to grips with the need to act prudently and to treat strategic vulnerability as a common problem to be solved cooperatively. One way or another, as technology and integration expose even the most powerful nations to growing threats from one another, the United States and China have strong interests to partner and special responsibilities to lead. We hope this book will prompt them to do so.

Notes

[1] The United States has spent on average $10 billion per year for the past 10 years on total missile defense (including research and development, military construction, and procurement). Doubling this expenditure for the next 10 years would put the missile defense program at $200 billion. A total of 424 satellites, 208 working, have been deployed with a total expenditure of $62.3 billion. At a low end cost of $147 million per launch, deploying an additional 200 satellites for redundancy would cost $30 billion. In the cyber domain, as technology gets better, expenses to defend U.S. critical networks will increase. U.S. Cyber Command, not fully operational until October 2010, requested $3.2 billion for its 2011 budget. Lacking personnel and facilities, this budget is likely to increase over the next 10 years to parallel increased cyber warfare capabilities. If the budget is tripled, expenditures would rise to $96 billion over a 10-year period, rivaling current costs of missile defense. Budget figures were derived from the Congressional Budget Office and Congressional Research Service.

[2] For instance, Robert J. Oppenheimer's insistence that U.S. use of atomic weapons against Japan be followed by a proposal to internationalize the knowledge control of nuclear power.

About the Authors

David C. Gompert is Distinguished Research Fellow in the Center for Strategic Research, Institute for National Strategic Studies, at the National Defense University (NDU), a Professor for National Security Studies at the U.S. Naval Academy, and an Adjunct Fellow of the RAND Corporation. From 2009 to 2010, he was Principal Deputy Director of National Intelligence. Mr. Gompert also has been a senior executive in the information technology industry, Vice President of the RAND Corporation and President of RAND Europe, Special Assistant to President George H.W. Bush and Secretary of State Henry Kissinger, and a senior official in the State Department. He has published extensively on international affairs, national security policy, and information technology. He holds a Bachelor of Science degree in Engineering from the U.S. Naval Academy and a Master of Public Affairs degree from the Woodrow Wilson School at Princeton University.

Phillip C. Saunders is a Distinguished Research Fellow and Director of Studies in the Center for Strategic Research, Institute for National Strategic Studies, at the National Defense University (NDU). He also serves as Director of the Center for the Study of Chinese Military Affairs. Dr. Saunders previously worked at the Monterey Institute of International Studies, where he was Director of the East Asia Nonproliferation Program from 1999 to 2003, and served as an officer in the U.S. Air Force from 1989 to 1994. Dr. Saunders has published numerous articles and book chapters on China and Asian security issues. He attended Harvard College and received his M.P.A. and Ph.D. in International Relations from the Woodrow Wilson School at Princeton University.